Ret
Me

Sociology of Health and Illness Monograph Series

Edited by Jonathan Gabe
Department of Social and Political Social Science
Royal Holloway
University of London

Current titles:

Medicine, Health and Risk
Edited by Jonathan Gabe

Health and the Sociology of Emotions
Edited by Veronica James and Jonathan Gabe

The Sociology of Medical Science and Technology
Edited by Mary Ann Elston

The Sociology of Health Inequalities
Edited by Mel Bartley, David Blane and George Davey Smith

Sociological Perspectives on the New Genetics
Edited by Peter Conrad and Jonathan Gabe

Rethinking the Sociology of Mental Health
Edited by Joan Busfield

Forthcoming title:

Sociological Perspectives on Health Care Rationining
Edited by Donald Light and David Hughes

Rethinking the Sociology of Mental Health

Joan Busfield

BLACKWELL *Publishers*

ISBN: 0631221859

Blackwell Publishers Ltd
108 Cowley Road
Oxford OX4 1JF, UK

Blackwell Publishers Inc
350 Main Street
Malden, Massachusetts 02148, USA

British Library Cataloguing in Publication Data has been applied for

Library of Congress Cataloging in Publication Data has been applied for

Typeset by Downdell
Printed and bound in Great Britain
By MPG Books, Bodmin, Cornwall

This book is printed on acid-free paper

Contents

Acknowledgements

We should like to thank all those involved in the various stages of producing this monograph. We are grateful to the individual contributors for responding swiftly to deadlines, comments and queries. The anonymous referees who read each of the chapters, usually two or three times, have helped the contributors enormously. Anthea Holme's copy-editing and Jackie Macmillan's administrative and proof-reading skills have also been invaluable.

1

Introduction: Rethinking the sociology of mental health

Joan Busfield

Recent advances in genetics, the neurosciences and pharmacology currently appear to be confirming the ascendancy of the natural sciences in contributing to the understanding of body and behaviour and, more particularly, to the explanation and treatment of both mental and physical ills. And in so doing they seem to be pushing aside the importance of social processes and any contribution from sociology to the understanding of mental health and disorder, a contribution that has been highly diverse and multi-faceted[1]. There are a number of reasons for the current predominance of genetic and biochemical understandings of mental disorder. First, and most obviously, the significant advances in these sciences during recent years, not least the progress in decoding the human genome, have drawn professional and media attention to the role of genetic factors in mental health and illness. Second, doctors still tend to be powerful, if not always the most powerful professionals within the mental health field, and, since medical training is still largely oriented towards the natural sciences, doctors usually give primacy to ideas and understandings based on the natural sciences over those from the human and social sciences. And third, explanations and understandings of mental disorder in terms of physical processes often have a number of attractions for other actors, including those with mental health problems, the lay public and politicians: they fit with medicine's widespread use of drugs in the treatment of mental disorder; they suggest a simple causal account of the condition – a faulty gene (see Conrad 1999); they seem to take away responsibility for being ill from the individual (the problem lies in the body rather than the mind or social relations); and they focus on what is going on within the body rather than on any deficiencies in society. But it is important to recognise that the situation is not entirely monolithic. In Britain, for instance, whilst researchers and media reports announce the discovery of new genes for different mental disorders (Conrad 1997), the Labour Government has given a new emphasis to health inequalities, including inequalities in mental health (Secretary of State for Health 1998), as well as the role of environmental factors, in generating these inequalities. It has also announced new Health Improvement Programmes. Whilst it is too early to assess the impact of these developments and there are grounds for caution, they do suggest some space for assertion by sociologists and others of the importance of the social.

Geneticists' reported claims notwithstanding, social processes are crucial to the understanding of mental health and disorder in a range of ways. First, social processes shape the very concepts of mental health and disorder, thereby setting the boundaries of what constitutes mental disorder and the categories that are used to distinguish one disorder from another. Second, social processes play an important part in the aetiology of mental disorders – any mental disorder is always a product of genetics *and* environment (Rutter and Plomin 1997). And third, social processes play a vital part in influencing mental health practice. It is essential, therefore, given the current tendency to eschew the social, to reassess the contribution sociology can make to understanding mental health and disorder, and to identify ways in which the relevance of sociology can be reaffirmed and its work advanced and, if necessary, redirected. We need to *rethink* the sociology of mental health. The aim of this introduction is to review the contribution sociology has made, and can continue to make, to understanding the sociology of mental health and disorder, and to look at possible ways of taking this knowledge and understanding forward. The chapters that follow then engage in this sociological work. I begin by considering the sociological contribution to understanding concepts of mental health and disorder.

Understanding concepts and categories of mental disorder

Sociologists have paid considerable attention to concepts of mental disorder and to the diagnostic categories with which psychiatrists and other mental health professionals operate. It is notable, for instance, that Derrol Palmer in this volume argues that this is the terrain par excellence where a sociological contribution can be made. Sociological work in this area can be traced back to the work of Emile Durkheim, and in particular to his work on the normal and pathological (1964 [1895]). His major insight is well-known: that the rules and standards that define what is pathological help to reinforce the norms and values of society – the normal and the pathological are mutually constitutive – and societies and social groups define the pathological in order to sustain and strengthen the normal. This observation, grounded in Durkheim's functionalism, has three corollaries. First, that rules that define the normal and pathological vary according to the values of the social group and in that respect what is constituted as mental disorder is socially and culturally relative[2]. Second, that there is always and necessarily an element of social control in the application of rules, including the rules as to what is normal and what pathological. And third, rules are necessary for the cohesion and smooth running of society.

Durkheim's analysis is clearly pertinent to understanding concepts of mental health and mental disorder: these become concepts that help to define what is acceptable conduct and action within society and his ideas have provided the foundation on which other authors have developed their ideas and analyses. The American sociologist, Talcott Parsons (1951), for example, argued that all illness can be viewed as a form of deviance since there are always motivational elements in any illness. A similar emphasis on viewing mental disorder as deviance is found in Thomas Scheff's (1999 [1967]) influential analysis of mental illness in terms of what he calls 'residual deviance'. In this case, however, deviance is not defined as rule breaking per se but, in terms of 'labelled' rule breaking as behaviour that has been *identified* as rule breaking. We can also see the influence of these ideas in the work of the anti-psychiatrists such as Thomas Szasz (1970) in the US, who viewed mental illness as the breaking of social, political and ethical norms.

Much sociological work on psychiatric classification and diagnosis in the US and Britain (see Brown 1990) has been shaped by such ideas, as well as by work on the sociology of science (see, for instance, Latour 1987). Phil Brown sees diagnosis and the work on diagnostic classifications, such as the American Psychiatric Association's *Diagnostic and Statistical Manual* (1994) or the World Health Organisation's *Classification of Mental and Behavioural Disorders* (1992), as central to psychiatry. There is a strong sociological tradition seeking to examine both the way in which new categories of mental disorder have emerged and others disappeared, and the way in which social and political factors have shaped these changes – a tradition represented in this volume by Nick Manning's discussion of psychopathic disorder. The classic case of the emergence of a psychiatric disorder, followed later by its exclusion from psychiatric classifications, is that of homosexuality (Spector 1972), but there has also been a range of sociological and other work on the development of other new psychiatric categories such as hyperactivity (Box 1984), now renamed Attention Deficit Disorder (ADD), pre-menstrual disorder (Figert 1996) and post-traumatic stress disorder (Young 1995).

An important feature of the sociological work, influenced directly or indirectly by Durkheimian ideas about the normal and the pathological, is the focus on *behaviour*. In that respect we can see such sociological analyses as assimilating mental disorder to the analysis of behaviour, in contrast to the bio-medical approaches dominant in psychiatry, which tend to assimilate mental disorder to the analysis of the body and bodily processes. However, the concentration on behaviour is not without its problems. On the one hand, it creates a major problem of how to differentiate the deviance characteristic of mental disorder from other types of deviance – a problem that no sociologist has solved at all satisfactorily without reference to judgements of mental processes[3]. On the other hand, it allows for no clear differentiation between disorders that are clearly defined around mental processes – thought and emotion – and those that have a more behavioural focus, such as alcohol problems or conduct disorders. Although the inclusion of these behavioural problems within the field of mental disorder has long been contested, they, along with the more obviously 'mental' disorders, are currently included in official psychiatric classifications[4].

However, Foucault (1967) has called the sociological focus on behaviour (and the bio-medical focus on the body) into question by defining mental disorder squarely in terms of mind, viewing it in terms of unreason and irrationality, and linking it to the affirmation of rationality that was a feature of Enlightenment thinking. Foucault's approach links well with concerns about the intelligibility of the thought, emotion and behaviour that is symptomatic of mental illness (see, Laing 1963, Jaspers 1963), and I have argued elsewhere (Busfield 1996: 71–4) that the conceptualisation has important advantages. This is because of the specific focus on mental processes rather than body or behaviour. These mental processes are often an important component of lay judgements of mental disorder and are held to underlie behaviour and to be intimately linked, but not coterminous, with it[5]. Within sociology these lay understandings have been explored by a number of writers, especially those influenced by phenomenology and ethnomethodology (Coulter 1973, Smith 1978, and Palmer in this volume).

The rethinking provoked by Foucault's analysis of madness in terms of reason is being taken in different directions by sociologists of the body and sociologists of the emotion, the former influenced by other aspects of Foucault's work. Sociology, in so far as it has tended to focus on behaviour and action, has paid remarkably little attention to the body, which has in effect been ceded to the natural sciences. Yet humans are embodied persons and our relations with our bodies are very important – the way we dress, our bodily sensations and so forth. Much consumption now focuses on the body – clothes, cosmetics, food, etc. Indeed, a key contemporary mental disorder that came into prominence in the second half of the 20th century is anorexia nervosa where problems around bodily shape are central. The disorder is seen by some as the archetypal mental disorder of late modern society with its concerns for regulating the body (see Giddens 1991: 103–8), though some have questioned the iconic status it has been attributed by such theorists (van't Hof and Nicholson 1996).

Equally sociology has itself tended to reflect Enlightenment thinking in concentrating its attention on thought and reason rather than emotion. Here again sociologists are attempting to redress the balance, through, for instance, discussions of the role of emotional work and emotional labour (Hochschild 1983), and the analysis of the gendering of emotional expression and so forth. Emotions are particularly important to mental health, and work in this area will undoubtedly contribute to a rethinking of the sociology of mental health (see Crossley 2000 and Simon Williams's chapter in this volume).

Foucault's ideas about reason and madness, though they shift the emphasis from behaviour to mind, retain the same emphasis on the social and cultural relativity of categories of mental disorder. This sociological emphasis has come to be expressed in a simple, shorthand form in the claim that mental disorder is a 'social construct' – a phrase now widely used by some mental health professionals, such as nurses and social workers, as well as sociologists. The phrase can mean a number of different things. On the one hand, it can mean little more than that mental disorder is a social category – that it is a product of how humans think about and act in the world – a proposition that is likely to be elaborated in terms of claims that what is so categorised, and the meanings attached to the categories, vary across time and place. On the other hand, it can be taken to incorporate an ontological claim that mental disorder is *only* a category and does not refer to any objective reality. This reading of the phrase social construct has been espoused not only by some symbolic interactionists when they adopt a conventionalist philosophy of the social sciences and argue that we cannot get beneath the realm of concepts, categories and experiences. It has also been espoused very forcefully by postmodern theorists who focus on the cultural analysis of texts and narratives and similarly suggest that we cannot get beyond such texts and narratives to any material reality. And it is this latter reading that is often assumed by non-sociologists when they hear or use the phrase 'mental disorder is a social construct'.

There can be little doubt of the importance of the contribution that has been made by those who use the language of social construction to think about the processes of social shaping that occur in the development and modification of categories of mental disorder, and there are no doubt many sociologists who wish to defend this language as well as espousing some of the more radical epistemological and ontological implications. However, there are alternative approaches. One is provided by Charles Rosenberg's (1992) notion of the 'social framing' of illness and disease. This conceptualisation has advantages, indicating, as it does, that the way we understand illness varies across time and place, but does not suggest any denial of the material reality of the phenomena that come to be constituted as disease or disorder. In that respect the language is consistent with the philosophical position of critical realism (Bhaskar 1998), whilst also recognising the importance of the social processes involved in the development of concepts and categories. Equally, reference to the social structuring of illness (see Figert 1996) is more consistent with a critical realist epistemology. In my view use of the terminology of 'framing' or 'structuring' would help to secure sociological insights and understandings of mental disorder rather more effectively than the language of social constructs. The notion of social construction has become very loose and imprecise and, because of its epistemological and ontological connotations, can generate hostility towards sociological ideas about mental disorder from doctors, patients and families who feel it rejects the reality of the pain, difficulty and suffering involved in mental disorder.

Sociology and explanations of mental disorder

The sociological contribution to understanding why individuals become disturbed has largely, though not exclusively, been grounded in epidemiology, with its focus on examining the distribution of diseases across populations as the starting point for aetiological exploration. In the 19th century the epidemiological approach, which has its roots in concerns about public health, was applied by asylum doctors, neurologists and alienists, as well as Commissioners in Lunacy, to examine and comment on the distribution of insanity across populations. In Britain, an important controversy in the late 19th century was over whether insanity was increasing, and if so why, since the numbers confined within asylums steadily increased as the movement to establish a network of asylums took hold. Writing in 1897, the Commissioners in Lunacy, having carefully examined the data, argued that insanity was not increasing, but that the establishment of the asylum system was bringing more cases of insanity to official attention and broadening the boundaries of cases thought to require asylum care. Nineteenth century writers also made a range of observations about the age, class, and gender of the asylum populations.

In the 20th century advances in epidemiology, including the use of more sophisticated statistical ideas, greater awareness of processes of selection, and surveys of broader groups of the population, were extended to psychiatric epidemiology in which sociologists played an important part. An early, influential sociological study was *Mental Disorders in Urban Areas* (1939) by two US sociologists, Robert Faris and Warren Dunham. Both were members of the Chicago School of Sociology. The study, describing itself as a study in social ecology, followed the traditions of that School in examining the distribution of all cases of mental disorder across the range of treatment facilities in the different residential zones of Chicago. The study is worth describing in some detail because it made the case for the need to study the role of social factors so effectively.

The authors noted in particular that whereas manic-depressive psychosis appeared to be randomly distributed across the city, suggesting the role of genetic factors in its aetiology, in contrast, cases of schizophrenia were concentrated in the poorer areas. This latter finding could not be accounted for by processes of geographical drift, in which those diagnosed with schizophrenia ended in the poorest zones of the city, since information on how long they had spent in the area showed that residence in the particular area usually preceded the onset of illness. The authors suggested that the high level of schizophrenia in these areas could well be due to the lack of community networks in the poorer localities and the high levels of social isolation. What was important, however, was the clear evidence provided by the study that genetic factors could not account for the observed distribution of schizophrenia and that social factors have to be brought into the aetiological accounts of schizophrenia. This conclusion has also been confirmed by genetic studies which show, for instance, that in the case of schizophrenia, genetic factors can only account for *some* of the variation in the incidence of schizophrenia (Gottesmann 1991, Trimble 1996).

Faris and Dunham's path-breaking study was followed by the equally influential American study, *Social Class and Mental Illness* (1958), by A.B. Hollingshead, a sociologist, and F.C. Redlich, a psychiatrist. Here the concern had shifted, following developments within the discipline of sociology, from geographical location to social class. The authors took great care to develop a satisfactory measure of social class and to identify all cases of mental disorder where there had been contact with any form of service. They showed that class was significantly related to the level of mental disorder, the type of mental disorder, the pathway into treatment, and the type of treatment received. Class V, the lowest social class, particularly stood out as experiencing more mental disorder, particularly psychosis, being more likely to enter treatment via the courts and official agencies, and being more likely to receive organic rather than psychological therapies.

The finding of the marked association between social class and mental disorder was replicated in other studies in the US, Britain and a range of other countries. They included studies that sought to identify mental disorder across the community independently of whether individuals were in contact with any form of mental health service (Langer and Michael 1963). Whereas Faris and Dunham had focused on social isolation as a possible aetiological factor, Hollingshead and Redlich adopted a more developmental approach, influenced by Freudian ideas then fashionable in American psychiatric circles. They suggested the possible role of a range of factors across the life cycle, particularly emphasising experience in early infancy. In contrast, many subsequent studies seeking to explore the relationship between class and mental disorder focused on social stress – defined in terms of immediate events or ongoing circumstances which individuals found difficult. This shifted the emphasis from early childhood experience to aspects of the more immediate social situation[6]. George Brown and Tirril Harris's well-known British community survey, *Social Origins of Depression* (1978), followed this approach, developing a model of stressful events and ongoing difficulties that interacted with socially generated vulnerability factors to account for class differences in levels of depression[7]. These aetiological ideas were developed in a range of subsequent work both on situational stresses, and on childhood experiences that may make individuals more vulnerable to mental illness, such as neglect (see, for instance, Bifulco and Moran 1998).

Drawing on the same traditions of psychiatric epidemiology, and influenced by both political and sociological developments including feminist scholarship, other sociologists from the late 1960s onwards explored gender and ethnic differences. In the US, Gove (see, for instance, Gove 1972, Gove and Tudor 1972) examined male-female differences in levels of mental disorder, attaching considerable importance to women's marital role in accounting for what was by then an over-representation of women amongst psychiatric patients. Although often critical of the details of Gove's arguments, subsequent work in Britain and elsewhere has continued to explore the impact of women's domestic work and paid employment (see Bartley *et al.* 1992), some considering the possible differential impact on women and men (Hunt and Annadale 1993). Equally, a number of writers identified an over-representation of blacks amongst psychiatric patients in both the US and Britain (Littlewood and Lipsedge 1997).

This strong epidemiological tradition is being continued by social scientists, including sociologists, across the world. In the US, the Epidemiologic Catchment Area Study carried out in the early 1980s has provided an invaluable source of data on the social distribution of mental disorder (Robins and Regier 1991). In Britain, the Office of Population Censuses and Surveys carried out a survey of psychiatric morbidity in the community in the early 1990s (Meltzer *et al.* 1995), and Nazroo (1997) has used the Survey of Ethnic Minorities in Britain to analyse ethnic differences in mental health. The novelty of recent work comes largely from improvements in measuring mental disorder, particularly through the use of more comprehensive and less biased measures.

Not all sociological work on explanations of mental disorder is grounded in social epidemiology. Some sociologists of deviance, especially writers of a symbolic interactionist persuasion, itself a development from the Chicago School, have paid particular attention to interpersonal dynamics in the development of disorder. A classic study here is Edwin Lemert's (1962) 'Paranoia and the dynamics of exclusion' in which he provided an account of the complex social processes involved in the development of paranoia. Lemert was a key figure in the development of labelling theory with his distinction between primary and secondary deviance, and other labelling theorists, notably Thomas Scheff (1999 [1967]), have stressed the importance of societal reaction in generating mental disorder. Whilst labelling theory is less influential than it was in the 1960s and 1970s, the tradition has continued to generate significant work that contributes to our understanding of mental disorder in individuals as, for instance, in Peggy Thoits's (1985) discussion of the role of self-labelling.

It is hard to overestimate the achievement of this type of explanatory research, particularly that grounded in social epidemiology, since it has shown so convincingly that social factors must be brought into the understanding of the causation of mental disorder at the individual level. For instance, the impact of the classic work of Hollingshead and Redlich, or the later work of Brown and Harris (1978), owes much to its careful and thorough use of quantitative techniques of data collection and analysis that conform to the scientific canons espoused by medical professionals, as well as to its theoretical underpinnings. The achievement of such work is recognised by some sociologists, especially those sympathetic to sound, theoretically informed, empirical work, both quantitative and qualitative. Gordon Marshall (1990), for instance, in his study *In Praise of Sociology*, includes the Brown and Harris (1978) study as one of the classic texts of postwar British sociology, emphasizing the contribution it has made to the understanding of the social origins of mental disorder.

Regrettably, however, the contribution of such studies is in danger of being swamped in the public and professionals' minds by new work in genetics. This is primarily, as I noted earlier, because any work on health and illness in the natural sciences tends to be given primacy over the social or behavioural sciences, on the assumption of a hierarchical ranking of the sciences – a view which is reinforced by the media who tend to portray genetic factors as offering *the* explanation of illness (see Conrad 1997). This contest over scientific knowledge is not helped by the critical, even hostile, attitudes of some sociologists to the work of social epidemiologists, with the argument that such work is insufficiently grounded theoretically. Such sociologists, particularly those of a postmodernist or post-structuralist persuasion, emphasise as I have noted, the social and cultural relativity of social categories, including concepts of mental health and illness. From this point of view, social epidemiology is not well-respected, since it is held to be guilty of some naivety and since it seems to take the status of concepts of mental illness and mental disorder for granted. The quality of such work, like other research, is of course variable and some is very poorly grounded theoretically. Yet, epidemiological research which accepts and operationalises definitions of mental disorder that hold for a particular time and place, is not incompatible with thinking critically about disorder, and the two approaches can be regarded as complementary (see Busfield 1988). It is notable, to take but one example, that Brown and Harris's research called the then common psychiatric distinction between endogenous and reactive depression into question by showing that social processes were similarly implicated in the origins of both[8]. What we need are both theoretically-informed critical thinking and sound empirical work, quantitative as well as qualitative. Without the sound empirical grounding which epidemiological studies provide, sociological claims about the importance of the social are considerably weakened. And there can be little doubt that the lack of support from some sociologists, particularly in Britain, for this work has tended to undermine rather than strengthen the case for the need for adequate attention to social factors in any examination of the aetiology of mental disorder. The sociological case is also not helped by the reluctance of many sociologists to engage in direct discussions about the relation between the biological and the social (see Benton 1991, Williams 1996), something which the recent attention to the sociology of the body has, in most cases, done little to remedy since the overriding focus of such work has been on cultural processes.

Professional practice and mental health services

The ways in which society responds to mental disorder is clearly and distinctively the terrain of sociology and the social sciences. Bio-medicine suggests some simple linkage between medical understandings of disorder and medical responses and treatments – between theory and practice. According to this view it is science and scientific advances that dictate practice. Sociologists seek a deeper and fuller understanding of both science and professional practice, showing how science is itself shaped by professional practice (see, for instance, Latour 1987) and how professional practice is in turn shaped by a range of social, political and economic forces.

Sociological work on professionalisation relates both to the understanding of concepts of mental health and illness and to all areas of psychiatric practice: the treatments that are used and the organisational context of psychiatric work. Here the focus shifts to the persons given formal responsibility for dealing with mental health and illness: psychiatrists and the expanding group of other mental health professionals, such as clinical psychologists, psychiatric social workers and psychiatric nurses. The importance of such work lies not only in the analysis of the changing power of mental health professionals, but also in understanding the way in which their activities and practices shape mental health services, and the concepts of disorder, aetiological accounts, and treatments they provide.

One theoretical influence has been the work of Durkheim. His analysis of the normal and the pathological not only contributes to our understanding of the category of mental disorder but also of how people respond to it, indeed they are two sides of the same coin. What his analysis suggests, as I have indicated, is the need to define and control the pathological in the interests of social solidarity and the maintenance of the normal. Such ideas were further developed by Parsons through his analysis of the social expectations governing what he called the sick role. Via the tradition of symbolic interactionism, they were also applied to the study of asylum life (Goffman 1961), as well as to the processes of stigmatisation, rejection and social exclusion that can follow being defined as mentally ill (see, for instance, Phillips 1963). Symbolic interactionist ideas have also informed studies of other aspects of mental health practice. For instance, there has been a range of research on the prescribing of tranquillisers and antidepressants which explores the meanings users attach to these (Gabe and Thorogood 1986) as well as the role of the media (Gabe and Bury 1991).

Weberian ideas have been just as, if not more, influential on sociological analyses of professionalisation and professional power. Freidson (1970, 1994) has been a major influence, developing a set of ideas that have been further developed and amplified by a range of sociologists – Larson (1977), Parkin (1979), Witz (1992), MacDonald (1995). Much of this work has not focused specifically on psychiatry and the mental health professionals, but some has. Notable here is Andrew Scull's (1975) early work on asylum doctors, as well as the work of some social historians influenced by sociological ideas such as Jan Goldstein's (1987) study of the French psychiatric profession in the 19th century.

Marxist ideas, and those derived from political economy, have also been very influential, emphasising the interests of different classes, in particular the value to the capitalist class of the regulation of different forms of deviance. Andrew Scull's (1977) analysis of the move from the asylum towards community care drew heavily on Marxist thinking, emphasising the changing costs of segregative forms of social control, whilst his analysis of the development of the earlier move to the asylum (1979) was influenced both by Marxism and a Weberian analysis of the professions. Similarly, Richard Warner (1994) used Marxist ideas to contend that the moves into and out of the asylum are linked to the state of the economy and the need for labour power. Though such ideas are now less fashionable within sociology than they were in the 1970s, Esping-Andersen's (1990) comparative analysis of welfare regimes in Europe, which draws on Marxist concepts, is having some impact on discussions of mental health services (see Goodwin 1997 and Carpenter this volume). Equally Light's (1995) discussion of countervailing powers allows for the incorporation of a range of actors: the professions, business corporations – notably the very powerful pharmaceutical companies – as well as the user groups which have come into prominence in the mental health field.

Foucault's ideas, both about the inseparability of power and knowledge, and about 'governmentality' (1991), have also had an impact on thinking about the development of professional practice and the mental health services. This work has been developed in France by Robert Castel (1988, Castel *et al.* 1982) who has sought to document the spread of psychological ideas and psychological professionals (the psy complex) into an ever-wider territory, and in Britain by writers such as Nikolas Rose (1999). Rose, like other Foucauldians, has been keen to emphasise the productive aspects of power, arguing that notions of social control suggest that power is repressive and embodies too strong a conception of agency, preferring terms such as regulation and management. Yet in practice these analyses still tend to emphasise repression and control much more than productivity.

More recently notions of risk have been used by a number of theorists of late modernity (Giddens 1991, Beck 1992), who have suggested that a focus on risk and risk assessment is a distinctive feature of late modern societies. Such ideas have obvious resonances in the mental health field where risk assessment is now an important feature of mental health work, and, in Britain, is often incorporated into the Care Programme Approach (CPA) (see Audit Commission 1994). Analysing such changes Castel (1991) has argued that there has been a shift from a notion of dangerousness, which was applied to individuals, to a notion of risk which is applied to populations and collectivities rather than individuals. Castel's thesis is contentious, not least because of the ongoing concern in services contexts about the risks posed by particular individuals as well as by the overall level of risk. Nonetheless the sociological analysis of risk undoubtedly provides a potentially fertile area for further rethinking about mental health.

What is clear from this account of the sociological work on mental health is the clear evidence it provides of the importance of social processes in a range of areas: in the definition, boundaries and categories of mental disorder; in any adequate understanding of the factors that give rise to mental disorder; and in the understanding of the character of mental health practice and the professionals and others who shape that practice together with the ideas that underpin it. Moreover, the overview not only provides evidence of the importance of careful, theoretically-informed empirical work, it also suggests new areas of sociological work on mental health and disorder where both theoretical and empirical research is needed. Whilst the character and direction of that research cannot be specified in advance, some areas where further work is likely to be fruitful can be suggested. These include the linkages between body and mind and the biological and the social, the sociology of the emotions, the analysis of risk, the role of the pharmaceutical industry and its relation to mental health practice, as well as the epistemological and ontological assumptions on which sociological work on mental disorder is grounded.

The chapters

The chapters in this volume seek to take thinking about the sociology of mental health forward. In the first section, Concepts and theories, the chapters explore aspects of theoretical approaches and concepts. Simon Williams begins with an exploratory chapter that discusses reason, emotion and embodiment, calling in particular for the development of a sociology of *emotional* health, a terminology that he suggests would be preferable to the standard language of mental health. Julie Mulvany then shifts the focus specifically to those with chronic mental ill-health, suggesting that ideas developed within the framework of social disability can be fruitfully applied to thinking about chronic mental disorder. Finally, in this section, Mick Carpenter looks again at theoretical debates about how we can best understand mental health policy since 1945, including the move to community care, and argues for the value of a social democratic approach.

The second section, Understanding symptoms and disorders, contains chapters on understanding particular mental disorders and specific symptoms. Nick Manning considers the category of personality disorder and relates it to issues of professional legitimacy, drawing on ideas from the sociology of science. Joyce Davidson examines agoraphobia, providing a phenomenological analysis of fear, and suggesting that the fear at issue is essentially fear of the social. And Derrol Palmer explores delusional discourse, using ideas from phenomenology and ethnomethodology and arguing, as I noted earlier, that it is in the identification of what is regarded as symptomatic of mental illness that sociology can make its most significant contribution. The third and final section, Policy issues, focuses on specific policy concerns. Bernadette Dallaire, Michael McCubbin, Paul Morin and David Cohen look at dangerousness and the intersection of the legal and psychiatric systems, contending, in particular, that violence and mental disorder are themselves intersecting concepts, and that mental disorder is increasingly defined in terms of dangerousness. Finally, Teresa Scheid explores the impact of managed health care arrangements in the United States on professional practice, showing how practice is compromised and limited by the system of managed care. All make a contribution to reasserting the importance of social processes, to understanding mental health and disorder and to rethinking the sociology of mental health. The task of sociology is not only to take this work forward, but to affirm the importance of the social, not only through their research, but by actively engaging in public debate about the interplay of the biological and the social.

Notes

1 I use the medical language here because of the predominance of the medical perspective in relation to understandings of what can also be termed psychological problems. Where possible I use the somewhat less medical term 'mental disorder' in preference to the term mental illness.
2 This point is discussed further below.
3 The best known example is Scheff's use of the concept of residual deviance, but this concept is very problematic (see Busfield 1986: 101–2).
4 The inclusion of behavioural disorders in psychiatric classifications has long been regarded as contentious.
5 The lay language of 'nerves' is interesting in this connection because of its connotations both of physical and mental processes.
6 Arguably a more distinctively sociological emphasis, given the way in which psychologists have tended to focus on early childhood experiences.
7 There has been considerable debate as to whether their vulnerability factors should be regarded as additional stresses and not as only having an impact in the presence of other stresses.
8 As the labels themselves suggest, the common psychiatric view was that whilst social factors played a part in the aetiology of reactive depression, genetic factors were crucial to the aetiology of endogenous depression.

References

American Psychiatric Association (1994) *Diagnostic and Statistical Manual of Mental Disorders*, 3rd Edition. Washington: APA.
Audit Commission (1994) *Finding a Place*. London: HMSO.

Bartley, M., Popay, J. and Plewis, I. (1992) Domestic conditions, paid employment and women's experiences of ill-health, *Sociology of Health and Illness*, 14, 313–43.

Beck, U. (1992) *Risk Society: Towards a New Modernity*. London: Sage.

Benton, T. (1991) Biology and social science: why the return of the repressed should be given a (cautious) welcome, *Sociology*, 25, 1–29.

Bhaskar, R. (1998) *The Possibility of Naturalism: a Philosophical Critique of the Contemporary Human Sciences*. 3rd Edition. London: Routledge.

Bifulco, A. and Moran, P. (1998) *Wednesday's Child: Research into Women's Neglect and Abuse in Childhood, and Adult Depression*. London: Routledge.

Box, S. (1984) Preface. In Schrag, P. and Divoky, D. *The Myth of the Hyperactive Child*. Harmondsworth: Penguin.

Brown, G. and Harris, T. (1978) *Social Origins of Depression*. London: Tavistock.

Brown, P. (1990) The name game: toward a sociology of diagnosis, *The Journal of Mind and Behavior*, 11, 385–406.

Busfield, J. (1986) *Managing Madness: Changing Ideas and Practice*. London: Hutchinson.

Busfield, J. (1988) Mental illness as social product or social construct: a contradiction in feminists' arguments? *Sociology of Health and Illness*, 10, 421–42.

Busfield, J. (1996) *Men, Women and Madness: Understanding Gender and Mental Disorder*. London: Macmillan.

Castel, R. (1988) *The Regulation of Madness: the Origins of Incarceration in France*. Oxford: Blackwell.

Castel, R. (1991) From dangerousness to risk. In Burchell, G., Gordon, C. and Miller, P. (eds) *The Foucault Effect*. Hemel Hempstead: Harvester Wheatsheaf.

Castel, R., Castel, F. and Lovell, A. (1982) *The Psychiatric Society*. New York: Columbia University Press.

Commissioners in Lunacy (1897) *Special Report on the Alleged Increase in Insanity*. London: HMSO.

Conrad, P. (1997) Public eyes and private genes: historical frames, new constructions, and social problems, *Social Problems*, 44, 139–54.

Conrad, P. (1999) A mirage of genes, *Sociology of Health and Illness*, 21, 228–41.

Coulter, J. (1973) *Approaches to Insanity*. London: Martin Robertson.

Crossley, N. (2000) Emotions, psychiatry and social order: a Habermasian approach. In Williams, S.J., Gabe, J. and Calnan, M. (eds) *Health, Medicine and Society: Key Theories, Future Agendas*. London: Routledge.

Durkheim, E. (1964 [1895]) *Rules of Sociological Method*. New York: Free Press.

Esping-Andersen, G. (1990) *The Three Worlds of Welfare Capitalism*. Cambridge: Polity Press.

Faris, R.E.L. and Dunham, H.W. (1965 [1939]) *Mental Disorders in Urban Areas*. Chicago: University of Chicago Press.

Figert, A.E. (1996) *Women and the Ownership of PMS: the Structuring of a Psychiatric Disorder*. New York: Aldine de Gruyter.

Foucault, M. (1967) *Madness and Civilisation*. London: Tavistock.

Foucault, M. (1991) Governmentality. In Burchell, G., Gordon, C. and Miller, P. (eds) *The Foucault Effect*. Hemel Hempstead: Harvester Wheatsheaf.

Freidson, E. (1970) *Profession of Medicine*. New York: Dodd, Mead.

Freidson, E. (1994) *Professionalism Reborn*. Cambridge: Polity Press.

Gabe, J. and Bury, M. (1991) Drug use and dependence as a social problem: sociological approaches. In Glass, L.B. (ed) *The International Handbook of Addiction Behaviour*. London: Tavistock Routledge.

Gabe, J. and Thorogood, N. (1986) Prescribed drug use and the management of everyday life: the experiences of black and white working class women, *Sociological Review*, 32, 524–46.

Giddens, A. (1991) *Modernity and Self-Identity*. Cambridge: Polity Press.

Goffman, E. (1961) *Asylums*. Harmondsworth: Penguin.

Goldstein, J. (1987) *Console and Classify*. Cambridge: Cambridge University Press.

Goodwin, S. (1997) *Comparative Mental Health Policy*. London: Sage

Gottesmann, I. (1991) *Schizophrenia Genesis: the Origins of Madness*. New York: Freeman.

Gove, W. (1972) The relationship between sex roles, marital status and mental illness, *Social Forces*, 51, 34–44.

Gove, W. and Tudor, J.F. (1972) Adult sex roles and mental illness, *American Journal of Sociology*, 78, 812–35.

Hochschild, A.R. (1983) *The Managed Heart: Commercialization of Human Feeling*. Berkeley: University of California Press.

Hollingshead, A.B. and Redlich, F.C. (1958) *Social Class and Mental Illness*. New York: Wiley.

Hunt, K. and Annandale, E. (1993) Just the job? Is the relationship between health and domestic and paid work gender-specific? *Sociology of Health and Illness*, 15, 643–64.

Jaspers, K. (1963) *General Psychopathology*. London: Manchester University Press.

Laing, R.D. (1963) *The Divided Self*. Harmondsworth: Penguin.

Langner, T.S. and Michael, S.T. (1963) *Life Stress and Mental Health*. Glencoe: Free Press.

Larson, M. (1977) *The Rise of Professionalism*. California: University of California Press.

Latour, B. (1987) *Science in Action*. Cambridge, Mass: Harvard University Press.

Light, D. (1995) Countervailing powers: a framework for the professions in transition. In Johnson, T., Larkin, G. and Saks, M. (eds) *Health Professions and the State in Europe*. London: Routledge.

Lemert, E. (1962) Paranoia and the dynamics of exclusion, *Sociometry*, 25, 2–20.

Littlewood, R. and Lipsedge, M. (1997) *Aliens and Alienists: Ethnic Minorities and Psychiatry*. 3rd Edition. London: Routledge.

MacDonald, K. (1995) *The Sociology of the Professions*. London: Sage.

Marshall, G. (1990) *In Praise of Sociology*. London: Unwin Hyman.

Meltzer, H., Gill, B., Petticrew, M. and Hinds, K. (1995) *The Prevalence of Psychiatric Morbidity amongst Adults Living in Private Households*. London: Office of Population Censuses and Surveys.

Nazroo, J. (1997) *Ethnicity and Mental Health*. London: Policy Studies Institute.

Parkin, F. (1979) *Marxism and Class Theory: a Bourgeois Critique*. London: Routledge and Kegan Paul.

Parsons, T. (1951) *The Social System*. New York: The Free Press.

Phillips, D. (1963) Rejection: a possible consequence of seeking help for mental disorders, *American Sociological Review*, 28, 963–72.

Robins, L. and Regier, D.A. (1991) *Psychiatric Disorders in America: the Epidemiologic Catchment Areas Study*.

Rose, N. (1999) *Governing the Soul: the Shaping of the Private Self.* 2nd Edition. London: Free Association Books.

Rosenberg, C.E. (1992) Introduction. In Rosenberg, C.E. and Gooden, J. (eds) *Framing Diseases: Studies on Cultural History.* New Brunswick: Rutgers University Press.

Rutter, M. and Plomin, R. (1997) Opportunities for psychiatry from genetic findings, *British Journal of Psychiatry*, 171, 209–19.

Scheff, T.J. (1999 [1967]) *Being Mentally Ill: a Sociological Theory.* 3rd Edition. New York: de Gruyter.

Scull, A. (1975) From madness to mental illness: medical men as moral entrepreneurs, *Archives Europeenes de Sociologies*, 16, 218–61.

Scull, A. (1977) *Decarceration: Community Treatment, a Radical View.* Englewood Cliffs: Prentice Hall.

Scull, A. (1979) *Museums of Madness.* London: Allen Lane.

Secretary of State for Health (1998) *Our Healthier Nation.* London: Stationery Office.

Smith, D. (1978) 'K is mentally ill': the anatomy of a factual account, *Sociology*, 12, 23–53.

Spector, M. (1972) Legitimizing homosexuality, *Society*, 14, 52–6.

Szasz, T.S. (1970) The myth of mental illness, *American Psychologist*, 15, 113–18.

Thoits, P. (1985) Self-labeling in mental illness: the role of emotional deviance, *American Journal of Sociology*, 91, 221–49.

Trimble, M. (1996) *Biological Psychiatry.* 2nd Edition. Chichester: John Wiley.

van't Hof, S. and Nicholson, M. (1996) The rise and fall of a fact: the increase in anorexia nervosa, *Sociology of Health and Illness*, 18, 581–608.

Warner, R. (1994) *Recovery from Schizophrenia.* 2nd Edition. London: Routledge.

Williams, S. (1996) Medical sociology, chronic illness and the body: a rejoinder to Michael Kelly and David Field, *Sociology of Health and Illness*, 18, 699–709.

Witz, A. (1992) *Professions and Patriarchy.* London: Routledge.

World Health Organisation (1992) *ICD-10 Classification of Mental and Behavioural Disorders.* Geneva: World Health Organisation.

Young, A. (1995) *The Harmony of Illusions: Inventing Post Traumatic Stress Disorder.* Princeton: Princeton University Press.

2

Reason, emotion and embodiment: is 'mental' health a contradiction in terms?

Simon J. Williams

Introduction

We should, according to psychologist Oliver James, be feeling 'much happier' and 'contented' than ever before. Far fewer of us in the Western world – atrocities such as the Balkan wars notwithstanding – are hungry and down-trodden than we were half a century ago. Yet James claims we are actually more 'miserable'; a 'happiness gap' produced through a 'chemical reaction' to the difference between the dreams we are sold and the daily reality of life in advanced capitalism. Embedded in this account is the notion of a 'low serotonin society', for which remedial measures include the development of an advanced capitalism which 'works for', rather than against, our 'mental' health (James 1998).

What, we may ask, is going on here? What issues does this raise about the nature of 'mental' health in particular and emotional life in general at the turn of century? What explanations predominate in these and other debates, and just how 'reasonable' a society is this to live in, given its supposed detrimental consequences to our health? It is these and other related issues that this particular chapter seeks to address through the specific lens of the emotions[1]. In doing so, I aim to re-examine the relationship between reason and emotions in other less 'unreasonable' terms, and critically to rethink the seemingly rigid categories and ossified conceptual forms within which they have been cast. A focus on emotions, I suggest, helps reanimate these issues, breathing new corporeal life into past and present debates, including a shift to a more fully-fledged focus on 'mental' health rather than illness. To focus on emotions moreover – as opposed to the more reified professional categories and disembodied notions of 'mental' health and illness – is to relocate them in the 'lifeworld' of the embodied agent and the 'communicative rationality' (Habermas 1986, 1987a,b) upon which it rests, however mediated this may have become (Crossley 1998). The reason, madness, mental disorder triumvirate, I suggest, has in large part 'co-opted' these debates, wittingly or otherwise, in ways that: (i) reinforce traditional views of emotions as somehow 'unreasonable' or 'unintelligible' from a dominant (*i.e.* instrumentally rational) viewpoint, and (ii) deflect attention away from the importance of emotions to the 'mental' health and 'rationality' of the individual agent alongside the 'rational functioning' of society as a whole. An 'unreasonable' position to be sure.

This of course, is not to say that these traditional viewpoints have themselves gone unchallenged, particularly through interpretative approaches to mental illness and the 'normalising' assumptions (*i.e.* mental illness as 'intelligible' from an alternative viewpoint) upon which they rest (Ingleby 1981). The anti-psychiatry movement, for example, provides ample evidence of these and other challenges, including a reversal of the traditional motivation-deviance equation (Gerhardt 1989, Sedgwick 1982, Scheff 1966, Laing 1965, Goffman 1961). Illness qua deviance, from these perspectives, becomes a (wholly) contingent affair: a product rather than cause of the (professional) labelling, with secondary deviance its (inevitable) sequelae. The aetiology of illness, in other words, has less to do with individual motivation than the framing or labelling process itself, as intelligible responses to seemingly absurd situations are all too often rendered unintelligible, and therefore pathologised. Important to be sure, these positions have nevertheless remained 'confined' if not 'trapped' within this particular dialogue with reason vis-a-vis broader debates on the positive role which emotions play in 'mental' health, social life and reason more generally.

In taking these issues forward, this chapter proceeds through a series of traditional divisions and debates, showing how emotions can facilitate new ways of thinking about these issues within the field of 'mental' health itself. My aim, in doing so, is not to question the utility of these categories as an analytical device, but rather to think about new ways of combining them through the emotions. A useful distinction can be drawn here at the outset between dual*ity*, as an *analytic* device, and dual*ism* as the *ideological* privileging, dominant throughout the course of Western culture and history, of one term over the other. As the process of Cartesian dualism suggests, it is only through an act of self-conscious reflection (*Cogito ergo sum*) that the split between mind and body is effected. Duality, to be sure, represents a stage in the development of human consciousness, but is nonetheless founded on a series of problematic assumptions about mind/body relations. This stage of development (*i.e.* duality), in turn leads to its own illusory appearance, the problem, that is, of dualism. As a doctrine, dualism turns duality into an 'ism', the mind/body split appearing somehow natural, rational and unconditional. Moreover, it spawns a number of other dualisms such as nature/culture, reason/emotion, public/private, and the associated baggage this involves. The critique of dualism, as a critique of the illusions of duality, and the critique of duality as a critique of a certain stage in the development of human consciousness, must therefore look forwards rather than backwards to a 'third stage' of development which is, as it were, prepared for by the previous stage(s). Doing so, I venture, compels and facilitates new ways of thinking, without (necessarily) falling into the reductionist or conflationary traps of the past.

In the first section of the chapter, I return to age-old debates over the relationship between reason and emotion, showing how the former, in large part, depends on the latter. The second section, building on these arguments, leads to the thorny question of biology and society, showing how emotions help bridge this divide in ways that re-embody the field of 'mental' health and illness as a whole. The third section picks up on issues of structure and agency, demonstrating again the micro-macro linkages which emotions provide in the aetiology of 'mental' health and illness. Under-pinning this lies a broader series of debates over the medicalisation-demedicalisation of society, including the current proliferation of drugs and therapies designed to help put us 'in touch' with, 'manage' or 'block out' our emotions. These issues are taken up in the final section of the chapter, through a call, following Craib (1994) and others, to take the 'importance of disappointment' seriously, as an inescapable facet of the human condition, without necessarily medicalising or pathologising these and other allegedly 'dysthymic' emotional states of existence. It is to the first of these issues that I now turn.

Reason versus emotion?

It is Foucault perhaps, more than any other theorist of his time, who has done most to open up the historically shifting dialogue between 'reason' and 'madness'. We no longer understand unreason today, Foucault declares, except in its 'epithetic form: the *Unreasonable*, a sign attached to conduct or speech, and betraying to the layman's eyes the presence of madness and all its pathological train' (1971: 83). Busfield too, building critically upon these Foucauldian insights, argues that the theorisation of mental disorder in terms of the regulation of 'reason' and 'rationality' provides the most 'useful conceptualisation for analyzing the boundaries of mental disorder, its regulation and its relation to gender' (1996: 69). The identification, that is to say, of ' "unreason" and "irrationality" through constructs of mental disorder, as an "affirmation of reason" ' (1996: 71)[2].

Undoubtedly, this is correct, extending to current debates over the '(un)reasonableness', if not 'irrationality' of a wide array of 20th century mental disorders such as anxiety, phobias, anorexia nervosa and drug addiction (Busfield 1996: 72). What it neglects without denying, however, is a sustained set of reflections on the contribution of emotions to 'mental' health and wellbeing as opposed to illness, and through this to the 'rationality' of the individual (Edwards 1981) and the 'rational functioning' of society as a whole (*i.e.* emotions as a functional prerequisite of both social order and social action (*cf.* Parsons 1951, Frank 1991))[3]. Emotions may at times wreak 'havoc' with processes of rational thought and decision-making, however defined. Their 'absence' however, as a variety of recent research has shown, is no less devastating (Damasio 1994). Society, in these and other respects, would indeed cease to function without emotion: a dull, empty affair without doubt. Emotions, from this perspective, are 'specific (*i.e.* "enchanted") ways of being-in-the-world' (*cf.* Sartre (1971/[1939]), thereby avoiding the tendency to view them negatively as failures in instrumental reasoning – a view which would 'consign everything from Platonic love to the passion of a football crowd, to the category of "pathological" or "dysfunctional"' (Crossley 1998: 29). Sartre to be sure, in referring to emotions as quasi-magical transformations of the world, imbues them with some highly regressive qualities. Alongside Merleau-Ponty (1962), however, the existential importance of emotions to our embodied being in the world is never lost sight of, paving the way therefore for a much more fully-fledged intersubjective and intercorporeal approach to emotions in social life (Crossley 1998).

Here we confront the thorny question of so-called 'appropriate' and 'inappropriate' emotions, itself related to the historically and culturally shifting nature and types of rationality, and the contextual circumstances within which they are embedded. At least three possible models, in this respect, suggest themselves: models, taking Barbalet's (1998) lead, I refer to as the 'conventional', 'complementary/critical' and 'convergent/radical' viewpoints respectively. The conventional or orthodox approach, dominant in Western culture, is one in which a wedge is firmly driven between reason and emotion – the latter banished to the margins of Western thought and practice. Traceable from Plato, Descartes and Kant, through Weber's 'incapacitating' fear of the irrational, to modern-day rational choice theory itself, emotion from this viewpoint 'perverts' the course of reason and the search for truth itself (*i.e.* 'outlaw' emotions as the 'saboteur' of instrumental rationality). To be rational, Plato declares, is truly to be 'master of oneself': a mastery based on unity, calm and collected self-possession. The realm of desire, in contrast, is deemed 'chaos', our souls 'torn apart' through a 'perpetual state of conflict' (Taylor 1989: 116). The Cartesian cogito, in a similar vein, turns reason into a somewhat disembodied process: a form of 'mental disengagement' (*Cogito ergo sum*) far removed from the corporeally-based 'passions of the soul'. Emotions, for Descartes, cannot be entirely 'controlled' by thinking. They can, however, be 'regulated' by thoughts, especially those that are 'true'. Reason in short, as Kant proclaimed, is 'sovereign': an independent faculty set in opposition to emotions qua nature[4].

A second, somewhat more 'tempered' or 'balanced' approach, sees this relationship in more complementary or 'critical' terms. Damasio (1994), for example, is a key contemporary exponent of this view. Reflective thought, he convincingly demonstrates, requires the 'tagging' of cognition with emotions. Without this capacity, decision-making itself becomes difficult if not impossible as there is no criterion with which to 'drive cognition' in a given direction. Emotions, it follows, are central to the 'effective deployment' of reason itself, providing it with salience, direction and purpose (i.e. goal formation) – see also de Sousa (1990). A classic example of this, as Damasio shows, is the case of Phineas Gage, a 19th century railroad worker whose frontal lobes were damaged when an iron bar shot through them by an accidental explosion. Along with the 'emotional deficits' which followed this damage, Gage had great difficulty in planning his ordinary life, making disastrous social decisions whilst dithering endlessly over inconsequential issues. A number of patients with similar damage have now been studied, the general conclusion being that it is this 'socio-emotional guidance system' which is affected, both in the brain of the original Phineas Gage and his modern-day counterparts. Emotions, this suggests, guide reason, furnishing us with priorities amongst multiple goals and options (Damasio 1994). What makes this a less than optimal position, as Barbalet notes, is that it remains somewhat 'apprehensive' about the possibility of emotion undermining reason, particularly its technical or instrumental forms (1998: 44). Emotion, that is, can only contribute so much: a more balanced assessment, to be sure, but one in which emotion continues to play a largely supportive if not subservient role, particularly in relation to technical and instrumental tasks[5].

Here we arrive at a third more 'convergent', or in Barbalet's (1998) terms 'radical', viewpoint: one in which the boundaries between reason and emotions themselves become wholly blurred. Instrumental reason, from this perspective, like any other form of reasoning, is itself founded on particular emotions (*i.e.* a passionately-held belief and a cherished ideal). James (1884, 1950/[1890]), for example, in an insightful essay entitled 'The sentiment of rationality' (1956/[1897]), emphasised the human passion for 'clarity' and 'order'. A passion, in his own terms, for 'generalising, simplifying and subordinating' (Barbalet 1998: 54, 1999). Emotion, from this viewpoint, is no mere adjunct to cognitive processes or the means to practical knowledge. Instead, it is woven into the very fabric of our reasoning; from scientific observation and the generation of hypotheses, to moral understanding and the 'communicative rationality' of Habermas' (1986, 1987a,b) lifeworld (*i.e.* emotions as 'accountable', 'contestable' and 'defeasible' (Crossley 1998)). We can, for example, in the main, be 'reasoned' both 'in' and 'out' of certain emotional states according to the communicatively rational criteria and 'validity claims' they raise. Even so-called 'emotional outbursts', Crossley points out, do not preclude the notion of 'communicative reasoning', nor the 'intersubjective reality' upon which it rests. Emotion, in short, from this latter more Habermasian viewpoint:

   ...is integrated within the order of communicative rationality...
   emotional responses raise validity claims which can be challenged or
   confirmed and...like any cognitive belief, an emotional response is

something that we believe we can talk people out of when they are wrong... Thus there is no reason why our social worlds cannot be simultaneously constituted through emotion and communicative rationality. Indeed, we can say that *emotion forms part of the sphere of communicative rationality* (Crossley 1998: 30, my emphasis).

Just as ('appropriate') emotions, however defined, may contribute to the development of knowledge, so too the growth of knowledge may contribute to the development of ('appropriate') emotions (Jaggar 1989). Rather than repressing emotion in Western epistemology therefore, it is necessary fundamentally to:

...rethink the relation between knowledge and emotion and construct conceptual models that demonstrate the *mutually constitutive* rather than oppositional relation between reason and emotion. Far from precluding the possibility of reliable knowledge, emotion as well as value must be shown as necessary to such knowledge (Jaggar 1989: 157).

Underpinning these latter two approaches – *i.e.* the 'complementary/ critical' and 'convergent/radical' viewpoints – is an attempt, as Barbalet (1998) notes, to bring emotions of a 'foreground' and 'background' nature into fuller focus, and to highlight the manner in which conventional understandings of both reason and emotion serve to 'mask' as much as they reveal, not simply about these terms themselves, but also their close relationship to one another (see also Heller 1990). The conventional opposition between reason and emotion, in this sense, may in large part be due to the 'cultural discounting of certain "background emotions"': emotions which 'underpin instrumental rationality but are seldom acknowledged or are seen as belonging to some other category (e.g. attitudes, customs) which fundamentally obscure their emotional nature' (Barbalet 1998: 29–30). Context, as noted above, is also crucial here, differing emotions, and the same emotions in different contexts, having different relations with reason itself, however defined (1998: 32). There is, in short, 'no one single rationality, but rather a set of traditions of rationality that are normatively governed and whose influence varies across time and place' (Busfield 1996: 73). Traditions, I have argued, which may not in fact be that 'reasonable'.

To this we may add a variety of other more 'radical' viewpoints, from feminisms to postmodernism, which both separately and in conjunction, champion new, more emotionally founded ways of being and knowing, as a challenge to dominant Cartesian traditions. Enough I hope has already been said to cast a long shadow over the first so-called 'conventional' or 'orthodox' approach, in which emotions are banished from Western thought and practice: driven out or pathologised by the steady hand of (male) disembodied reason (Seidler 1998, 1994, Rose 1994, Lloyd 1993). This, however, is merely one preparatory step in a broader attempt to bring emotions, and the body to which they are so closely tied, back in to debates on 'mental' health and illness. The next step is to tackle, head on, the traditional division between biology and society, mind and body, through a focus on *embodiment*.

Biology versus society?

Perhaps one of the main challenges in the field of 'mental' health and illness, given developments in biopsychiatry and the dominance of biochemical explanations, is to rethink the relationship between biology and society, and associated terms such as mind and body, without slipping into former reductionist or conflationary traps of the past. The consequences of modern life for individuals, as Lyon comments, are increasingly defined and treated through illness constructions grounded in the 'neurochemical features of individuals': developments reinforced through the marketing of new so-called wonder drugs such as Prozac for an infinite array of 'problems' associated with supposed 'defects' in our serotonin levels (1996: 64).

To this increasingly narrow/reductionist neurochemical search for explanation, we may add sociology's own reluctance to re-open the biology-society debate, given the socio-biological baggage of the past – preferring instead to concentrate on the socio-cultural aspects of health and illness. To the extent that it is addressed at all, biology has in large part been 'discursively co-opted', so to speak, through the relativist spirals of 'social constructionism', including full-blown Foucauldian scholarship. The tendency, as Lyon puts it, to 'flip-flop between these two distinct types of explanation depending on the "dimension" in question, or simply to grant primacy to one form of explanation and ignore the other, does little to encourage the exploration of new models which may bridge or obviate this division and lead to new forms of analysis' (1996: 56). What is needed in other words, are approaches which, whilst respecting the 'discrete *analytic* potential' of sociological and biological modes of explanation, find new ways of *'combining the two'* (Kelly and Field 1994: 36). Within the biological sciences themselves for example, as Benton reminds us, there are 'numerous competing conceptualisations', including 'several well-articulated alternatives to reductionist materialism available for use as philosophical means in the attempt to re-think the biology/society relationship' (1991: 18). Rose (1997) too, himself a biologist, points to a series of promising new ways forward in making biology 'whole again' – see also the feminist biologist Birke (1999).

It is no longer a question therefore of biological versus social accounts of 'mental' health and illness. Mental disorder, as Busfield comments, may indeed be a ' "label", in the sense that it is, like all words, a social construct; but it is not "merely" a label. It has a referent that has an *ontological reality...beyond the multiplicity of "voices"* to which we must attend' (1996:

60, my emphasis). This in turn requires us to abandon traditional mind/ body divisions[6] – of which medicine and psychiatry, not to mention sociology, have contributed much – and to:

> confront the question of how the social realm itself is *embodied*: a notion which can give form to the relationship between the social structural milieu in which humans live, their subjective experience, and the *flesh* through which that existence is lived (Lyon 1996: 69, my emphasis).

It is this dilemma, as Lyon herself notes, for which the study of emotions, qua bodily *and* social phenomena, provides one possible 'solution'. What then are emotions precisely and how do they contribute to these debates? As thinking, moving, feeling complexes, emotions, I suggest, are *irreducible* to any one domain or discourse. Emergent human compounds, located at the intersection of biology and society, they involve a complex mixture of physiological correlates/substrates, lived bodily feelings, experiences and expressions, as well as cognitive appraisals/antecedents[7]. Factors which, in turn, are linked to on-going relational practices of a socio-cultural kind, (including 'emotion talk' (Heelas 1986) itself). Whilst basic, so-called 'primary' emotions are doubtless involved here – rooted in our evolutionary biological make-up and shared amongst all human beings qua embodied agents – they are endlessly elaborated, like colours on a painter's palette, across time and place, history and culture, including fundamental social processes of differentiation and socialisation, management and change (Gordon 1990).

Emotions, from this perspective, display a 'deep sociality' (Wentworth and Yardley 1994), forged within a social habitus (*cf.* Bourdieu 1984, Mauss 1973), which is at once both communicative and embodied (*cf.* Merleau-Ponty 1962). Consciousness and intentionality however, as existential phenomenologists such as Merleau-Ponty (1962) remind us, need not necessarily entail self-awareness as such. It is possible, for example, to be angry, sad or jealous without being self-consciously aware of it – at least that is until others draw it to our attention. Nor does this preclude the possibility of other (unconscious) elements of human motivation and desire: dimensions, returning to former conventional or orthodox viewpoints discussed above, which display a continual 'resilience' in the face of rational attempts at (emotion) management and control (*cf.* Hochschild 1983). Emotions, as lay discourses show, are 'fluid', rather than 'static' (Lupton 1998), including a series of literal and metaphorical associations with notions of 'heat', 'pressure' and the like (Lakoff 1987, Johnson 1987).

Viewing emotions in this way enables us to grapple with the seemingly problematic fact that whilst, in some sense, they always have a social or worldly referent – even, as Freud's classic case-studies reveal, when repressed or unconscious – they also appear, at times at least, to possess a peculiar 'life of their own', including: 'feelings we cannot express to our satisfaction'; feelings we can 'express but that others find difficult to understand'; and, perhaps most importantly of all, the 'regular experiencing of contradictions between our thoughts and our feelings' (Craib 1995: 153). The place of emotions in the explanation of human behaviour, as this suggests, is both complex and contradictory. This should not however, to re-emphasise, blind us to the fact that a world without emotions is no world at all. Rational or irrational, pathological or healthy, emotions provide our individual and collective lives with purpose and direction, contributing both to order and chaos, stability and change. To focus simply on their 'subversive' potential therefore is to confuse part for whole; perpetuating the dominant (*i.e.* orthodox) Western viewpoint referred to above.

The emphasis here, as this suggests, is on the active, emotionally 'expressive' body, in sickness and in health, as the basis of self, sociality, meaning and order, set within the socio-cultural realms of everyday life and the ritualised forms of interaction and exchange they involve. The interactive, *relational* character of lived emotional experience and expression (Burkitt 1997, 1998), in turn, offers us a way of moving 'beyond' micro-analytic, subjective, internal or individualistic analyses towards more 'open-ended horizons' in which embodied agency, as the existential basis of culture and self (Csordas 1994), can itself be understood not merely as 'individual' but also 'institution-making' (Csordas 1994: 14, Lyon and Barbalet 1994). It is to these latter connections and linkages that I now turn.

Micro-macro relations

From classic sociological concepts such as alienation (*cf.* Marx) and anomie (*cf.* Durkheim), to Scheff's (1990a,b, 1994) account of pride, shame and the 'social bond'; and from Hochschild (1983) and Flam's (1990a,b, 1993) deliberations on corporate actors/emotion management, to Kemper's (1990) structural analysis of emotions and social relations and Collins' (1975, 1981, 1990) analysis of stratification, emotional energy, and the transient emotions, a rich seam of emotional insights are there to be mined concerning these micro-macro links. What emerges from this literature, as Barbalet's (1998) perceptive analysis of class and resentment reveals, is a view of emotions as inhering simultaneously in individual experience and the social structures and relationships within which individuals are embedded. Emotion that is ritually based or not connects 'different phases of social structure through time' (Barbalet 1998: 65). In these and other respects moreover, their socially *constituted*, as opposed to socially *constructed*, character should not be confused: the latter (qua discourse) is merely a part of the former.

A potentially useful concept here, as I have argued elsewhere, is the Bourdieuesque notion of 'emotional capital' (Williams 1998). 'Emotional capital' is a concept which readily translates notions of 'emotional energy' (*cf.* Collins 1990) into a more thorough-going socio-economic frame of reference (*i.e.* the 'social patterning' or distribution emotions according to key features of social structure)[8]. From this viewpoint, accumulations of positive and negative emotional experiences, including feelings of pride and shame, mesh more or less closely with broader patterns of structured social (dis)advantage, power, status and prestige across historical time and space. It also captures the underlying link between the habitus (Bourdieu 1984), body techniques (Mauss 1973 [1934]) and more general struggles for social distinction in the criss-crossing fields which together constitute society. This in turn, suggests some interesting linkages between the social inequalities and life-events literature, particularly in terms of current 'mental' health debates. This, of course, is not the end of the matter, for emotions, as we have seen, appear at times to possess a 'peculiar life of their own'. Here we return to the Janus-faced nature of emotions as both structure and process, stability and flux. Emotions, as these and other observations suggest, are never simply structured 'things' or static properties. They also, perhaps most importantly, possess a social efficacy (Barbalet 1998) and dynamic (if not 'transgressive') potential in their own right – one which is never entirely a 'gift' or product of society.

The crucial issue here for our purposes, taking Freund (1990, 1998) as our lead, is that differing modes of emotional being – physical and psychic states which can be either 'pleasant' or 'unpleasant' (Buytendijk 1950) – are, in effect, different felt ways of feeling empowered or disempowered: feelings which are very much linked to people's material and psychosocial conditions of existence throughout their embodied biographies. More precisely, a person's social position and status will determine the resources they have at their disposal in order to define and protect – through 'status shields' (*cf.* Hochschild 1983) and various other means – the boundaries of the self, and to counter the potential for invalidation by powerful and significant others. An extremely powerless social status, for instance, 'increases the likelihood of experiencing "unpleasant" emotionality or emotional modes of being' (Freund 1990: 466). Less powerful people, therefore, face a 'structurally in built handicap' in managing social and emotional information; one which, in turn, may contribute to existential fear, anxiety and neuro-physiological perturbation of many different sorts (1990: 466). Here Freund poses two extremely important questions: first, 'how "deep" can the social construction of feelings go?', and secondly, 'can emotion work eliminate the responses of an unconsciously knowing body?' The implications of his argument – including notions of 'dramaturgical stress' (*cf.* Goffman 1959) and the 'ontologically insecure self' (*cf.* Laing 1965) – seem to suggest that society affects us, both emotionally and physically, deep within the recesses of the human body although, as the concept of 'schizokinesis' implies (Kelly 1980), the 'mind', consciously at least, may be unaware of the 'body's' response.

Certainly there is plenty of evidence to support these contentions, including a growing life-events and illness literature (*e.g.* Brown and Harris

1978, 1989). This, coupled with other recent research within the inequalities paradigm on the 'psychosocial pathways' to disease (Wilkinson 1996) – pathways in which the salubrious/deleterious effects of 'social relativities' loom large – suggests some promising new links between the field of 'mental' health and illness and the sociology of emotions. Emotions, to repeat, whilst never entirely a 'gift' from society, inhere simultaneously in structured social relations and actions, elaborated over time. They also, as mentioned earlier, possess a socially constituted vis-a-vis social constructed character (Greenwood 1994): one in keeping with realist principles of 'stratification' and 'emergence' (Bhaskar 1989, Archer *et al.* 1998, Archer 1995). 'Mental' health and illness from this perspective – given former 'social product' versus 'social construct' debates (Busfield 1988) – are part and parcel of the dialectical interplay between 'personal troubles' and broader 'public issues of social structure' (*cf.* Mills 1959). A 'deep' sociological relationship elaborated across time and forged through emotions qua embodied modes of praxis. Emotional health and well-being, in short, like mental illness itself, is intimately linked to our socially structured conditions of existence, including the positive as well as negative effects of social hierarchies and relativities. In these and other respects, as this and the following section suggest, things could indeed be 'otherwise'.

Medicalisation-demedicalisation

A crucial issue, underpinning much of the discussion so far, has been the now familiar debates over the 'medicalisation-de-medicalisation' of society. It is not my intention to rehearse these again here, nor the problems of sociological as well as medical 'imperialism' they raise (Strong 1979)[9]. Suffice to say that what we are currently witnessing, trends and counter-trends notwithstanding, are creeping forms of 'mental disorder', including a range of supposedly 'dysthymic' emotional states, which lend themselves in various ways to 'professional help' in one form or another. The boundaries of the category of 'depression' for example, as Lyon comments, continue to expand, as does the:

> ...list of other types of 'disorders' for which Prozac is prescribed. According to some commentators, Prozac is commonly prescribed for persons who do not at all fit the criteria of depression, but who are labelled as 'dysthymic' or even 'sub or borderline dysthymic' (*i.e.* emotion 'inappropriate' to the circumstances) (1996: 61).

To these 'cosmetic' forms of 'psychopharmacology' and the 'chemically assisted' selves they promote (Lyon 1996) we may add the broader array of so-called 'psy therapies' which currently litter the field. From self-help books to agony aunts, counsellors and psychotherapists to celebrity status doctors and holistic healers, we are increasingly advised and instructed, encouraged and cajoled, on how best to manage ourselves and ride the emotional waves of everyday life, both at home and in the workplace. As Hochschild comments:

> While the counsel of parents, grandparents, aunts and uncles, ministers, priests and rabbis holds relatively less weight than it would have a century ago, that of professional therapists, television talk show hosts, radio commentators, video producers, magazine and advice book authors assumes relatively more weight (1994: 2).

Not only have the number of so-called experts in the field mushroomed in recent years, but lay people themselves are increasingly coming to frame their problems in '(proto)-professional' terms (de Swaan 1990). Authors of advice books, for example, like other commercially-based advice-givers, act as 'emotional investment counsellors', recommending 'how much, and in whom, to "invest" emotional attention' (Hochschild 1994: 2). Others, however, pitch their message much wider, extending far beyond the realms of personal relationships to success, via notions such as *Emotional Intelligence*, in all walks of life (Goleman 1996).

In this and countless other ways the individual, as Rose (1990) observes, is not some 'isolated automaton' to be dominated and controlled by others. Rather s/he is a 'free citizen', endowed with personal desires and enmeshed, for better or worse, in a dynamic network of relations with others: a 'therapeutic culture of self', including expert-led techniques of 'self-inspection and self-rectification', which 'measures the psyche' with ever increasing precision. It is in the space opened up *between* the imposition of controls upon conduct by public powers and the forms of life adopted by each individual that the:

> ...vocabularies and techniques of these psycho-sciences operate...These technologies for the *government of the soul* operate not through the crushing of subjectivity in the interests of control and profit, but by seeking to align political, social and institutional goals with individual pleasures and desires, and with the happiness and fulfilment of the self. Their power lies in the capacity to offer means by which *regulation of selves* – by others and by ourselves – can be made consonant with contemporary political principles, moral ideals and constitutional exigencies. They are, precisely, *therapies of freedom* (1990: 257, my emphasis).

Within these therapies, Craib (1994) notes, a strong emphasis is placed on the achievement (if not maximisation) of personal 'happiness' and 'fulfilment', whatever that means, through processes of 'self-discovery', 'self-assessment' and 'self-actualisation'. The public face of psychotherapy and counselling, in this sense – itself an index of more thorough-going processes of social reflexivity in late modernity (Giddens 1990, 1991) – is a comforting, understanding one, enabling people more generally to 'find themselves, take responsibility for themselves and satisfy their needs' (Craib 1994: 6). In doing so however, psychotherapy itself becomes caught up in the very ideology of late modernity which, from client to client, it is called upon to disentangle – one based on powerful illusions of 'personal growth' and 'fulfilment' which are never quite 'achievable'. As Craib (with his psychotherapist's hat on) states:

> The cultural pressures, often normal pressures which have to do with wanting to help people, to ease suffering, to be effective, to be good at our jobs, make us vulnerable to the denial of the necessity and inevitability of certain forms of human suffering. We set out to cure and we construct blueprints of what people ought to be feeling, ought to be like, and we can too easily set about trying to manipulate or even force people into these blueprints (1994: 8).

It is important therefore, given these late-modernist imperatives, to emphasise the 'negative' message(s) of psychoanalytic theory. Predicated as it is on the fatal 'flaws' of the human condition, psychoanalysis cannot, Craib argues, be offered as a guide to 'the good life', nor as a 'cure' that is bound to work. There are no guarantees or miracle cures, it takes a long time, and if it is to work, invariably involves some painful, anxiety-provoking moments: a process in which notions of happiness and personal fulfilment may indeed seem little more than ideological ideals, late modernist or otherwise (1994: 190). A central paradox therefore emerges. In order to protect the values threatened by the changes we are currently living through, psychoanalysis may have to reject its popularity, so to speak, 'holding on' to the very 'principles for which it is so often criticised' (1994: 192)[10]. More broadly what this suggests, given current debates over 'mental' health, is that far from being 'unhealthy' or 'pathological', it is indeed quite normal if not healthy to feel dissatisfied, disillusioned or even downright depressed at times; not simply due to prevailing ideologies of happiness and personal fulfilment, but also because of the embodied dilemmas and existential predicaments we all, qua human beings, inevitably face. We must not, in other words, confuse or equate issues of emotional health with happiness and wellbeing. Emotional health, in this sense, may indeed run the gamut of emotions, including those currently deemed 'treatable' by whatever means.

Whether, in short, through a 'designer chemical self' or a lengthy dose of talking-therapy, ours is an age in which we are seduced, via myths of (unfulfilled) 'happiness' and the 'good life', into thinking that our emotional lives are somehow faulty, deficient or lacking, or that something is wrong with us if we feel disappointed or dissatisfied with our lot in life. In certain cases, of course, this may well be unwarranted, if not unreasonable or pathological. In many other instances, however, it is not: it is an authentic existential marker and entirely realistic assessment of our feelings in an alienating, 'runaway world' of 'manufactured risks' and uncertainties (Giddens 1994). More generally what it testifies to, returning to Crossley's (1998) previous Habermasian arguments, is a 'colonisation' of the lifeworld and the 'communicatively rational' claims upon which it rests, by other more system-oriented concerns and forms of expertise. A situation, in the current biopsychiatric era of Prozac and other powerful mind-altering drugs (*cf.* Huxley's 1982/[1932]) *Brave New World*) in which a pragmatics of human understanding, including understandable unhappiness, gives way to the push for an endlessly 'happy meal' – a 'McDonaldized' (Ritzer 1995, 1997) recipe dished out to the masses in handy 'bite-sized chunks' (Mĕstrović 1997). The resilience of emotions within such contexts to rational management and control (*i.e.* the recalcitrant language of the '(un)managed heart' (Hochschild 1983)) is both healthy and reasonable: an 'authentic' response or critical mode of resistance (Smart 1999), if ever truly possible, in an inauthentic or postemotional age (Mĕstrović 1997).

Discussion and concluding remarks

Let me take this opportunity to recap here on some of the central arguments of the chapter as a whole. Emotions, I have argued, in shifting the focus somewhat, are central to 'mental' health as well as illness, just as they are to reason itself in its manifold guises. Janus-faced to be sure, both order and chaos, stability and flux, emotions (whilst never simply a 'gift' or product of society) are the sine qua non of social life. The enchanting glue that binds us together (Maffesoli 1995); the animating principle in all sociality (*cf.* Simmel 1971); the well-spring of human ethics and morality; the fountain of Durkheimian 'collective effervescence' and the font of 'bloody revenge' (Mellor and Shilling 1997). Taking this line has enabled us to tackle a number of associated conceptual problems and debates along the way, including the persistent division between reason and emotion, the biological and the social – itself exacerbated through current developments in biopsychiatry and the new genetics on the one hand, and the constructionist/linguistic turn on the other – the micro and the macro, alongside current debates over the medicalisation-demedicalisation of society.

To continue to co-opt consideration of emotions, in large part, within the framework of mental illness and the irrational is, therefore, to neglect their key role in the *health* and wellbeing of individuals and society more generally; including issues of social cohesion, integration and solidarity. It is also, to repeat, to downplay the crucial role of emotions in reason and rationality itself, however defined, confusing part (*i.e.* their potentially 'subversive' potential) for whole, and perpetuating dominant Western views (themselves 'unreasonable') along the way. Emotions, as the critical and radical viewpoints discussed earlier suggest, are no mere intruders into the bastion of (male) reason and (instrumental) rationality. They are instead central to its very constitution as well as its a/effective deployment. Key ways forward, in this respect, include a more explicit focus on the 'mindful', emotionally 'expressive' body (Schepper-Hughes and Lock 1987, Freund 1990), in sickness *and in health*, as the existential basis of culture and self (Csordas 1994), together with a defence of the 'communicatively rational' (*i.e.* intersubjective, intercorporeal) claims of the lifeworld vis-a-vis the system-oriented imperatives and 'colonising' ambitions of expert attempts at containment, prediction and control (*i.e.* medicalisation) – processes aided and abetted by powerful new genetic and biochemical 'fixes' or 'technologies of self'. Within all this is a call to: (i) rethink and re-embody reason in other less 'unreasonable' terms; (ii) reinsert emotions more positively into current sociological debates on health and social life; (iii) critically question prevailing ideologies and expert-led discourses of personal growth, fulfilment and happiness as themselves (all too often) 'unhealthy', promoting rather than mitigating our discontent. The paradox, that is to say, that prevailing discourses of happiness and the good life themselves breed unhappiness; feelings, in many cases, which are (entirely) reasonable if not healthy. In these and other ways my call has been to bring emotions 'back in', so to speak, to current debates over health and reason – including the all too easy equation of emotional health with happiness and wellbeing – freeing them along the way from the strait-jacket of both irrationality and pathology.

More broadly what this suggests, is some promising new linkages, not simply between the sociology of so-called 'mental' health and the sociology of emotions, but also to a more emotionally-founded, if not passionate, sociology in general (Game and Metcalfe 1996): a sociology, contra rationalist 'myths' of dispassionate or disembodied enquiry, which takes the embodiment of its practitioners as well as those it seeks to study seriously. As a reflexive social discipline/discipline of the social, a passionate sociology:

> ...celebrates an *immersion in life, a compassionate involvement with the world and with others*...An engaged or passionate sociology involves *a sensual, full-bodied approach to knowing and to practices of knowledge* such as reading, writing, teaching...passion, social life and sociology only exist in the in-between, in specific, moving social *relations* (1996: 5, my emphasis).

Not only would this serve to 're-animate' the sociological imagination (*cf.* Mills 1959), breathing new emotional life into its classically rationalist bones, it may also help to dispel, once and for all, the 'irrational passion for dispassionate rationality' to which we all, at times, pay homage. In these and other ways, the sociology of 'mental' health, alongside the sociology of emotions, has much to contribute.

Let me conclude, however, on a somewhat more critical note; one, as the sub-title of this chapter suggests, which may sit uneasily alongside some of the other contributions within this issue. If as I have argued, we need a *full bodied*, if not sensual or passionate, approach to emotions in social life – one which no longer falls into irrational traps, pathological ruses or mind/body divides – then the very notion of a sociology *of* 'mental' health becomes something of a contradiction in terms. By this I mean it perpetuates rather than slips the very divisions which, throughout this chapter, we have been trying to escape; particularly the mind/body divide. Moreover, like the sociology *of* the body, it creates yet further subject-object divides in which we (qua disembodied, objective?) sociologists reflect on the minds, bodies and feelings of those we seek to study, carving the world up (again) into neat and tidy analytic categories and divisions of labour. My call, in this sense – one very much in keeping with the principles of a passionate, embodied sociology outlined above – would be to rethink these issues more in terms of emotional health, itself a fully embodied phenomenon, than a sociology of 'mental' health. Appeals to emotional health, echoing the above points, help: (i) avoid the somewhat 'medicalised' ring of mental health, restoring emotions to the meaningful, intersubjective, intercorporeal domains of everyday life and communicative praxes; (ii) put minds back into bodies, bodies back into society and society back into the body, and (iii) bring emotions to the fore in *all* discussions of health, including the 'afflictions' of inequality. Herein lies my reason throughout this chapter of putting the mental in quotes: a Cartesian deception to be sure which notions such as the 'mindful' (Schepper-Hughes and Lock 1987), emotionally 'expressive' body (Freund 1990) effectively lay to rest once and for all (see also Johnson 1987). We should also of course, in taking up this call, resist the all too easy equation of issues of emotional health with prevailing notions of happiness and wellbeing. For some this may seem an attractive, if not compelling option. For others, no doubt a hopeless ideal, based on yet another unworkable theoretical proposition. At the very least I suggest, in the spirit of reflexive inquiry, it demands a critical engagement with the constraints as well as opportunities which a sociology of 'mental' health affords: not simply for practitioners but for those it seeks to study. The danger or risk in not doing so is that the sociology of 'mental' health becomes yet another 'strait-jacket', wittingly or otherwise, in keeping with two centuries of 'unreasonable' Western thought and practice. Let us hope not.

Notes

1   The sociology of emotions is a burgeoning new area of study. See, for example, Williams (2000), Bendelow and Williams (1998), Williams and Bendelow (1998)

and Barbalet (1998) for recent discussions of the nature and status of this field, including current lines of development and debate. See also James and Gabe (1996) for other applications to health.

2   For other interesting discussions of these and related matters, see Radden (1985) and Edwards (1981): the latter focusing more specifically on issues of 'mental health *as* rational autonomy'.

3   Health, for Parsons, involves the 'teleonmic' capacity of an organism, or its 'propensity', to successfully undertake 'goal oriented' actions – see, Frank (1991) for a useful reconstruction of the Parsonian 'health' as opposed to the 'sick role'. A component of 'mental illness' in contrast, as Gerhardt points out, is a characteristic of every (Parsonian) illness, since 'sick people' are in various ways 'emotionally disturbed' (1979: 232). Illnesses, in short, may be conceptualised on a 'continuum' between the most completely 'mental of mental illnesses', through various 'psychosomatic' conditions to the category of 'completely somatic' (1979: 232).

4   Even within the rationalist tradition itself, however, the division between reason and emotion has never in fact been absolute. Plato, for example, compared reason to a 'charioteer' and emotions to galloping horses. Without the galloping horses, however, the skill of the charioteer, he noted, would be 'worthless' (Jaggar 1989). Aristotle and Spinoza, likewise, accorded emotions more than a peripheral role in their respective rationalist philosophies: emotions helping clarify and understand, both morally and spiritually, our place in the world and relationship to others. The 'potentialities of human emotions that are in us', Aristotle proclaimed in the *Poetics*, 'give delight in moderation, are satisfied and purified by this means, are stopped by persuasion and not by force'. For Weber too, the rational and the irrational were maintained through 'creative activity'; something, he believed, which could result in one 'intensifying the other'.

5   Hume, in many ways, takes a far more 'critical' approach here. 'Passions', he proclaimed, 'direct the will, and reason serves the passions' (1969/[1739/40]: 462). Reason, from this 'counter' viewpoint, is well and truly the 'slave' of the passions. Again however, what this amounts to, in common parlance, is the notion that emotion, qua passion, drives or directs reason, and that without passion reason is lost. Hume, moreover, raises a further possibility, one which feeds directly into the next convergent/radical viewpoint. In differentiating between so-called 'calm' and 'violent' passions – associating Reason more with the former than the latter through the 'tranquil actions of the mind' – he points to a view in which emotion, qua passion, does not simply 'drive' or 'direct' but, in an important sense, constitutes Reason (properly understood) itself. 'Control', in other words, contrary to conventional viewpoints, is exercised not strictly by reason – as 'improperly' understood – but by a 'calm and reflective form of passion – an enlightened self-interest' with gendered (*i.e.* 'masculine') connotations (Lloyd 1993: 55).

6   The notion of 'mental disorder', Busfield states, 'embodies (sic) a clear dualism of mind and body', one which, whilst widely contested, remains a 'fundamental feature of medicine and lay discourse' (1996: 54): on the latter see Lupton's (1998) recent study. Even Laing (1960) it seems, ends up endorsing this position: associating (severe) mental illness, through the agency of 'ontological insecurity', with the patently 'false', yet deceptively 'real', feelings of the 'unembodied' self.

7   The role of cognition in emotion can be traced back to Aristotle. Cognition, for example, may 'trigger' an emotion. Emotion, in contrast, may 'influence' a cognition. A cognition may also have emotion as its intentional or propositional 'object'. See for example, Elster (1999), and the Lazarus (1984, Lazarus and Lazarus 1984)–Zajonc (1984) debate.

8   The argument here is for an approach which emphasises the patterning or distribution of emotions in more or less enduring ways throughout the social order, and the links this provides with associated Bourdieuesque notions of the habitus and body-techniques: those enduring socio-cultural dispositions and 'unchosen principles of choice' (Williams 1995). In these and other ways, appeals to notions of emotional 'capital' should not be confused with more instrumentally oriented approaches such as those associated with rational choice theory (RCT).

9   In some cases, as Busfield notes, 'problems widely recognised, but not viewed as mental or health matters, come to be viewed as *"medicalized"* – that is they come to be subject to the medical gaze. In other cases, such as neurasthenia and hysteria, conditions virtually *disappear* from the psychiatric lexicon and are *declassified*; in yet others one medical problem is *transformed* into another, both being seen as suitable for professional attention' (1996: 56).

10 For other feminist critiques of psychotherapy and associated forms of psychological and psychiatric intervention see Showalter (1987) and Ussher (1991) – both of whom champion women's own voices and experiences in patriarchal society and misogynist culture, past and present. See also Horgan (1999) for a more general critique of the 'ineffectiveness' of all these interventions to date.

References

Archer, M., Bhaskar, R., Collier, A., Lawson, A. and Norrie, A. (1998) *Critical Realism: Essential Readings*. London: Routledge.

Archer, M. (1995) *Realist Social Theory: the Morphogenetic Approach*. Cambridge: Cambridge University Press.

Aristotle (1968) *Poetics* (transl. by Janko, R.). Indianapolis/Cambridge: Hackett Publishing Company.

Barbalet, J. (1998) *Emotion, Social Theory and Social Structure*. Cambridge: University Press.

Barbalet, J. (1999) William James's theory of emotions: filling in the picture. *Journal for the Theory of Social Behaviour*, 29, 3, 251–66.

Bendelow, G. and Williams, S.J. (eds) (1998) *Emotions in Social Life: Critical Themes and Contemporary Issues*. London: Sage.

Benton, T. (1991) Biology and social science: why the return of the repressed should be given a (cautious) welcome. *Sociology*, 25, 1, 1–29.

Bhaskar, R. (1989) *Reclaiming Reality*. London: Verso.

Birke, L. (1999) *Feminism and the Biological Body*. Edinburgh: Edinburgh University Press.

Bourdieu, P. (1984) *Distinction: a Social Critique of the Judgement of Taste*. London: Routledge.

Brown, G.W. and Harris, T.O. (1978) *The Social Origins of Depression: a Study of Psychiatric Disorder in Women*. London: Tavistock.

Brown, G.W. and Harris, T.O. (eds) (1989) *Life Events and Illness*. London: Hyman Unwin.

Burkitt, I. (1997) Social relationships and emotions, *Sociology*, 31, 1, 37–55.

Burkitt, I. (1998) Bodies of knowledge: beyond Cartesian views of persons, selves and minds, *Journal for the Theory of Social Behaviour*, 28, 1, 63–82.

Busfield, J. (1988) Mental illness as social product or social construct: a contradiction in feminists' arguments, *Sociology of Health and Illness*, 10, 521–42.

Busfield, J. (1996) *Men, Women and Madness: Understanding Gender and Mental Disorder*. London: Macmillan.

Buytendijk, F.J.J. (1950) The phenomenological approach to the problem of feelings and emotions. In Reymert, M.C. (ed) *Feelings and Emotions: the Mooseheart Symposium in Cooperation with the University of Chicago*. New York: McGraw Hill Company Inc.

Collins, R. (1975) *Conflict Sociology: Towards an Explanatory Science*. New York: Academic Press.

Collins, R. (1981) On the micro-foundations of macro-sociology, *American Journal of Sociology*, 86, 984–1014.

Collins, R. (1990) Stratification, emotional energy, and the transient emotions. In Kemper, T.J. (ed) *Research Agendas in the Sociology of Emotions*. New York: State University of New York Press.

Craib, I. (1988) *Psychoanalysis and Social Theory: the Limits of Sociology*. London: Harvester Wheatsheaf.

Craib, I. (1994) *The Importance of Disappointment*. London: Routledge.

Crossley, N. (1998) Emotions and communicative action. In Bendelow, G. and Williams, S.J. (eds) *Emotions in Social Life: Critical Themes and Contemporary Issues*. London: Routledge.

Csordas, T.J. (1994) Introduction: the body as representation and being-in-the-world. In Csordas, T.J. (ed) *Embodiment and Experience: the Existential Ground of Culture and Self*. Cambridge: Cambridge University Press.

Damasio, D. (1994) *Descartes' Error: Emotion, Reason and the Human Brain*. New York: Putnam.

de Sousa, R. (1990) *The Rationality of Emotion*. Cambridge, MA: MIT Press.

de Swaan, A. (1990) *The Management of Normality: Critical Essays in Health and Welfare*. London: Routledge.

Edwards, R. (1981) Mental health as rational autonomy, *The Journal of Medicine and Philosophy*, 6, 309–22.

Elster, J. (1999) *Alchemies of the Mind: Rationality and the Emotions*. Cambridge: Cambridge University Press.

Flam, H. (1990a) '"Emotional Man"': the emotional 'man' and the problem of collective action, *International Sociology*, 5, 1, 39–56.

Flam, H. (1990b) 'Emotional "Man"': corporate actors as emotion-motivated emotion managers, *International Sociology*, 5, 2, 225–34.

Flam, H. (1993) Fear, loyalty and greedy organizations. In Fineman, S. (ed) *Emotion in Organizations*. London: Sage.

Foucault, M. (1971) *Madness and Civilization*. London: Tavistock.

Frank, A.W. (1991) From sick role to health role: deconstructing Parsons. In Robertson, R. and Turner, B.S. (eds) *Parsons: Theorist of Modernity*. London: Sage.

Freund, P.E.S. (1990) The expressive body: a common ground for the sociology of emotions and health and illness, *Sociology of Health and Illness*, 12, 4, 452–77.

Freund, P.E.S. (1998) Social performances and their discontents: reflections on the biosocial psychology of role-playing. In Bendelow, G. and Williams, S.J. (eds) *Emotions in Social Life: Critical Themes and Contemporary Issues*. London: Routledge.

Game, A. and Metcalfe, A. (1996) *Passionate Sociology*. London: Sage.

Gerhardt, U. (1979) The Parsonian paradigm and the identity of medical sociology, *Sociological Review*, 27, 2, 229–51.

Gerhardt, U. (1989) *Ideas about Illness: an Intellectual and Political History of Medical Sociology*. London: Macmillan.

Giddens, A. (1990) *The Consequences of Modernity*. Cambridge: Polity Press.

Giddens, A. (1991) *Modernity and Self-Identity: Self and Society in the Late Modern Age*. Cambridge: Polity Press.

Giddens, A. (1994) *Beyond Left and Right*. Cambridge: Polity Press.

Goffman, E. (1959) *The Presentation of Self in Everyday Life*. New York: Doubleday.

Goffman, E. (1961) *Asylums: Essays on the Social Situation of Mental Patients and Other Inmates*. New York: Doubleday Anchor.

Goleman, D. (1996) *Emotional Intelligence: Why it can Matter more than IQ*. London: Bloomsbury.

Gordon, S. (1990) Social structural effects on emotions. In Kemper, T. (ed) *Research Agendas in the Sociology of Emotions*. New York: State University of New York Press.

Greenwood, J.D. (1994) *Realism, Identity and Emotion: Reclaiming Social Psychology*. London: Sage.

Habermas, J. (1986) *The Theory of Communicative Action, Vol. 1. Reason and the Rationalisation of Society* (transl. McCarthy, T.). Cambridge: Polity Press.

Habermas, J. (1987a) *The Theory of Communicative Action, Vol. II: Lifeworld and System: a Critique of Functional Reason* (transl. McCarthy, T). Cambridge: Polity Press.

Habermas, J. (1987b) *Knowledge and Human Interests*. Cambridge: Polity Press.

Harré, R. (ed) (1986) *The Social Construction of Emotions*. Oxford: Basil Blackwell.

Heelas, P. (1986) Emotion talk across cultures. In Harré, R. (ed) *The Social Construction of Emotions*. Oxford: Basil Blackwell.

Heller, A. (1990) *Can Modernity Survive?* Cambridge: Polity Press.

Hochschild, A.R. (1983) *The Managed Heart: the Commercialisation of Human Feeling*. Berkeley CA: University of California Press.

Hochschild, A.R. (1994) The commercial spirit of intimate life and the abduction of feminism: signs from women's advice books, *Theory, Culture and Society*, 11, 1–24.

Horgan, J. (1999) *Undiscovered Minds: How the Brain Defies Explanation*. London: Weidenfeld and Nicolson.

Hume, D. (1969/[1739/40]) *A Treatise of Human Nature*. Harmondsworth: Penguin.

Huxley, A. (1982/[1932]) *Brave New World*. Essex: Longman Group Ltd.

Ingleby, D. (ed) (1981) *Critical Psychiatry*. Harmondsworth: Penguin.

Jaggar, A. (1989) Love and knowledge: emotion in feminist epistemology. In Bordo, S. and Jaggar, A. (eds) *Gender/Body/Knowledge: Feminist Reconstructions of Being and Knowing*. New Brunswick/London: Rutgers University Press.

James, O. (1998) *Britain on the Couch: Why We're Unhappier than We Were in the 1950s – Despite Being Richer*. London: Arrow.

James, V. and Gabe, J. (eds) (1996) *Health and the Sociology of Emotions*. Oxford: Blackwell.

James, W. (1884) What is an emotion? *Mind*, 9, 188–205.

James, W. (1950/[1890]) *Principles of Psychology*. New York: Dover Publications.

James, W. (1956/[1897]) The sentiment of rationality. In *The Will to Believe and Other Essays in Popular Philosophy*. New York: Dover Publications.

Johnson, M. (1987) *The Body in the Mind*. Chicago: University of Chicago Press.

Kelly, D. (1980) *Anxiety and Emotions*. Springfield Ill: Charles C. Thomas Publishers.

Kelly, M. and Field, D. (1994) Comments on the rejection of the biomedical in sociological discourse, *Medical Sociology News*, 19, 2, 34–7.

Kemper, T.D. (1990) Social relations and emotions: a structural approach. In Kemper T.D. (ed), *Research Agendas in the Sociology of Emotions*. New York: State University of New York Press.

Laing, R.D. (1965) *The Divided Self*. Harmondsworth: Penguin.

Lakoff, G. (1987) *Women, Fire and Dangerous Things*. Chicago: University of Chicago Press.

Lazarus, R. (1984) Thoughts on the relations between emotion and cognition (Reprinted). In Scherer, K.R. and Ekman, P. (eds) *Approaches to Emotion*. Hillsdale, New Jersey and London: Lawrence Erlbaum Associates, Publishers.

Lazarus, R. and Lazarus, B.N. (1994) *Passion and Reason: Making Sense of our Emotions*. New York: Oxford University Press.

Lloyd, G. (1993) *The Man of Reason: 'Male' and 'Female' in Western Philosophy*. London: Methuen.

Lupton, D. (1998) *The Emotional Self*. London: Sage.

Lyon, M. (1996) C. Wright Mills meets Prozac: the relevance of 'social emotion' to the sociology of health and illness. In James, V. and Gabe, J. (eds) *Health and the Sociology of Emotions*. Oxford: Blackwell.

Lyon, M. and Barbalet, J. (1994) Society's body: emotion and the 'somatization' of social theory. In Csordas, T.J. (ed) *Embodiment and Experience: the Existential Ground of Culture and Self*. Cambridge: Cambridge University Press.

Maffesoli, M. (1995) *Time of the Tribes*. London: Sage.

Mauss, M. (1973/[1934]) Techniques of the body, *Economy and Society*, 2, 70 88.

Merleau-Ponty, M. (1962) *The Phenomenology of Perception*. London: Routledge and Kegan Paul.

Mĕstrović, S.G. (1997) *Postemotional Society*. London: Sage.

Mellor, P. and Shilling, C. (1997) *Re-Forming the Body*. London: Sage.

Mills, C. Wright (1959) *The Sociological Imagination*. New York: Oxford University Press.

Parsons, T. (1951) *The Social System*. London: Routledge and Kegan Paul.

Pilgrim, D. and Rogers, A. (1999) A sociology of mental health and illness: developing an agenda or taking stock? *Medical Sociology News*, 25, 2, 41–3.

Radden, J. (1985) *Madness and Reason*. London: George Allen and Unwin.

Ritzer, G. (1995) *The McDonaldization of Society: An Investigation into the Changing Character of Contemporary Social Life*. London: Sage.

Ritzer, G. (1997) *The McDonaldization Thesis: Explorations and Extensions*. London: Sage.

Rose, H. (1994) *Love, Power and Knowledge: Towards a Feminist Transformation of the Sciences.* Cambridge: Polity Press.

Rose, N. (1990) *Governing the Soul: the Shaping of the Private Self.* London: Routledge.

Rose, S. (1997) *Lifelines.* Harmondsworth: Penguin.

Sartre, J.P. (1971/[1939]) *Sketch for a Theory of the Emotions* (transl. Mairet, P. with Preface by Warnock, M.). London: Methuen and Co. Ltd.

Scheff, T.J. (1966) *Being Mentally Ill.* London: Weidenfeld and Nicolson.

Scheff, T.J. (1990a) Socialization of emotions: pride and shame as causal agents. In Kemper, T.D. (ed) *Research Agendas in the Sociology of Emotions.* New York: State University of New York Press.

Scheff, T.J. (1990b) *Microsociology: Discourse, Emotion and Social Structure.* Chicago and London: University of Chicago Press.

Scheff, T.J. (1994) *Bloody Revenge: Emotions, Nationalism and War.* Boulder, Colorado and Oxford: Westview Press.

Scheper-Hughes, N. and Lock, M. (1987) The mindful body: a prolegemonon to future work in medical anthropology, *Medical Anthropology Quarterly*, 1, 1, 6–41.

Sedgwick, P. (1982) *Psychopolitics.* London: Pluto Press.

Seidler, V. (1994) *Unreasonable Men: Masculinity and Social Theory.* London: Routledge.

Seidler, V. (1998) Masculinity, violence and emotional life. In Bendelow, G. and Williams, S.J. (eds) *Emotions in Social Life: Critical Themes and Contemporary Issues.* London: Routledge.

Showalter, E. (1987) *The Female Malady.* London: Virago.

Simmel, G. (1971) *On Individuality and Social Forms (Selected Writings)* (Edited with an Introduction by Levine, D.N.). Chicago/London: University of Chicago Press.

Smart, B. (ed) (1999) *Resisting McDonaldization.* London: Sage.

Strong, P. (1979) Sociological imperialism and the profession of medicine: a critical examination of the thesis of medical imperialism, *Social Science and Medicine*, 13A, 199–215.

Taylor, C. (1989) *Sources of the Self: the Making of Modern Identity.* Cambridge: Cambridge University Press.

Ussher, J. (1991) *Women's Madness: Misogyny or Mental Illness?* London: Harvester Wheatsheaf.

Wentworth, W.M. and Yardley, D. (1994) Deep sociality: a bioevolutionary perspective on the sociology of emotions. In Wentworth, W.M. and Ryan, J. (eds) *Social Perspectives on Emotion.* Greenwich, Connecticut/London: JAI Press Inc.

Wilkinson, R.G. (1996) *Unhealthy Societies: the Afflictions of Inequality.* London: Routledge.

Williams, S.J. (1998) 'Capitalising' on emotions? Rethinking the inequalities debate, *Sociology*, 32, 1, 121–39.

Williams, S.J. (2000) *Emotion and Social Theory: Corporeal Reflections on the (Ir)Rational.* London: Sage.

Williams, S.J. and Bendelow, G. (1998) *The Lived Body: Sociological Themes, Embodied Issues.* London: Routledge.

Zajonc, R.B. (1984) The interaction of affect and cognition. In Scherer, K.R. and Ekman, P. (eds) *Approaches to Emotion.* Hillsdale, New Jersey and London: Lawrence Erlbaum Associates, Publishers.

3

Disability, impairment or illness? The relevance of the social model of disability to the study of mental disorder

Julie Mulvany

Introduction

As a result of major changes in mental health policy most people with a severe mental disorder now live in the community. The experience of severe mental disorder is frequently associated with economic hardship, unemployment, a breakdown in social relationships and a lowered standard of living. Sociological theory and research has not provided either a much-needed analysis and critique of the major changes taking place in mental health policy or fostered any recent social policy directed towards improving the quality of life for people diagnosed as suffering from severe mental illness who live in the community.

There is a long tradition of sociological work in the area of mental health and illness (Busfield 1996, Pilgrim and Rogers 1993). The earliest sociological work addressed the influence of social and economic factors on the development and distribution of 'disorders of the mind' (see, for example, Hollingshead and Redlich 1958, Faris and Dunham 1939)[1]. During the 1960s and 1970s the social constructionists examined both psychiatric[2] and community understandings of mental illness, and their impact on those labelled as mentally ill (see Scheff 1966, Schur 1971, Strauss *et al.* 1964). Other sociologists, such as Prior (1993) and Scull (1979), have traced the changing modes of treatment of the mentally ill over the last century. More recently a number of sociologists (see, for example, Rose 1996, De Swaan 1990) drawing on Foucault, have studied changes in the ideology and practices of psychiatry in a postmodern society. The increasing psychiatric interest in the relationship between violence and mental disorder and the introduction of techniques of risk assessment and management have also been analysed (see Castel 1991 and McCallum 1997).

While recognising the value of much of this work, this chapter argues that sociologists appear to have abandoned the study of serious mental illness[3].

Although labelling theorists and members of the anti-psychiatry movement asked many important questions, their responses were often crude and unsophisticated. The blanket condemnation of psychiatric intervention and the determination to portray all mental disorders as social constructs, led their work into disrepute. The more recent theoretical focus on the 'discursive practices' of psychiatry, although important, has less relevance for the study of serious psychiatric disorders (Pilgrim and Rogers 1994).

The focus in this chapter on people with serious mental disorders is based on the assumption that for a small, but significant category of people, mental disorder is associated with severe restrictions on social, psychological and physical wellbeing. Although the severity of the symptoms associated with serious mental disorders may fluctuate, for many people they remain chronic. People suffering from severe mental disorders are likely to attract one of a number of medical diagnoses listed in traditional psychiatric classification systems such as the Diagnostic and Statistical Manual of Mental Disorders (DSM-IV). These diagnoses include major psychotic conditions such as schizophrenia and affective psychoses, involving mood disorders such as manic-depression and major depression. They may also include serious anxiety disorders including obsessive-compulsive disorders and phobias. These diagnostic categories, though problematic, do enable a distinction between serious psychiatric disorders and other milder mental health problems[4].

Disability theory

This chapter argues that sociologists should re-visit the study of serious mental disorder and suggests that a direction forward can be found in the writings of the disability theorists. Developments in disability theory have emerged largely from the work of a group of British writers and researchers (see, for example, Barton 1996)[5]. This work is often referred to as the 'social model of disability' (Drake 1999: 10) or the 'social barriers model of disability' (Finkelstein 1993: 36). However, as work in this area is constantly being developed and refined by writers from a range of different theoretical backgrounds, it is more appropriate to refer to the work as 'the social approach to disability' (Barnes *et al.* 1999: 27). There is an increasing diversity of views about how theorising in this area should proceed; nonetheless there are a number of defining characteristics of the approach.

Writers challenge conventional 'individualist and deficit views of disability' (Barton 1993: 235). A distinction is made between impairment and disability. As one of the best-known theorists Michael Oliver writes: '[disability is] the disadvantage or restriction of activity caused by a contemporary social organisation which takes no or little account of people who have physical impairments and thus excludes them from the mainstream of social activities' (1990: 11). Impairment, on the other hand, refers to some bodily defect, usually constituting 'a medically classified condition' (Barnes *et al.* 1999: 7). This location of the conceptualisation and analysis of disability within a social framework redirects analysis from the individual to processes of social oppression, discrimination and exclusion. The disadvantage experienced by disabled people is seen to be 'institutionalised throughout society' (Oliver 1996: 33).

The social approach to disability demands an identification and analysis of the social, political and economic conditions that restrict the life opportunities of those suffering from an impairment. Central to this work is a focus on the rights of people with disabilities and the consequences of the development of a collective identity for social action and social change. Thus, in addition to promoting new ways of conceptualising and analysing disability, the social approach to disability has an ideological component. A focus on political action gives 'disabled people a feeling of self-worth, as well as offering them a collective identity and a stronger political organization' (Butler and Bowlby 1997: 412).

Although disability theorists have rarely included psychiatric disability in their work[6], their ideas can be used to inject new vigour and direction into an analysis of the plight of people suffering from mental illness. The application of the social approach to disability to the study of mental ill health orients research and theoretical development towards an analysis of the complexity and multiplicity of the social restrictions faced by people diagnosed as 'mentally ill', and the social disadvantage and oppression they face. It directs sociologists to identify the sites and the mechanisms of institutionalised oppression. This focus moves far beyond the work of symbolic interactionist theorists, such as Scheff (1966), whose concern with societal reaction was largely restricted to the use of diagnostic stereotypes by psychiatrists. Goffman's work on stigma (1961) is also narrowly focused on 'the defensive, anxiety-ridden and largely doomed manoeuvrings of stigmatized individuals, and of their acceptance of the negative label' (Barnes *et al.* 1999: 47).

The focus on institutionalised oppression would extend the sociology of mental health beyond the study of psychiatry and medical treatment to an examination and identification of the social barriers that deny or restrict access for people with a serious psychiatric disability to the rights of citizenship[7]. This focus would include the analysis of urban space (Imrie 1998), housing (Morris 1993), education (Roulstone 1993), recreation (Fullager and Owler 1998) and employment (Baron *et al.* 1998). The implications of ideologies of economic rationalism, consumerism and neoliberalism for the delivery of medical and welfare services for people with a psychiatric disability would be examined. The reality of systems of 'community care' for people with psychiatric disabilities in an era dominated by managerialism, privatisation, the introduction of the market ideology and the mixed economy of welfare would be assessed (Pilgrim *et al.* 1997). A focus on oppression, citizenship and rights within the sociology of mental health challenges sociologists to ground the relevance of their theoretical and empirical work in the lives of people suffering from serious psychiatric disorders.

The social approach to disability provides a framework from within which to analyse social policy of relevance to people with psychiatric disabilities. Writers in the disability area are concerned to draw out the implications of their analysis for the development of social policy and the growth of the disability movement (Barnes and Oliver 1995, Shakespeare 1993). Disability theorists' examination of the current policy focus on needs instead of rights (Sullivan and Munford 1998), the linkage of rights and responsibilities of citizens (Barton 1993), and the analysis of the gap between the rhetoric of inclusive citizenship and the reality of resource delivery (Davis 1998) remain highly relevant to an examination of the experience of living with a serious psychiatric disorder. The social approach to disability also calls for a reassessment of the role of legislation as a vehicle for social change (Barnes and Oliver 1995).

Existing mental health policy is based on the assumption that the major problems and 'medical symptoms' faced by people with serious psychiatric disabilities result from their illness. Broader social structural factors that affect an individual's experiences of illness, such as poverty, inequality, discrimination and exclusion are not targeted[8]. People with mental disorders have been excluded from generic disability programmes in areas such as employment and training, housing and accommodation support, generic social support, recreation and disability services. The relevance of narrow mental health legislation which primarily regulates the delivery of medical services in hospitals, to the needs of people living in the community has not been challenged. The sociology of mental health has done little to clarify the nature of the social barriers faced by people with serious psychiatric disorders living in the community.

The social approach to disability is, however, still being developed and refined (Barton 1993, Oliver 1996, Shakespeare and Watson 1997). For instance, although Oliver's model is built on a materialist theoretical perspective, social approach theorists are increasingly drawing on a range of theoretical perspectives, including social constructionism and post-modernism. One of the major attractions of this body of work, however, is the use of theory to both understand 'why things are the way they are' and to establish 'a future agenda for social change' (Riddell 1996: 103). Whilst the model does not offer a comprehensive theoretical framework within which work in the sociology of mental health should proceed, the recent work of disability theorists identifies a range of highly pertinent questions of relevance to the study of mental disorder.

Writers drawing on the social approach to disability share a commitment to explaining the structural constraints that create disability. There is, however, much lively debate about how the approach should be developed and refined (Shakespeare and Watson 1997, Oliver 1996, Barton 1993, Butler and Bowlby 1997, Watson 1998). This chapter argues that these debates highlight issues and dilemmas of major relevance to the study of psychiatric disability. Three areas of controversy with disability theory will be examined. First, the relative importance of incorporating an understanding of the differences that exist between disabled people is a source of tension between theorists. A second concern relates to the importance of theorising impairment, as well as a concern to examine the relationship between impairment, identity, disability and empowerment. Finally, disability theorists have questioned the applicability of work in the sociology of health and illness to the study of disability.

Significance of difference

A major debate within disability theory relates to the importance of acknowledging differences between people with disabilities. Some argue that the social approach to disability should focus on the common social oppression which people with disabilities face, and on their need to unite politically to fight this oppression (Oliver 1996). Others contend that the conceptualisation of disability as a monolithic experience ignores differences that exist between people with disabilities based on class, gender, race and ethnicity, sexual orientation and age (Barton 1993, Crow 1996, Hearn 1991, Lloyd 1992).

Associated with this failure to acknowledge difference, it is claimed, is a disinterest in people's perceptions of living with impairment and disability. This lack of focus on disabled people's experiential knowledge detracts from the relevance of the social approach for many people with disabilities (French 1993, Morris 1992, Crow 1996). An analysis of people's experiences of impairment and disability, it is argued, will both enhance theoretical understandings of the nature and impact of social barriers for people with disabilities (Thomas 1997) while simultaneously providing insight into the differential impact of these restrictions on different categories of disabled people.

These concerns by some disability theorists, to link the importance of acknowledging personal differences with detailed analysis of individual experience, are highly relevant to the sociology of mental health. Ironically, whilst the work of interpretive sociologists in labelling theorists, and more recent Foucauldian theorists, has provided a critique of psychiatry and its impact on 'mental patients', this work has actually reinforced some of the worst aspects of medicalisation. The person with a mental illness is constructed as the 'other' (Peters 1996: 218). Labelling theorists, although highlighting the social process of stigmatisation and exclusion, portrays the 'deviant' as a victim (see Becker 1963, Lemert 1962). This 'oversocialised' view ignores the 'bodily identity, personhood, and transformative potentials' of the stigmatised individual (Peters 1996: 218). This kind of research ignores the diversity of experience existing between people suffering from mental disorders.

An exploration of how these experiences might differ depending on factors such as age, gender, ethnicity or even attributed psychiatric diagnoses has rarely been done[9]. The consequences of this failure to explore difference limits the ability of sociological research to analyse and explore the complexity, subtlety and diversity of disabling barriers faced by people suffering from mental disorders. Additionally, the tendency to conceptualise 'mental patients' as an undifferentiated group of victims restricts the potential of sociological research and theorising to both analyse and support the interests of the developing mental health consumer movement. As Barnes and Shardlow (1996: 131) point out, 'it is important to understand and to theorise personal responses of mental distress in order to make the link between such experiences and collective action'[10].

There are, however, some notable exceptions to these failures that suggest possibilities for future research. Two recent qualitative studies of the experiences of users of mental health services (Rogers *et al.* 1993, Wadsworth and Epstein 1998) address the importance of understanding the perceptions of individuals accessing mental health services. These studies explore the interface between medical services and the users of these services. While this focus is understandable, given the importance of medical treatment in the lives of people suffering from serious psychiatric disorders, the social location of the individual and their perceptions of the significance of their mental health problems in terms of their wider life experiences, is not, unfortunately, addressed.

Barham and Hayward (1991) explore the wider significance of a mental disorder in the lives of a small group of people diagnosed as suffering from a schizophrenic illness. A particularly significant aspect of this qualitative study is the researchers' inclusion of their participants as active collaborators in the research process. The research identifies both the participants' perceptions of the difficulties they face in negotiating their illness and its treatment, as well as their active attempts to maintain or create an identity as a person rather than as a mental patient. More research like this, that compares the experiences of different categories of people living in the community with serious mental disorders is essential.

Impairment and disability

Disability theorists are divided in their views about the importance of theorising impairment. For many disability theorists, the distinction between impairment and disability is fundamental. They argue that there are ideological reasons for not focusing on impairment (Oliver 1996). They are concerned that the acknowledgement of the pain of impairment will lead to a renewed focus on physical limitations (Shakespeare 1996). A return to the ascendancy of the medical model, with its focus on blaming the victim will lead to the dissipation of the disability political movement (Shakespeare and Watson 1997).

Conversely, those theorists advocating a focus on the differences between people with disabilities are concerned to ensure that the social approach to disability incorporates an analysis of impairment. They argue that to ignore impairments is to ignore the 'reality' of the lived experiences of people with disabilities (see, for example, Crow 1996, French 1993, Hughes and Paterson 1997, Shakespeare and Watson 1995). It is argued that the effect of pain, physical restrictions on movement, loss of function and exhaustion can be as frustrating and depressing as ridicule, abuse, stigma and discrimination (Butler and Bowlby 1997, Pinder 1995). As Williams argues, disability is 'at some level, undeniably to do with the pain or discomfort of bodies, and this is a dimension of the oppressive quality of chronic illness and disability for large numbers of people' (1996: 205–6).

Sociological work in the area of mental disorder has largely ignored issues of impairment[11]; the individual's experience of illness is disregarded. The anti-psychiatrists explicitly deny the possibility of 'illness' (Szatz 1961) and the post-structuralists portray mental illness as the product of discourse (Seymour 1998). The focus of the research of labelling theorists is on the nature of the social reaction, rather than on the perceptions of those labelled (see, for example, Lemert 1962, Sampson et al. 1962). Labelling theorists who make a distinction between primary and secondary deviance disregard impairment and focus only on those aspects of a person's identity believed to be related to the social reaction to their condition. The major argument of these theorists is that the role of the mental patient is consolidated by the social reaction of friends, relations and medical professionals (Goffman 1968).

A focus on mental impairment appears to pose a greater challenge for sociologists than a focus on physical impairment. An acceptance of the mind/body dualism has allowed sociologists generally to take as unprob-lematic the existence of physical illness and impairment (without impeding the study of the contribution social structural factors make to the devel-opment of these conditions). The ontological status of madness has been viewed, however, as far more problematic. Although the portrayal of mental disorders as social constructions has provided a much-needed challenge to the essentialist view of the body portrayed in medical science, it has placed major limitations on sociological inquiry.

Sociologists working in the area of mental health have been loath to confront the possibility that a range of mental impairments exists which make the performance of certain activities difficult for people who suffer from these impairments. Traditionally, sociologists have avoided the dilemmas of confronting the implications that may flow from an acknowledgement that some people experience severe pain and discomfort as a result of dis-organised thinking, racing thoughts, fixed paranoid delusions, inability to control thought processes or perceptions of external thought control. This makes their work increasingly irrelevant for many people experiencing serious mental distress. Barnes and Shardlow (1996: 130) provide a succinct summary of this failure when they argue that the sociology of mental health has not been able to develop 'an alternative model (equivalent to the social model of disability) which can provide the basis for both understanding the origin and nature of distress and providing enabling and empowering assistance to those experiencing such distress'.

Embodied impairment

Sociological work can gain from examining the writings of disability theorists attempting to grapple with the consequences of including impairment in their theorisation of disability. A number of disability theorists, concerned to incorporate the significance of impairments into the social approach to disability, have drawn on work from the sociology of the body to refine their analysis of the relationship between impairment and disability. These theorists argue that the social approach must see impairment as 'embodied', rather than as presenting a biologically reductionist depiction of the body where the body is seen as separate from society (Butler and Bowlby 1997: 418)[12]. One's experience of embodiment, it is argued, is the result of a complex relationship between society and corporeality. As the body is both a corporeal and a social construction, so our experience of embodiment is both sensory and 'shaped by social relations and ideas' about normal bodily form (Butler and Bowlby 1997: 416). Similarly an individual's identity is partly a product of their experience of embodiment (1997: 416). The mind/body dualism has discouraged an exploration of how people make sense of their physicality and corporeality and how this in turn impacts on their identity. If we accept these arguments we are led to acknowledge that 'selves', identity and agency cannot be studied independently of bodies, whether impaired or otherwise.

Theorists in the sociology of the body have ignored the mind or brain. There has been no attempt to apply the concept of embodied impairment to intellectual and psychiatric disability. The concept of embodied impairment can, however, include mental impairments. We can speak of 'embodied irrationality'. The concept of embodiment dissolves the mind/body distinction. In so doing, it also eliminates the need to distinguish between physical and mental impairments. As Seymour points out: 'If sociology is the interpretative understanding of social action, then embodied human beings, human personality and consciousness embodied in human material, are engaged in that action' (1998: 9).

The concept of embodiment allows sociologists to see the body as both a 'biological phenomenon' and a 'social production' (Seymour 1998: 12). A focus on 'embodied irrationality' encourages the study of how people make sense of the bodily experiences of insanity without falling back on a biologically determinist view of 'madness'. With the increased scientific interest in the genetic basis of mental illness and the development of

new antipsychotic medications the relevance of the social to an understanding of mental distress faces new challenges. The concept of embodied
irrationality provides a focus for a sociological contribution to the understanding of the complex relationship between biological and social factors.
This conceptualisation allows 'the possibility of interdisciplinary research between traditional enemies, the biological and the social sciences'
(Seymour 1998: 13) rather than conceding this territory to the biological
sciences.

An area of major concern for many people suffering from serious mental
disorders is the assessment by psychiatrists that the person lacks 'insight'
into his/her illness. Research into people's explanations of the significance,
meaning, and status they attribute to what appear to be psychotic symptoms, such as hallucinations, is an example of an area where the concept of
embodied irrationality could be pursued (Barrett 1996). It is also an area in
which the relationship between sociocultural, psychological and neurological influences could be examined. Similarly research into 'disease outcomes'
should not be the sole province of medical researchers. Sociologists must
challenge concepts such as 'the natural history of schizophrenia', but must
do so within a framework that allows for the incorporation of ideas about
'biological disorder', cultural meanings, professional ideologies and social
structural constraints.

A number of disability writers argue that the concept of embodied
impairment allows for a more sophisticated analysis of people's experience
of disabling environments. These theorists have made explicit the relationship between impairment, disability and environment. Butler and Bowlby
(1997), for example, examine the use of public space by people with visual
impairments. By focusing on individuals' perceptions of their experiences in
public spaces the researchers analyse the different way people with visual
impairments confront and negotiate a range of social and physical barriers.
They also emphasise, though, 'the reflexive relationship between bodily and
social experience' (1997: 422). They illustrate how shared understandings
and expectations about disability affected their respondents' 'embodied
experience of being in public space and how their physical experiences
interact with their views of themselves and their relationship to others'
(1997: 422). Pinder (1995) looks at the experiences of people with chronic
arthritis in managing paid work. She explores her respondents' attempts to
accommodate their episodic and unpredictable arthritic symptoms with
employment that demands regular hours of employment.

Research that analyses the negotiation of disabling environments by
people with serious mental disorders must be undertaken. Research in
Australia, for example, has shown that university students suffering from
psychiatric disorders face major problems in completing their courses, partly
due to impairment-related factors. In addition to stigmatising treatment by
staff and fellow students, many encountered problems in completing assessment tasks within the stipulated time frames or in regularly attending classes

because of their fluctuating symptoms (National Centre for Vocational Education Research, 1999). Avoidance of the issues of impairment means that researchers in the sociology of mental health rarely undertake sophisticated analyses of the relationship between impairment, disability and environment, or identify the policy implications that flow from such analyses.

The work of disability researchers highlights first, the limitations of conceptualising social barriers in crudely simplistic and determinist terms and secondly, the importance of acknowledging impairment, agency and difference. People's management of their lives will vary depending partly on the nature of their impairment, their self perceptions, their immediate social and physical context and the broader social, cultural, economic and political environment (Butler and Bowlby 1997: 421). Social policy developments, it is argued, must be built on this recognition.

These disability theorists seek to combine a focus on structure, agency and meaning. They argue that the focus on individuals' understandings of how impairment and disability is experienced (Hughes and Patterson 1997) restores a focus on agency and identity. They are particularly interested in how positive self-identity can be established and how the experience of impairment can lead to empowerment rather than disempowerment (Shakespeare 1996, Barnes and Shardlow 1996). The application of these ideas to an analysis of, for example, 'psychiatric system survivor' movements (Beresford 2000) presents a particular challenge for the sociology of mental health.

The contention that the study of disability should include both the analysis of disabling environments and the experience of embodied impairment (which cannot be separated) has major relevance for the study of psychiatric disability, which has generally failed to link personal experience to structural issues. These ideas provide a framework within which to study the impact of disabling barriers on people living with embodied irrationality.

Recent work by Parr, informed by a social approach to disability perspective, examines some of the problems people with mental disorders face in accessing public space and 'negotiating a "mentally ill" identity within the city' (1997: 441). By privileging 'the voice of the individual' Parr is able to detail individuals' reflections on how they negotiate survival in social spaces where a range of social barriers restrict their activities (1997: 436)[13]. They face marginalisation, exclusion and stigmatisation in their negotiation of public areas of the city (1997: 440). They seek out what Parr coins 'insane space' places: 'a bedroom, a park, a café, a pavement – momentary fleeting "insane spaces" where people can simply be themselves' (1997: 442). Parr's data suggest that his respondents' identities were influenced both by their interpretation of their mental attributes and the 'common sociocultural codings and understandings of how the self should be presented in everyday life' (1997: 451). An interesting part of Parr's data is the way his respondents identify those aspects of their behaviour that they see as causing concern in the community. They speak, for example, of feeling 'high', losing inhibition or having thinking that is 'a bit warped' (1997: 441)[14].

Medical sociology and the study of disability

Another set of issues raised by disability theory relates to the contribution medical sociology can make to the study of disability. Most disability theorists accept that there are some similarities between impairment and chronic illness and acknowledge that disabled people may require medical assistance from time to time (Barton 1993, Oliver 1996). All impairment should not, though, be studied from 'an illness perspective' (Barnes and Mercer 1996: 5). They are concerned that a focus on illness will restrict the ability of the social approach to disability to move from an individualistic to a social structural analysis of disability (Barton 1993). Oliver (1996), for example, contends that a focus on illness can lead to the posing of a causal relationship between chronic illness and disadvantage.

Many disability theorists are critical of the contribution medical sociologists can make to the study of chronic illness and disability. They argue that although research which examines the way people make sense of living with illness or impairment is important, it highlights the negative aspects of illness and neglects the structural context within which meanings are shaped (Williams 1996: 202). This reinforces the 'victim' image of the person with a disability and a negative sense of self and identity (Barnes and Mercer 1996: 5). The social approach to disability, in contrast, focuses on empowerment and the development of an active disability rights movement committed to major social change (Oliver 1996).

Some disability theorists argue, however, that work in the sociology of health and illness can help address the failure of disability theorists generally to acknowledge the bodily discomfort and pain experienced by some people with disabilities. They point out that interpretative studies of chronic illness provide an alternative understanding to the experience of living with a chronic illness to that of professionals (Williams 1996: 203). Williams cites the work of Zola as an example of how 'a phenomenological and interactionist analysis of disability' could be located within 'a collectivist framework'[15].

Many disability theorists also argue that the social approach should be principally concerned with critiquing medical intervention only in those areas of a person's life that are unrelated to impairment or illness. They see much of the work within medical sociology, which is concerned with the interaction between medical personnel and their patients, as irrelevant to the study of disability. They are more concerned to critique medical and paramedical professionals' decision-making in areas of disabled people's lives including termination of pregnancies, sterilisation, access to employment, housing, welfare benefits and schooling (Oliver 1996: 36).

Not all disability theorists, however, endorse these views. While accepting the general thrust of these propositions a number of concerns have been raised. It is argued that the essentialist conceptualisation of the body within the social approach limits any challenge to medical dominance. As Hughes and Patterson point out, although the social approach critiques the medical model, it 'concedes the body to medicine and understands impairment in terms of medical discourse' (1997: 326). While the social disability theorists have avoided the mistake made by the anti-psychiatrists in their assertions that psychiatric impairments were total social constructions, they appear to have acceded too much to medicine. By so doing, they ignore the possibility of exploring the complex relationship existing between embodied impairment and disability. They also retreat from a critical analysis of all aspects of medical involvement in the lives of people with disabilities. Bury extends these arguments further with his claim that 'a full picture of disablement in contemporary populations inevitably exposes its health and illness dimensions' (Bury 1996: 22). The recognition of a link between illness, impairment and disability would include an acknowledgement that some people with disabilities will and do seek medical treatment. The distinction between impairment and disability, it is argued, leads theorists to ignore the 'legitimate' medical work related to the treatment of disease and illness for people with a disability. The social approach to disability must acknowledge the legitimacy of medical activities while, at the same time, critiquing these activities where appropriate if it is to identify the full range of social barriers people with disabilities face.

The dilemmas raised in the above debate have direct relevance for the study of mental health. I have already discussed the importance of the concept of impairment to the sociology of mental health and the need to give prominence to the accounts given by people with mental disorders (Barnes and Shardlow 1996) of living with impairment and disability. The preceding discussion both cautions against research approaches that result in the reinforcement of a 'victim' identity for the person with the disability, and encourages research approaches that locate the individual's narratives within a broader structural context. These debates also suggest the need for sociologists to revisit their critiques of the medicalisation of mental disorders. The work of disability theorists suggests that such a sociological analysis will need to take a number of directions. The first of these would involve a re-examination of the operation of medical social control in the post-deinstitutionalisation era.

In the aftermath of the rather unsubtle social control theories of psychiatry developed in earlier decades (see, for example, Scull 1979), the analysis of 'the destructive and oppressive features of modern psychiatry' has been abandoned (Pilgrim and Rogers 1994: 525). Most recent work is being done by post-structuralists who analyse the increasing dispersal of discursive psychiatric and psychological practices of control among the 'worried well' (Rose 1990). While acknowledging the importance of this work, Pilgrim and Rogers (1994) are concerned that the pendulum has swung too far. They point out that the dominant response by institutional psychiatry to people with serious mental disorders still utilises preventative detention and a range of 'hospital-centred biological treatments' (1994: 531). The dominant mode of treatment for most people suffering from serious mental disorders is the prescription of psychotropic medication. This medication frequently has major side-effects that can severely restrict the ability of the user to engage in a range of social activities, including paid employment. The fact that medication is often enforced by the use of compulsory community treatment orders further complicates the effects of this treatment regime on the lives of those involved. The impact of the increasing use of mandatory community-based treatment in England, America and Australia, on the lives of people with serious mental disorders needs careful appraisal (Mulvany 1994).

A second direction in the analysis of medicalisation would be the examination of the influence of medical ideology on the formulation of mental health policy and its implementation. The disability experiences of people with a mental disorder are closely related to the conceptualisation of their 'problems' as essentially medical. Even in the post-deinstitutionalisation era, mental health policies still emanate predominantly from health departments, and focus primarily on the way clinical services should be provided (Peck and Parker 1998, Australian Health Ministers 1992). The impact of a policy focus, located within a medical framework, on the lives of people living with a chronic illness in the community must be assessed. There is, of course, an increasing acknowledgement in policy documents, of the relevance of social factors in the lives of people living with major mental disorders and the necessity to develop links between health services and generic social support and welfare services. The critique emanating from the work of the social approach disability theorists suggests, however, that issues of control, discrimination, dependency creation and exclusion will not dissipate with the development of such partnerships. Detailed analysis of the social barriers and constraints faced by people with serious mental disorders in their negotiation of these government sectors must be undertaken.

Finally, the work of the disability theorists suggests that a balance must be reached between acknowledging the ideological and conceptual disadvantages associated with a focus on illness, while recognising individuals' experiences with and concerns about impairment. Debates within disability theory have identified tensions and dilemmas associated with this recognition. One of these relates to the status to be given to the demands of the emerging health consumer groups for the improved delivery of medical services (see Barnes and Shardlow 1996). The concerns of consumers of psychiatric services include lack of access to medical services and acute hospital beds for people with serious psychiatric disorders. Consumers are particularly keen to identify ways of improving the delivery of health services to reduce stigmatisation, dependency and disempowerment (National Mental Health Strategy Evaluation Steering Committee 1997). Should these concerns be taken seriously or should they be seen as reflecting an uncritical acceptance of medical discourse regarding illness and diagnosis

(Parr 1997, Chadwick 1996)? There has been little sociological analysis of the problems people with psychiatric disabilities may face both in accessing medical treatment and in the delivery of medical treatment within the community. Clearly for some people medicalisation provides meaning, understanding and legitimisation of their experiences of impairment (Broom and Woodward 1996). Sociologists should also, then, reassess medicalisation critiques in terms of the meaning of both disability and impairment in the lives of mental health consumers.

Conclusion

It is not suggested that the work of disability theorists holds all the answers. It is, however, an area in which interesting and challenging ideas are being developed. The social approach developed by disability theorists offers a way forward for analysis of the situation of people suffering from major psychiatric disabilities and provides a coherent analytical framework within which to examine the social creation of psychiatric disability. A number of issues being debated by disability theorists have particular significance for the sociology of mental disorder and psychiatry. A major challenge facing the sociology of mental health is how to deal with the concept of mental impairment and how to link this with the study of the social production of disability.

A related challenge is to sharpen the analysis of the medicalisation of mental disorder, while at the same time recognising the need to broaden the focus of sociological concern well beyond issues of medicalisation. An examination is required of the myriad of ways in which people with mental disorders are disabled in the post-deinstitutionalisation era, whilst still acknowledging serious illness and impairment. Disability theorists have unashamedly become involved in social change, policy critique and policy development. If medical sociology is to have significance in the new millennium, medical sociologists must embrace with renewed vigour the practical and policy implications of their theorising for those they study. Coincidentally, such an embrace may contribute to the quality of life of the psychiatrically disabled whose lives remain untouched by loftier theories.

Notes

1 Sociological work in this area has continued (see, for example, Busfield 1996, Vega and Rumbaut 1991 and Warner 1985).
2 See Barrett 1996 for a fascinating recent analysis of the social construction of schizophrenia in a state psychiatric hospital in Australia.
3 See Cook and Wright 1995 for possible explanations for this lack of interest.
4 Some writers would prefer to make distinctions of the basis of the severity of the problems associated with mental illness, regardless of the psychiatric diagnosis.

See, for example, the distinction made by the Australian Psychiatric Disability Coalition between 'serious mental illness' and 'serious mental health care problems' (National Community Advisory Group on Mental Health, 1994: 10).

5   There is also a vibrant disability studies literature developing in America (see, for example, Davis 1997).

6   A number of writers begin their discussions with a reference to impairments of the mind and body (see Butler and Bowlby 1997: 412), but most go on to discuss physical disability only. Others ignore mental disabilities altogether (e.g. Shakespeare and Watson 1997).

7   Some work in this area has commenced. See Barham and Hayward 1991 who examine the transition from 'patient' to 'person' and Goodwin 1997 who looks at citizenship rights in the context of mental health service usage.

8   The Australian National Mental Health Strategy, for example, is squarely located in the Mental Health Branch of the Commonwealth Department of Health and Family Services. Part of the Strategy focuses on linking needy individuals into support services, rather than addressing structural disadvantage through the development of policies that straddle and link government departments concerned with housing, education, employment and training.

9   Some important exceptions are research on the link between sexism (Busfield 1996, Miles 1988) and racism (Fernando 1988, Renshaw 1988) and the experience of psychiatric disability.

10   There has been little interest by sociologists in the study of the mental health user movement. For two exceptions see Barnes and Shardlow 1996 and Rogers and Pilgrim 1991.

11   There has, of course, been a small but long research tradition in the area of what Busfield (1989) calls 'the social causation' strand. Researchers, although often highlighting problems associated with the use of secondary data, acknowledge the existence of 'illness' while focusing on identifying the contribution social factors make to the patterns and occurrence of particular categories of mental illness.

12   Comparisons are made with the feminist movement. Its critique of the dualistic notion of sex and gender is compared to the distinction made between impairment and disability (Hughes and Paterson 1997: 333).

13   The ultimate example of the difficulties they may have in accessing public space is found in mental health legislation that allows people to be removed from both public and private places and confined involuntarily in a mental institution.

14   See Davies and Jenkins (1997) for a study of the construction of self-identity in young people with learning difficulties. The research highlights the complex inter-relationship between identity, discourse and bodily experiences.

15   See Thomas' 1997 study of the mothering experiences of women with disabilities and her identification of the 'attitudinal, ideological and material' social barriers faced by the women.

References

Australian Health Ministers (1992) *National Mental Health Policy*. Canberra: Australian Government Publishing Service.

Barham, P. and Hayward, R. (1991) *Relocating Madness: from the Mental Patient to the Person.* London: Free Association Books.

Barnes, C. and Oliver, M. (1995) Disability rights: rhetoric and reality in the UK, *Disability and Society*, 10, 1, 111–16.

Barnes, C. and Mercer, G. (eds) (1996) *Exploring the Divide: Illness and Disability.* Leeds: The Disability Press.

Barnes, C., Mercer, G. and Shakespeare, T. (1999) *Exploring Disability: a Sociological Introduction.* Oxford: Polity Press.

Barnes, M. and Shardlow, P. (1996) Identity crisis: mental health user groups and the 'problem of identity'. In Barnes, C. and Mercer, G. (eds) *Exploring the Divide: Illness and Disability.* Leeds: The Disability Press.

Baron, S., Riddell, S. and Wilkinson, H. (1998) The best burgers? The person with learning difficulties as worker. In Shakespeare, T. (ed) *The Disability Reader: Social Science Perspectives.* London: Cassell.

Barrett, R. (1996) *The Psychiatric Team and the Social Definition of Schizophrenia: an Anthropological Study of Person and Illness.* New York: Cambridge.

Barton, L. (1993) The struggle for citizenship: the case of disabled people, *Disability, Handicap and Society*, 8, 3, 235–48.

Barton, L. (ed) (1996) *Disability and Society: Emerging Issues and Insights.* Essex: Addison Wesley Longman.

Becker, H. (1963) *Outsiders: Studies in the Sociology of Deviance.* New York: Free Press.

Beresford, P. (2000) What have madness and psychiatric system survivors got to do with disability and disability studies? *Disability and Society*, 15, 1, 167–72.

Broom, D. and Woodward, R. (1996) Medicalisation reconsidered: toward a collaborative approach to care, *Sociology of Health and Illness*, 18, 3, 357–78.

Bury, M. (1996) Defining and researching disability: challenges and responses. In Barnes, C. and Mercer, G. (eds) *Exploring the Divide: Illness and Disability.* Leeds: The Disability Press.

Busfield, J. (1989) Sexism and psychiatry, *Sociology*, 23, 3, 343–64.

Busfield, J. (1996) *Men, Women and Madness.* London: Macmillan.

Butler, R. and Bowlby, S. (1997) Bodies and spaces: an exploration of disabled people's experiences of public space, *Environment and Planning D: Society and Space*, 15, 4, 379–504.

Castel, R. (1991) From dangerousness to risk. In Burchell, G., Gordon, C. and Miller, P. (eds) *The Foucault Effect: Studies in Governmentality.* London: Harvester Wheatsheaf.

Chadwick, A. (1996) Knowledge, power and the Disability Discrimination Bill, *Disability and Society*, 11, 1, 25–40.

Cook, J. and Wright, E. (1995) Medical sociology and the study of severe mental illness: reflections on past accomplishments and directions for future research, *Journal of Health and Social Behaviour*, (Extra Issue), 95–114.

Crow, L. (1996) Including all of our lives: renewing the social model of disability. In Morris, J. (ed) *Encounters with Strangers: Feminism and Disability.* London: The Women's Press.

Davies, C. and Jenkins, R. (1997) 'She has different fits to me': how people with learning difficulties see themselves, *Disability and Society*, 12, 1, 95–109.

Davis, L. (ed) (1997) *The Disability Studies Reader.* New York: Routledge.

Davis, L. (1998) Rights replacing needs: a new resolution of the distributive dilemma for people with disabilities in Australia? In Hauritz, M., Sampford, C. and Blencowe, S. (eds) *Justice for People with Disabilities: Legal and Institutional Issues*. Sydney: The Federation Press.

De Swaan, A. (1990) *The Management of Normality: Critical Essays in Health and Welfare*. London: HMSO.

Drake, R. (1999) *Understanding Disability Policies*. Basingstoke: Macmillan.

Faris, R. and Dunham, H. (1939) *Mental Illness in Urban Areas*. Chicago: University of Chicago Press.

Fernando, S. (1988) *Race and Culture in Psychiatry*. London: Croom Helm.

Finkelstein, V. (1993) Disability: a social challenge or an administrative responsibility? In Swain, J., Finkelstein, V., French, S. and Oliver, M. (eds) *Disabling Barriers – Enabling Environments*. London: Sage.

French, S. (1993) Disability, impairment or something in between? In Swain, J., Finkelstein, V., French, S. and Oliver, M. (eds) *Disabling Barriers – Enabling Environments*. London: Sage.

Fullagar, S. and Owler, K. (1998) Narratives of leisure: recreating the self, *Disability and Society*, 13, 3, 441–50.

Goffman, E. (1961) *Stigma*. Harmondsworth: Penguin.

Goffman, E. (1968) *Asylums: Essays on the Social Situation of Mental Patients and Other Inmates*. Harmondsworth: Penguin.

Goodwin, S. (1997) *Comparative Mental Health Policy*. London: Sage.

Hearn, K. (1991) Disabled lesbians and gays are here to stay. In Kaufman, T. and Lincoln, P. (eds) *High Risk Lives: Lesbian and Gay Politics after the Clause*. Bridport: Prism Press.

Hollingshead, A. and Redlich, F. (1958) *Social Class and Mental Illness*. New York: Wiley.

Hughes, B. and Patterson, K. (1997) The social model of disability and the disappearing body: towards a sociology of impairment, *Disability and Society*, 12, 3, 325–40.

Imrie, R. (1998) Oppression, disability and access in the built environment. In Shakespeare, T. (ed) *The Disability Reader: Social Science Perspectives*. London: Cassell.

Lemert, E. (1962) Paranoia and the dynamics of exclusion, *Sociometry*, 25, 1, 2–20.

Lloyd, M. (1992) Does she boil eggs? Towards a feminist model of disability, *Disability, Handicap and Society*, 7, 3, 207–21.

McCallum, D. (1997) Mental health, criminality and the human sciences. In Petersen, A. and Bunton, R. (eds) *Foucault, Health and Medicine*. London; Routledge.

Miles, A. (1988) *Women and Mental Illness: the Social Context of Female Neurosis*. Brighton: Wheatsheaf.

Morris, J. (1992) Personal and political: a feminist perspective on researching physical disability, *Disability, Handicap and Society*, 7, 2, 157–66.

Morris, J. (1993) Housing, independent living and physically disabled people. In Swain, J., Finkelstein, V., French, S. and Oliver, M. (eds) *Disabling Barriers – Enabling Environments*. London: Sage.

Mulvany, J. (1994) Medicalization, marginalization and control. In Waddell, C. and Petersen, A. (eds) *Just Health: Inequality in Illness, Care and Prevention*. Melbourne: Churchill Livingstone.

National Centre for Vocational Education Research (1999) *The Learning Support Needs of Students with Psychiatric Disabilities Studying in Australian Post-secondary Institutions*. Melbourne.

National Mental Health Strategy Evaluation Steering Committee (1997) *Evaluation of the National Mental Health Strategy: Final Report*. Canberra: Mental Health Branch, Commonwealth Department of Health and Family Services.

Oliver, M. (1990) *The Politics of Disablement*. London: Macmillan.

Oliver, M. (1996) *Understanding Disability: from Theory to Practice*. London: Macmillan.

Parr, H. (1997) Mental health, public space, and the city: questions of individual and collective access, *Environment and Planning D: Society and Space*, 15, 435–54.

Peck, E. and Parker, E. (1998) Mental health in the NHS: policy and practice 1979–98, *Journal of Mental Health*, 7, 3, 241.

Peters, S. (1996) The politics of disability identity. In Barton, L. (ed) *Disability and Society: Emerging Issues and Insights*. Essex: Addison Wesley Longman.

Pilgrim, D. and Rogers, A. (1993) *A Sociology of Mental Health and Illness*. Buckingham: Open University Press.

Pilgrim, D. and Rogers, A. (1994) Something old, something new...: sociology and the organisation of psychiatry, *Sociology*, 28, 2, 521–38.

Pilgrim, D., Todhunter, C. and Pearson, M. (1997) Accounting for disability: customer feedback or citizen complaints? *Disability and Society*, 12, 1, 3–15.

Pinder, R. (1995) Bringing back the body without the blame? The experience of ill and disabled people at work, *Sociology of Health and Illness*, 17, 5, 605–31.

Prior, L. (1993) *The Social Organization of Mental Illness*. London: Sage.

Renshaw, J. (1988) *Mental Health Care to Ethnic Minority Groups*. London: Good Practices in Mental Health.

Riddell, S. (1996) Theorising special educational needs in a changing political climate. In Barton, L. (ed) *Disability and Society: Emerging Issues and Insights*. Essex: Addison Wesley Longman.

Rogers, A. and Pilgrim, D. (1991) 'Pulling down churches': accounting for the British Mental Health Users Movement, *Sociology of Health and Illness*, 13, 2, 129–48.

Rogers, A., Pilgrim, D. and Lacey, R. (1993) *Experiencing Psychiatry, Users' Views of Services*. London: Macmillan.

Rose, N. (1990) *Governing the Soul: the Shaping of the Private Self*. London: Routledge.

Rose, N. (1996) Psychiatry as a political science: advanced liberalism and the administration of risk, *History of the Human Sciences*, 9, 2, 1–23.

Roulstone, A. (1993) Access to new technology in the employment of disabled people. In Swain, J., Finkelstein, V., French, S. and Oliver, M. (eds) *Disabling Barriers – Enabling Environments*. London: Sage.

Sampson, H., Messinger, S. and Towne, R. (1962) Family processes and becoming a mental patient, *American Journal of Sociology*, 68, 88–96.

Scheff, T.J. (1966) *Being Mentally Ill*. London: Weidenfeld and Nicholson.

Schur, E. (1971) *Labelling Deviant Behaviour*. New York: Harper and Row.

Scull, A. (1979) *Museums of Madness: the Social Organization of Insanity in 19th Century England*. London: Allen Lane.

Seymour, W. (1998) *Remaking the Body: Rehabilitation and Change*. Sydney: Allen and Unwin.

Shakespeare, T. (1993) Disabled people's self-organisation: a new social movement? *Disability, Handicap and Society*, 8, 3, 249–64.

Shakespeare, T. (1996) Disability, identity and difference. In Barnes, C. and Mercer, G. (eds) *Exploring the Divide: Illness and Disability*. Leeds: The Disability Press.

Shakespeare, T. and Watson, N. (1997) Defending the social model, *Disability and Society*, 12, 2, 293–300.

Strauss, A., Schatzman, L., Bucher, R., Ehrlich, D. and Sabahin, M. (1964) *Psychiatric Ideologies and Institutions*. Glencoe, IL: Free Press.

Sullivan, M. and Mumford, R. (1998) The articulation of theory and practice: critique and resistance in Aotearoa New Zealand, *Disability and Society*, 13, 2, 183–98.

Szasz, T.S. (1961) *The Myth of Mental Illness*. New York: Hoeber-Harper.

Thomas, C. (1997) The baby and the bath water: disabled women and motherhood in social context, *Sociology of Health and Illness*, 19, 5, 622–43.

Vega, W. and Rumbaut, R. (1991) Ethnic minorities and mental health, *Annual Review of Sociology*, 17, 351–83.

Wadsworth, Y. and Epstein, M. (1998) Building in dialogue between consumers and staff in acute mental health services, *Systemic Practice and Action Research*, 11, 4, 353–79.

Warner, R. (1985) *Recovery From Schizophrenia*. London: Routledge and Kegan Paul.

Watson, N. (1998) Enabling identity: disability, self and citizenship. In Shakespeare, T. (ed) *The Disability Reader: Social Science Perspectives*. London: Cassell.

Williams, G. (1996) Representing disability: some questions of phenomenology and politics. In Barnes, C. and Mercer, G. (eds) *Exploring the Divide: Illness and Disability*. Leeds: The Disability Press.

4

'It's a small world': mental health policy under welfare capitalism since 1945

Mick Carpenter

Introduction: moving beyond Anglo-American analysis

A stronger emphasis upon comparative analysis is one of the most striking developments in social science since the 1990s. Clearly this is in large measure a response to changes in the real world, as globalising processes accelerate and become a focus of concern. This chapter explores the connections between these processes and mental health policies, arguing that many of the classic debates about the rise and decline of the asylum have generalised from Anglo-American contexts, and need placing within a broader comparative framework. My method is first of all briefly to review and assess the three major Anglo-American sociological 'positions' in relation to deinstitutionalisation and community care – social democratic, neo-Marxian and poststructuralist. While each are seen as having strengths they are nevertheless all found lacking in some respects. I therefore argue, theoretically, for the possibility of synthesis, and, ideologically, for not completely rejecting social democratic claims that the shift from the asylum to the community has had genuine benefits. This is particularly relevant in a British context where, at the time of writing, mental health policy under New Labour is being framed by claims that 'community care has failed'. Rather than agreeing that 'deinstitutionalisation has gone too far', I therefore seek to explore within a comparative framework what conditions might lead it to have the most beneficial consequences.

Two main sources serve as my launching pad, both of which seek to construct a comparative approach to mental health policy by applying models developed for other purposes. Goodwin (1997) has applied the 'three worlds of welfare capitalism' approach developed by Esping-Anderson (1990), while Pilgrim and Rogers (1990), apply the approach to the 1990 British health reforms developed by Mohan (1996). I suggest that combining these two approaches opens up the possibility of a new synthesis. Mohan's model enables us to explore both local and global influences within national regimes, while Esping-Anderson's approach facilitates the more systematic comparison of national policy systems. In developing my evaluation of regimes, I acknowledge that everywhere community care in mental health has at best had mixed results. Yet, without romanticising Sweden and Italy, where policies emerged from a fusion of radical critiques and reformist politics, I claim that they offer more support for a positive assessment than neoliberal Britain or the USA.

Anglo-American approaches reconsidered

What I will first try to show is that each of the three major Anglo-American sociological approaches to deinstitutionalisation and community care also connect to broader political commentaries on welfare capitalism. Informed with this awareness, I then proceed to evaluate their strengths and weaknesses, before broadening the debate outwards in a comparative direction.

The three main positions
There are broad areas of agreement between each approach. For example, each acknowledged that the lunatic asylum became an institution of social control of the poor and socially disadvantaged within industrial capitalism, though disagreeing on whether this was integral to the project (Foucault 1967, 1977, Scull 1979, 1993, Rothman 1971) or a diversion from the path of reform (Jones 1972). They also concur that the shift to the community that visibly took place from the 1950s onwards in Britain and the USA, can at best only be partially accounted for technologically by a 'drugs revolution' which controlled florid symptoms and made earlier discharge possible. France developed the drug Largactil, but was in fact slow to deinstitutionalise (Sedgwick 1982: 198). In their different ways, they see community care as located within broader shifts towards welfare capitalism after 1945, though offering markedly different interpretations on the origins and effects of policy shifts.

The *social democratic* or 'social conscience' approach, most associated with Jones (1972), views that the state and its professional agents as essentially neutral and benevolent. The mentally ill are seen as a naturalistically identifiable group of people in need of communal support and help. A combination of Enlightenment humanism and rationality helps to 'illuminate' them as a pressing social problem – stir the public conscience and, through the development of expert knowledge allied to political action, produce appropriate and effective public responses. Thus, Jones regards the 'drugs revolution' as subordinate to a broader 'administrative' revolution absorbing the mental health services into the NHS and welfare state, leading to new therapeutic regimes and supportive services outside the hospital. This is capped by a 'legislative' revolution associated with the 1959 Mental Health Act which emphasises voluntaristic treatment under medical discretion, combined with access to community provision as a right of social citizen-ship. Hers is therefore a distinctly Whiggish account, although she does not see progress as inevitable. She is particularly critical of civil libertarian traditions and modern 'social constructionist' critiques of institutional psychiatry (which she problematically tends to lump together in one oppo-sitional camp). She blames civil libertarianism for producing the late Victorian custodial asylum system which sought to protect the liberties of the sane and permanently exclude the mad. She feared that the emerging 'social control' critiques of psychiatry of the 1960s were having the effect of helping to knock down asylums without putting anything in their place, playing into the hands of right-wing, cost-cutting politicians. In these ways her work can be read as the product of the historical moment when the British postwar 'welfare consensus' was breaking down, accompanied by a plea for it to be shored up.

The two main alternative approaches considered here both broke with the social democratic consensus. *Marxist structuralism* is on the whole an economic reductionist theory that is cynical about the reasons for policy shifts, and generally pessimistic about the possibility of progressive change within capitalism. It sees changes in the psychiatric system as primarily a reflection of external political economic pressures. Thus Brenner (1973) sees the mental hospital as in large measure an institution mopping up the 'surplus' unemployed, expanding during the Depression despite the costs of maintaining people in the asylum, discharging people in the Keynesian era of high employment demand. Thus Scull (1979) initially portrayed the asylum as an institution which sought to instill and normalise attitudes to wage labour, before it degenerated into a purely custodial institution for the containment of labour market casualties. The consequent shift to the community was made possible by welfare capitalism's provision of social security benefits, which provides a cheap alternative to refurbishment of decaying hospitals in an era of 'fiscal crisis', or inability to meet expanding social demands through the tax system (O'Connor 1973). As adequate community provision is not funded, community care rapidly becomes community neglect (Scull 1977). Although strongly economic deterministic, Scull does recognise that segregative institutions have become politically less acceptable, although the implications of this insight are not pursued.

Poststructuralist [1] or 'discursive' accounts of the shift to the community have recently become influential, often drawing on Foucault but developing the analysis further. In broad terms they can be seen as modern inheritors of the libertarian tradition in mental health. Within this framework 'normal-isation' is seen as something more diffuse than socialisation into wage labour, which helpfully facilitates analysis of gender and 'race/ethnicity' issues. Rose (1985, 1986) associates this trend with the development of the 'psycomplex' constituting 'the discipline of mental health', incorporating but extending beyond psychiatry to encompass a broader range of psycho-logical and psychotherapeutic professions. These prescribe behavioural norms and sets of interventions or 'technologies of the self' which frame human problems as 'mental health' issues. The shift to the community is therefore seen in critical terms as a 'widening of the net' of social control, rather than unmitigated progress, but through a co-optative rather than a purely repressive process.

These developments are traced some way further back than the 1950s, to the innovations in psychology and psychiatry from the early years of the 20th century, from which the origins of 'community care' are seen to spring (Prior 1993). Rather than resulting from top-down pressures from capitalism, such discourses are seen as being mobilised by various kinds of professional 'experts'. A shorthand way of summarising this approach might be that community care increasingly equals community control or 'governmentality', as the 'panopticon' (power based on the certain knowledge of surveillance (Foucault 1977)) ceases to operate solely in the institution and becomes transferred to the whole of society through a process of 'psychiatrisation' of distress. Within this the hospital and compulsory intervention remains important but part of a differentiated set of interventions aimed at reconstructing subjectivity. Poststructuralist analysis is less obviously connected to a political 'tendency' than the approaches outlined so far. Nevertheless, following Foucault, exponents often dispute the Marxian notion of structural power as shaped by the requirements of capital. Greater, even prime emphasis is given to the mediative role of professions and associated forms of expert knowledge which generate standards of normality which justify disciplinary power. However this power is seen as diffuse and contingent, and subject to slippage and resistance (Rabinow 1984). This in turn resonates with an increasingly influential qualitative critique of the social democratic welfare state which, though not neoliberal, is equally critical of socialist collectivism and radical programmes or 'grand narratives' of social change (Lyotard 1984). In any case, society is seen as moving in postindustrial and post- or late-modern directions. Class has become less of a central issue and new social movements, including those around forms of disability and self-help, figure more. Contested forms of scientific and professional knowledge become the major sources of conflict in society, as people become increasingly individualised and politics becomes dominated by issues of 'risk', rather than traditional 'left-right' class struggles over distribution (Giddens 1991, Beck 1992).

Assessing the three main positions
It should now be apparent that each of the three main commentaries on community care is also engaged in a broader dialogue on the merits and demerits of welfare capitalism and its discourse of 'progress'. Nevertheless, there are also immediate questions about their empirical adequacy as specific narratives on the decline of the traditional mental hospital and as the development of new policy approaches.

The particular strength of Jones's account is an awareness of how ideology and political developments shape the development of mental health policy. However, while often perceptive, she fails to relate political currents to social interests when, for example, she identifies links between Conservative politics and medicalisation, and those of Labour with a broader approach to community care. Also problematic is her tendency to dismiss social constructionism and radical critiques as entirely subversive of a reformed mental health system, simply seeing them as 'ideologies of destruction' (Jones 1993: 159), because she is not prepared to acknowledge the relationship between professional power and social control. The strength of Scull's analysis is its ability to relate developments in the psychiatric system to broader structural trends in society. The tendencies towards reductionism are much less pronounced in his account of the development of the asylum system, than his account of its demise, as the former puts considerable emphasis on the mediative effects of professional power. Unfortunately then, contemporary change is pictured as being entirely top-down and externally imposed. He also completely ignores issues such as 'race'/ethnicity, gender and age inequality and how these are reproduced through the psychiatric system (for which see Pilgrim and Rogers 1999).

Scull's deterministic Marxism was in fact criticised early on by other leftist commentators. Matthews (1979) disputed Scull's economistic approach, suggesting that it was political struggle by workers that necessitated a shift to the 'more flexible non-segregative forms of control' represented by community psychiatry. Sedgwick (1982) and Busfield (1986) both pointed out that Scull's timing was problematic, as the initial shift to the community occurred in the 1950s, and fiscal crisis did not become a pressing issue until the 1970s. Busfield showed how in Britain rationalisation also connected to professional agendas, as biomedical psychiatrists welcomed the concentration in Britain on slimmed down general hospital units. Sedgwick (1982: 205–6) argued that there was a progressive and democratic impulse behind the initial shift to the community, given by 'conditions of political possibility'. He attributed this generally to the radicalising impact of World War II, and more specifically to socially-oriented military psychiatry in both the USA and Britain. Subsequently, however, this impulse diminished and in alliance with biological psychiatry, politicians of the right sought to use community care as an early 'testing bed' for neoliberalism (notably Powell in the UK and Reagan as Governor of California). In fact, in the USA, the Community Mental Health Centres (CMHCs) established by a reforming President Kennedy represented the continuation of a more radical social vision than the Powellite cost-cutting put in place in Britain between 1959 and 1961, and never fundamentally reversed by subsequent Labour governments up to 1979.

Fiscal pressures undoubtedly started to bite from the oil crisis years of mid-1970s onwards, and have certainly served as the *pretext* for a rationalisation of the mental health system involving rapid run-down and closure as a cost-cutting measure. The traditional system has mainly been replaced by a medically dominated 'downsized' public psychiatric system, giving increasing priority to treatment and containment of seriously disordered users, partly pressured (as Scull predicted) by public concerns about risk and 'dangerousness'. Alongside it has been a significant growth in private sector acute services and contracted out 'transinstitutionalisation' of the long term disabled to privatised care homes, as well an increase in the mentally disturbed prison population (Brown 1985). This emerging post-asylum system represented the abandonment of social democratic aspirations to create a universal mental health system. It emerged more markedly in the USA through Reagan's funding cuts to CMHCs of the early 1980s, and repeal of the 1980 Mental Health Services Act. In Britain the formal commitment to social citizenship rights was not rescinded, even if it was never backed by adequate resources in either health or welfare. However some of the worst effects associated with the US experience, where there is no universal health care or social assistance (Income Support) programme, have been avoided (Bachrach 1997, Trieman *et al.* 1999).

Two conclusions can be drawn from this brief review. First, that it was not fiscal crisis alone, but its combination with neoliberal political control that accelerated the emergence of a downsized psychiatric system in both countries. Second, the differences as well as similarities between the two countries indicate that the institutional inheritance of social democracy made a positive impact in Britain even in a neoliberal era. A sophisticated political economic analysis in fact more satisfactorily views mental health policy as moulded by the *interaction* between external and internal influences, in contrast to the excessively *inside-outwards* focus of discourse theory. Nevertheless, discursive approaches not only show how changing forms of professional knowledge play a central role in restructuring the mental health system, but also how a 'modernised' community-based psychiatry may not represent unmitigated progress but involve the extension of technocratic power over people's lives. Their most important insight is that psychiatry is not just a repressive but also a manipulative system of power which is more effective by becoming 'internalised' through lay collaboration with psychiatric discourses. The widening of the social democratic net can therefore pose a threat to autonomy, self-reliance and genuine self-development. However, this tendency to excessive negativity has been criticised by Matthews (1987) who suggests that appropriate intervention, where state and professionals work in genuine collaboration with communities, might in fact enhance personal autonomy.

In any case, this focus on the 'softer' features of psychiatric intervention, though important, can detract attention from the fact that much psychiatric practice is overtly disciplinary, and that increased political focus on 'risk' and 'dangerousness' is reinforcing these traditional features in a post-asylum setting. The preference for punishment over welfare is a pronounced feature of neoliberalism, and is associated with a declining or even 'zero tolerance' of all forms of deviance. Fiscal pressures apparently do not prevent massively increased expenditure on prisons, particularly in Anglo-Saxon countries (Stern 1998). This is not just the property of the new right but has also often been taken up for electoral reasons by centre-left parties, led by the 'New Democrats' in the USA, and enthusiastically emulated by 'New Labour' in Britain.

Rather than assuming in quasi-functionalist terms that these are necessary adaptations to changed circumstances, there is a need to identify whether such Anglo-American trends are universal. Have countries like Italy and Sweden, which from the 1970s sought to take a different path by forging systems combining the radical critique of psychiatry with a reformist approach to politics, managed to sustain the momentum in an increasingly neoliberal world order?

Three worlds of welfare, many, or only one?

The most influential vehicle for analysing comparative social policy in recent years has undoubtedly been that developed by the Scandinavian social scientist Esping-Anderson (1990). This is social democratic in orientation, but incorporates elements of neo-Marxian structural analysis as the foundation upon which variations in class mobilisation occur, giving rise to 'three worlds' of welfare capitalism, 'Liberal', 'Conservative' and 'Social Democratic'. Social democratic regimes like Sweden, through effective political mobilisation of both manual and salaried workers behind reformist socialism, had by 1980 achieved high universal social security benefits as a 'citizenship right' with few overt conditions and strong redistributive effects. The strength of labour in 'Conservative' social insurance regimes in continental Europe was weakened by religious political mobilisation on the right by Christian Democracy. As a result, a universal system of generous benefits emerged, but the middle class did better through a strong emphasis on earnings-related benefits. Labour's collective strength was weakest in 'liberal' regimes such as the USA. As a result the middle class often resorted to private arrangements, leading to high emphasis on residual welfare for the poor rather than universal social security, low benefits and strict means testing. Thus, there is wide variation in the types of welfare system compatible with capitalism. In social democratic regimes, Esping-Anderson argues, labour is highly 'decommodified', with generous benefits enabling people to live comfortably outside the labour market, contradicting orthodox Marxist expectations about capitalist social discipline.

While there is not sufficient space here for a full critical assessment of Esping-Anderson's model, a major concern is the lack of focus given to gender and 'race' issues (Langan and Ostner 1993, Williams 1995), as well as the fact that he generalises from social security benefits to welfare states, thus excluding health and social services provision. Another problem is that it is an 'outside-inwards' theory in which the welfare state is seen largely as a reflection of external political forces, in contrast with the interactive approach advocated above, which sees state institutions and professions associated with them as actors in their own right. The most serious difficulty however, is that the notion of 'three worlds' may be too simplistic. While the USA, Germany and Sweden are clearly representative types, others cannot be so easily categorised. Thus Ginsburg (1992) argues that Britain is a hybrid 'liberal collectivist' regime, incorporating elements of liberalism and social democracy, and this certainly seems to fit British mental health policy. Others have suggested that there are more worlds than three, variously identifying Australasian, East Asian and southern European regimes as distinct types in their own right. The last, identified by Leibfried (1993) is highly relevant to this chapter as Italy can be regarded as a hybrid Conservative/Southern regime, with poorer and less 'progressive' health and social welfare provision in the southern regions.

Ironically, however, against the notion that there is more diversity than Esping-Anderson acknowledged, is a quite opposite claim which can perhaps be called the new 'convergence theory', that in the contemporary era 'globalisation' is rapidly eroding the differences between welfare capitalisms that existed up to 1980, and we are rapidly travelling on the road towards 'one' neoliberal model. These arguments have been generally reviewed elsewhere (eg Esping-Anderson 1996, Rhodes 1996), and only one or two relevant points will be made here. First, while real change is occurring, it is important not to exaggerate the extent to which national variation is disappearing in the contemporary world, or fail to notice the basic convergence against which national variation occurred in the past. The other problem is that such arguments often rest on quasi-functionalist, productivist assumptions, from which welfare policy is then read off. National variation was said to be shaped by 'Fordist' mass production for national markets, facilitating labour mobilisation, full employment and welfare states, while 'post Fordist' non-standard production requires 'flexible' organisation of labour, global rather than national production, weakening labour and national states, resulting in higher unemployment, welfare retrenchment and disciplinary welfare (*e.g.* Jessop 1994). The general problem with this theory, as Navarro (1991) points out, may be to mistake consequences for causes, downplaying the role of class politics and ideology in shaping production and welfare rather than the other way round. Williams' (1994) critique adds new social movements into the equation, and argues that British mental health policy is an object-lesson in how policy cannot be read off from production relations, as the shift from bureaucratic to 'flexible' provision commenced in the 1950s and was influenced by political struggle by reform movements.

A possible way forward is to keep regime types in mind, but to look at policy developments within national settings in ways that bring both global and local issues into view. Such an approach has recently been developed by

Mohan (1996) in relation to the British NHS reforms of the 1990s, which looks at policy issues at the international, 'Macro-' (international), 'Meso-' (national) and 'Micro-' (local) levels. As Mohan points out, the British reforms occurred in an international context in which there was pressure to converge towards cost-containment, and institutional change encouraging decentralisation and choice. However, these macro pressures towards convergence do not explain why in Britain this took the particular form adopted by the 1990 NHS and Community Care Act, which Mohan attributes more to an (albeit politically constrained) Conservative pursuit of neoliberal and anti-collectivist principles in health. At the micro level, pressures such as the interplay of managerialism, professionalism, labour market shifts, technological changes and consumerism may also operate. Mohan's analysis is promising but reads like 'work in progress' and he acknowledges that there are problems in separating analysis into three levels (Mohan (1996: 692). There is, therefore, a need to develop a theoretical and empirical account of how local, national and transnational levels *interrelate* and, in particular, the relative role of structural and political influences at all levels.

An outline analysis of comparative mental health policy under welfare capitalism

I shall now explore the extent to which the regime analysis pioneered by Esping-Anderson can be combined with the multi-tiered approach of Mohan, acknowledging structure and process at all levels, building on the efforts of Goodwin (1997) and Pilgrim and Rogers (1999).

Goodwin (1997) makes the first significant attempt to apply the 'regime theory' of Esping-Anderson (1990) to the mental health sector. His account acknowledges the role of psychiatric discourse in redefining mental health needs that widened the potential clientele and the possibilities for treatment. In turn it helps to create a political imperative to widen access to reintegrate people into the labour market, that became particularly pressing in the high Keynesian era of full employment. The traditional mental hospital, catering for all the needs of a defined group, was not suitable for these purposes. Therefore greater 'specialisation' occurred, that is dispersion of sites to more acute short-stay units, community-based facilities and voluntary, private and informal care. At the same time, however, formally provided care remained 'skewed' towards institutional treatment (Goodwin 1997: Chapter 5). Thus Goodwin sees the shift as primarily a rationalisation measure, in which controlling and economic priorities were strong, rather than primarily a product of humanitarianism or social progress. There are thus arguably still economically reductionist tendencies in his argument. He puts considerable emphasis on outside pressures, not least because he suggests that psychiatrists often resisted a wholesale shift to the community in order to protect their institutional base (Goodwin 1997: 35).

However, against these convergent trends, his analysis recognises that the varying political nature of welfare regimes has significantly mediated pressures to social control and economic rationalisation. He argues that these are most pronounced in 'liberal' regimes ruled by market ideology and limited welfare rights, where there is an early shift to the community in the 1950s and '60s, presumably referring to Britain and the USA. In the 'conservative' continental regimes of Europe, by contrast, pressures to deinstitutionalise do not emerge so rapidly (*i.e.* not until the 1970s) because the asylum survives as an institution of social control, and the development of specialisation is restricted by principles of 'subsidiarity' which define community provision as the responsibility of voluntary organisations, churches and families. Strongly social democratic regimes in Scandinavia also deinstitutionalised late, but Goodwin argues that in this case it is because generous entitlement to citizenship welfare (high 'decommodification' in Esping-Anderson's terms) meant that there was less pressure to reinforce labour market participation. Policy provision to expand mental hospital beds from the 1950s was based on a principle of extending entitlements and from the 1970s, this changed in response to the critique of institutions and proposal of alternative services based on 'normalisation' and a right to social participation in the community, within a network of means of supportive provision.

Goodwin's analysis is promising, but arguably sticks too closely to the Esping-Anderson script, rather than adapting it to the context of specific regimes and their distinctive mental health policy features. Policies are politically contested within regimes and do not always conform exactly to type and it is hard to sustain the argument that liberalism was the initial impetus to change in the 1950s among the early innovators of Britain and the USA. It was, as Jones (1988: 5) argues, a movement which was rooted in 'left wing humanism' and later developed 'fresh momentum by right wing cost-cutting'. In Britain the foundations for a neoliberal, downsized mental health system had already been laid by Enoch Powell as Conservative Minister of Health, even if its fuller implementation became delayed until the 'fresh momentum' 1980s. By contrast, the innovations of the Kennedy-Johnson era in the USA can be seen as part of broader moves towards constructing a social democratic social policy through an alliance between the Democratic Party and black voters, that sought to respond to the unrest associated with the civil rights movement. The reforms in both mental health and social policy generally were hesitant and only made partial inroads into the American liberal tradition. This project was stymied almost immediately by the costs of the Vietnam War and derailed by the oil recessions of the 1970s.

In the case of Germany and Sweden which are, respectively, 'classic' Conservative and Social Democratic regimes, Goodwin's analysis fits up to a point. However in the case of Germany, the attachment to the Esping-Anderson model leads to an understatement of the effects of institutional pressures in the health system, particularly the ways in which the rigid separation between primary and secondary care inhibited the transfer of mental health care across hospital-community boundaries (Mangen 1985). Institutional pressures are also arguably significant in explaining why reform may have been delayed in Sweden up to the 1970s, and why it took the turn towards 'normalisation' afterwards. Swedish politics is associated with conflict in the parliamentary sphere and efforts to achieve consensus in the policy arena. As a result reforms in health took a long time to emerge, because medical resistance slowed them down. A NHS did not appear until 1955 and mental hospitals were only transferred from central government to the counties in 1967 (Garpenby 1993, Immergut 1999). Goodwin's own analysis of Sweden suggests strongly that ideological shifts played a significant part in reform in the 1970s, which was clearly linked to the emergence of new professional discourses, such as those developed by Nirje (see Brown and Smith 1992). The wider political context of the shift to the left in Swedish social democracy associated with the 'Equality Movement' of the late 1960s (see Ginsburg 1992) was also important in ensuring that these new discourses led to political action. Another fact facilitating reform was the late appearance of fiscal crisis, as the Swedish economy largely weathered the problems of the 1970s and most of the 1980s, that acutely affected other capitalist economies.

This situation changed dramatically in the 1990s as the Swedish economy was finally pitched into fiscal crisis by the combination of slow decline and predatory global economic forces. This has led to the substantial erosion of many social security benefits, putting the future of the welfare state in question. However, social services expenditure by municipalities has been relatively protected, with commitments to extend the rights to social provision for older, disabled and mentally ill people (Gould 1996). There was official awareness that provision often fell short of the expectations of users and relatives, with a pronounced hospital bias in all health care, and poor co-ordination between separated county health and municipal social services. In response, the Swedish government embarked on major reforms, in 1992, extending the legal rights of users in relation to compulsory treatment and, in 1995, introduced financial incentives to transfer responsibility for mental health to social services in order to create a system more responsive to the wishes of users and relatives (Brusén *et al.* 1999). Even in a period of fiscal crisis, then, and despite inroads by neoliberalism into the Swedish welfare state, considerable efforts are being made to extend both the legal and social rights of mentally ill people, modelled on UN guidelines. However, against this, poststructuralists might identify a less benign side to Swedish social democracy which has shown itself less tolerant of deviance. Eugenicist policies were responsible for the forcible sterilisation of 63,000 people with learning disability or mental health problems between 1936 and 1976 (Sone 1997), and today Sweden has provision for compulsory treatment of drug users and people with AIDS.

Goodwin himself acknowledges that mental health policy in Italy, the country in which the 'left humanist' critique of psychiatry has received most official recognition, does not conform to type. It demonstrates the influence of ideology and political contestation against the grain of a 'Conservative' regime, particularly when, at a moment of social turbulence, it was allied to local experimentation in northern Italy and a strong campaigning organisation (*Psichiatrica Democratica*) linked to trade unions and left parties. The movement's charismatic figurehead, Franco Basaglia, had previously worked as a psychiatrist in the USA and been influenced by Goffman, Laing and Scheff and advanced practices such as crisis intervention, therapeutic community and CMHCs. Political luck also played a part in enabling a petition by the Radical Party to panic the government into instituting Law 180 of 1978. This forbade new admissions to mental hospitals, initiated a mental hospital closure programme and provided for the development of alternative, community-based services (Ramon 1983, 1991). It was not however an isolated reform but alongside it in the same year was the creation of a National Health Service into which the psychiatric reform was consolidated in 1983.

The Italian reform has attracted considerable international interest, both friendly (*e.g.* Ramon 1983) and critical (*e.g.* Jones 1988), although unfortunately it has not been properly monitored and evaluated within Italy itself. It can be said to have some inherent problems and that it has been poorly and patchily implemented. The reform had limited scope, in that the forensic hospitals were excluded from it, as well as services for substance abusers (Samele and Bologna 1991). There has been a lack of emphasis on retraining of staff, which has sometimes perpetuated custodial attitudes. At its best, particularly in some areas of northern Italy like Trieste, most sources agree that it works well as an effective community-based alternative to the traditional model, implementing World Health Organization (WHO) guidelines of best practice. In contrast to Sweden, the reforms appear more embedded in civil society, achieving fuller social integration. One of the few official evaluations of the system showed that in 1984, 53 per cent of new facilities were in northern regions, while only 20 and 27 per cent respectively had been developed in central and southern regions (cited Pergami 1992). Despite attempts to develop a new system, 80 per cent of psychiatric expenditure went on maintaining the old mental hospitals (Samele and Bologna 1991). In the early 1990s there were efforts to modify Law 180 to deal with some of the criticisms that had emerged, providing support for families of users, and imposing sanctions on local authorities for non compliance (Pergami 1992). The major problems have therefore been implementation, due to a fragmented, inefficient and often corrupt state structure, and differences of culture and economic capacity between north and south. These have been exacerbated by the appearance of serious economic malaise and fiscal crisis in the 1980s which led in 1992 to a health reform modelled on the British purchaser provider split, as an attempt to rein in the growth in public expenditure (Niero 1996).

In the analysis of Sweden and Italy developed above, the interaction of national, local and international influences has already been traced, with global pressures clearly exerting themselves. Sometimes these were operating in conflicting directions. On the one hand, the pressures to improve and extend provision in line with the WHO and UN, on the other, the constraints exercised by global economic forces. These internationally-mobilised influences come into stronger focus in the preliminary efforts by Pilgrim and Rogers (1999) to apply Mohan's approach to mental health policy. They point out that at the macro level, the 'risk' of violence and disorder by mentally disturbed people has been a significant (often disproportionate) policy concern leading to delegation to professional groups and debates about procedures and rights. At the same time there has been considerable national variation in the way that this has affected particular mental health policy regimes, in which interest groups and the mass media have played a significant role. They make the important point that civil liberties issues have figured strongly in the USA illustrating the strength of 'liberal' traditions, whereas professional discretion has been a stronger feature of British and European systems. In both Britain and the USA a strong 'anti-psychiatry' tradition emerged which also portrayed mental health users as the victims and not just the perpetrators of violence. As well as working through issues of risk and violence, Pilgrim and Rogers present a chart which offers the prospect of developing a more systematic approach to comparative mental health policy at the transnational level, from which I have extracted four key elements:

- Fiscal crisis of the capitalist state, leading to deinstitutionalisation;
- Biomedical dominance in treatment of 'serious mental illness', leading to enduring dominance of physical treatments;
- Concerns with cost-effectiveness, quality control and evidence-based treatments, leading to critical evaluation of treatment regimes;
- Rise of user movements and anti-psychiatry, and demands for more self-determination in health.

This list of influences provides a useful starting point for an analysis of transnational influences which could be refined and further developed. For example, what is meant by 'biomedical dominance' and how is it produced at the international level? The psychiatric profession – like the medical profession as a whole (Turner 1987) – is an international political force operating through various institutional mechanisms, seeking mainly to reproduce biomedical dominance. Both also often operate in alliance with the transnationally-organised pharmaceutical industry. There is thus also a 'psychiatric-industrial complex' whose most important globalising base today is the USA. The psychiatric-industrial complex does not only seek to expand its remit in relation to serious mental illness, but also promotes the psychiatrisation of 'minor' distress through 'branded' drugs such as Prozac,

Viagra and Ritalin (for childhood behavioural difficulties). This expansionary project operates within a discursive environment in which human distress and difference are increasingly being defined in psychiatric terms. The most influential way in which this is happening is through the Diagnostic and Statistical Manual of Mental Disorders. Now in its fourth version (DSM-IV), it promotes US conceptions of normality and disorder as the standard international tool kit for professionals, with unceasing efforts at improvement, revision and splitting, reminiscent of the wider processes of 'McDonadlization' associated with American capitalism (Ritzer 1996). DSM-I emerged in 1952, the brainchild of Adolf Meyer, one of the leading architects of the interwar American Mental Hygiene movement. Things were very different then and its categories were strongly influenced by psychoanalytic theories and war-time social psychiatry. These influences have been largely expunged by DSM-IV and patient subjectivity progressively eliminated, as anti-holistic biological psychiatry grew in influence (Wallace 1994, Mishara 1994). A fundamental aspect of US globalisation is that the world observes its preferred standards and groundrules (in this instance, over the WHO's International Classification of Diseases (ICD)). DSM-IV is thus the psychiatric equivalent of the World Trade Organization (WTO), promoting the principles of American universalism as objective standards that are beyond reproach.

The global level is not therefore a 'structure' within which national variations occur, but is itself politically constructed. A number of authors have criticised discourses of globalisation for often having politically-disabling tendencies towards determinism, by picturing it as an end-state rather than a contested process (Dicken 1998, Held et al. 1999). In this respect, developments such as fiscal conservatism and biomedical dominance can be regarded as part of a process of 'globalisation from above' involving influential actors such as financial interests, multinational corporations, the medical profession and drug companies. The user movement can be seen as part of a wider international challenge to these processes, part of an emerging 'globalisation from below' (Brecher and Costello 1994), which is arguably gaining in significance in the wake of protests against globalisation such as those in Seattle in 1999.

This discussion enables us to begin developing an outline account of globalising processes throughout the post World War II period. The internationalisation of mental health was something which emerged within the wider left-liberal climate of anti-fascism, reform of the world economy and creation of institutions associated with new attempts to promote security through the United Nations. Out of this geopolitical climate the World Federation for Mental Health formed and the Mental Health Committee of the WHO was established. This latter was strongly influenced by the 'advanced' models that had been pioneered by British-American war-time psychiatry, in conditions that had immensely boosted the profession's scope and reputation (Bourke 1998). The WHO then sought to universalise their approaches through its international blueprint of 1953 for transformation of mental health services towards greater specialisation and differentiation, a professionally dominated model of community care in mental health that was first implemented (with significant national variations) in Britain and the USA. However, since the 1970s 'fiscal crisis', combined with the growing power of the new right, have narrowed the scope for the development of universalist citizenship-based welfare and biomedical psychiatry, though contested, has regained the initiative. Both have sought to extend their global influence from the US heartland. The general influence of the new right has ensured that parallel processes of centralisation and decentralisation have taken place. Financial discipline operates at the global level through finance markets that exercise control over nation states, while at the local level producer-provider splits and other techniques allow operational discretion and diversity within certain limits. These can be seen as new forms of political economic control that differ from those of the social democratic era, but whether or not we should associate with 'post-Fordism' (Hogget 1994) is another matter. Within this framework, the neoliberal emphasis on consumerism and suspicion of professional as well as state monopoly, paradoxically creates some space for user-movements to contest biologistic psychiatry, but at the risk of playing into the shift from welfare to punishment, *i.e.* from softer to harder forms of social control.

Conclusion: the theory and politics of possibility

The foregoing analysis has hopefully demonstrated the advantages of developing a comparative approach to mental health policies under welfare capitalism. It has emphasised the need both to contextualise Anglo-American traditions of analysis and to move beyond them. A critical application of welfare regime analysis, sensitive to the specifics of national cultures and mental health policy contexts and their contested character, offers potentially rich theoretical veins that have yet to be fully exploited. However, this form of analysis also needs to be linked to a political-economic analysis of the global contexts of reform. As we have seen, these have discursive elements, sets of rules and procedures, whether of DSM-IV or the WTO, but in neither case do these operate independently of political-economic influences. A broader frame of analysis is also important in the assessment of progress or otherwise in community care. It is true that universally the tendency is for rhetoric to promise more than is provided in reality. Nevertheless, the rather different experiences of Sweden and Italy show how popular political movements involving a synthesis of social democracy with more radical elements can have a broadly beneficial effect on community care reform. Though a poststructuralist critique is undoubtedly relevant to uncovering their more negative features, these somewhat different models represent significant achievements with remarkable powers of survival. They provide evidence that not everywhere, at least, can community care be claimed to have been a failure, and even in Britain and the USA real benefits have been delivered to many users.

Note

1   Although strongly influenced by Foucault's social history of the asylum and disciplinary power, the Foucauldian analysis of the modern mental health system considered here is a British product.

References

Bachrach, L.L. (1997) Lessons from the American experience in providing community based services. In Leff, J. (ed) *Care in the Community: Illusion or Reality?* Chichester: John Wiley and Sons.

Beck, U. (1992) *Risk Society: towards a New Modernity.* London: Sage.

Bourke, J. (1998) Disciplining the emotions: fear, psychiatry and the Second World War. In Cooter, R., Harrison, M. and Sturdy, S. (eds) *War, Medicine and Modernity.* Stroud: Sutton.

Brecher, J. and Costello, T. (1994) *Global Village or Global Pillage: Economic Restructuring from the Bottom Up.* Boston: South End Press.

Brenner, H. (1973) *Mental Illness and the Economy.* Cambridge, Mass: Harvard University Press.

Brown, H. and Smith, H. (eds) (1992) *Normalization: a Reader for the 1990s.* London and New York: Routledge.

Brown, P. (1985) *The Transfer of Care: Psychiatric Deinstitutionalization and its Aftermath.* London: Routledge and Kegan Paul.

Brusén, P. et al (1999) *Welfare and Freedom of Choice? Final Report from the Evaluation of the 1995 Psychiatric Reform.* Stockholm: National Board for Health and Welfare (in Swedish, English summary available http:/www.sos.se/)

Busfield, J. (1986) *Managing Madness: Changing Ideas and Practice.* London: Unwin Hyman.

Dicken, P. (1998) *Global Shift: Transforming the World Economy.* London: Paul Chapman, third edition.

Esping-Anderson, G. (1990) *The Three Worlds of Welfare Capitalism.* Cambridge: Polity.

Esping-Anderson, G. (1996) After the golden age? Welfare state dilemmas in a global economy. In Esping-Anderson, G. (ed) *Welfare States in Transition: National Adaptations in Global Economies.* London: Sage.

Foucault, M. (1967) *Madness and Civilization: a History of Insanity in the Age of Reason.* London: Tavistock.

Foucault, M. (1977) *Discipline and Punish: the Birth of the Prison.* London: Allen Lane.

Garpenby, P. (1993) From ideology to reality: mental health care in Sweden, *European Journal of Public Health,* 3, 296–8.

Giddens, A. (1991) *Modernity and Self-Identity: Self and Society in the Late Modern Age.* Cambridge: Polity.

Ginsburg, N. (1992) *Divisions of Welfare: a Critical Introduction to Comparative Social Policy.* London: Sage.

Goodwin, S. (1997) *Comparative Mental Health Policy: from Institutional to Community Care.* London: Sage.

Gould, A. (1996) Sweden: the last bastion of social democracy. In George, W. and Taylor-Gooby, P. (eds) *European Welfare Policy: Squaring the Welfare Circle.* Basingstoke: Macmillan.

Held, D., McGrew, A., Goldblatt, D. and Perraton, J. (1999) *Global Transformations: Politics, Economics and Culture.* Cambridge: Polity.

Immergut, E. (1999) Historical and institutional foundations of the Swedish health care system. In Powell, F.D. and Wessen, A.F. (eds) *Health Care Systems in Transition: an International Perspective.* Thousand Oaks, London, Delhi: Sage.

Jessop, B. (1994) The transition to post-Fordism and the Schumpeterian welfare state. In Burrows, R. and Loader, B. (eds) *Towards a Post-Fordist Welfare State?* London and New York: Routledge.

Jones, K. (1972) *A History of the Mental Health Services.* London: Routledge and Kegan Paul.

Jones, K. (1988) *Experience in Mental Health: Community Care and Social Policy.* London: Sage.

Jones, K. (1993) *Asylums and After. A Revised History of the Mental Health Services: from the Early 18th Century to the 1990s.* London: Athlone.

Langan, M. and Ostner, I. (1993) Gender and welfare: towards a comparative framework. In Room, G. (ed) *Towards a European Welfare State?* Bristol: SAUS.

Leibfried, S. (1993) Towards a European welfare state? On integrating poverty regimes in the European community. In Jones, C. (ed) *New Perspectives on the Welfare State in Europe.* London and New York: Routledge.

Lyotard, J.-F. (1984) *The Postmodern Condition: a Report on Knowledge.* Manchester: Manchester University Press.

Mangen, S. (1985) Germany: the Psychiatry Equete and Its Aftermath. In Mangen, S.P. (ed) *Mental Health Care in the European Community.* London: Croom Helm.

Matthews, R. (1979) 'Decarceration' and the fiscal crisis. In Fine, B., Kinsey, R., Lea, J., Picciotto, S. and Young, J. (eds) *Capitalism and the Rule of Law: from Deviancy Theory to Marxism.* London: Hutchinson.

Matthews, R. (1987) Decarceration and social control: fantasies and realities. In Lowman, J., Menzies, R. and Palys, T. (eds) *Transcarceration: Essays in the Sociology of Social Control.* Aldershot: Gower.

Mohan, J. (1996) Accounts of the NHS reforms: macro-, meso- and micro-level perspectives, *Sociology of Health and Illness,* 18, 5, 675–98.

Mishara, A.L. (1994) A phenomenological critique of commonsensical assumptions in DSM-III-R: the avoidance of the patient's subjectivity. In Sadler, J.Z., Wiggins, O.P. and Schwartz, M.A. (eds) *Philosophical Perspectives on Psychiatric Diagnostic Classification.* Baltimore and London: Johns Hopkins University Press.

Navarro, V. (1991) Production and the welfare state: the political context of reforms, *International Journal of Health Services,* 21, 4, 585–614.

Niero, M. (1996) Italy: right turn for the welfare state. In George, V. and Taylor-Gooby, P. (eds) *European Welfare Policy: Squaring the Welfare Circle.* Basingstoke: Macmillan.

O'Connor, J. (1973) *The Fiscal Crisis of the State.* New York: St. Martin's.

Pergami, A. (1992) Towards an implementation of the Italian model of community psychiatry, *Psychiatric Bulletin,* 16, 90–2.

Pilgrim, D. and Rogers, A. (1990) *A Sociology of Mental Health and Illness.* Buckingham and Philadelphia: Open University Press, second edition.

Pilgrim, D. and Rogers, A. (1999) Mental health policy and the politics of mental health: a three tier analytical framework, *Policy and Politics,* 27, 1, 13–24.

Prior, L. (1993) *The Social Organization of Mental Illness.* London: Sage.

Rabinow, P. (ed) (1984) *The Foucault Reader: an Introduction to Foucault's Thought.* Harmondsworth: Penguin.

Ramon, S. (1983) Psichiatria democratica: a case study of an Italian community mental health service, *International Journal of Health Services,* 13, 2, 307–24.

Ramon, S. (1991) Introduction. In Ramon, S. and Giannichedda, M.G. (eds) *Psychiatry in Transition: the British and Italian Experiences.* London: Pluto.

Rhodes, M. (1996) Globalization and West European welfare states: a critical review of recent debates, *Journal of European Social Policy* 6, 4, 305–27.

Ritzer, G. (1996) *The McDonaldization of Society: an Investigation into the Changing Character of Contemporary Social Life* (2nd Edition). Thousand Oaks: Pine Forge Press.

Rothman, D.J. (1971) *The Discovery of the Asylum: Social Order and Disorder in the New Republic.* Boston: Little, Brown and Company.

Rose, N. (1985) *The Psychological Complex: Politics and Society in England 1869– 1939.* London: Routledge and Kegan Paul.

Rose, N. (1986) Psychiatry: the discipline of mental health. In Miller, P. and Rose, N. (eds) *The Power of Psychiatry.* Cambridge: Polity.

Samele, C. and Bologna, C. (1991) Italy: the post-1978 reform era – difficulties, dilemmas and future directions. In Appleby, L. and Araya, R. (eds) *Mental Health Services in the Global Village.* London: Gaskell.

Scull, A. (1977) *Decarceration: Community Treatment and the Deviant – a Radical View.* Englewood Cliffs, New Jersey: Prentice Hall.

Scull, A. (1979) *Museums of Madness.* Harmondsworth: Penguin.

Scull, A. (1993) *Museums of madness* revisited, *Social History of Medicine,* 6, 2, 3–23.

Sedgwick, P. (1982) *Psycho Politics.* London: Pluto.

Sone, K. (1997) The body political, *Community Care,* 9–15 October, 18–19.

Stern, V. (1998) *A Sin Against the Future: Imprisonment in the World.* Harmondsworth: Penguin.

Trieman, N., Leff, J. and Glover, G. (1999) Outcome of long stay psychiatric patients settled in the community: prospective cohort study, *British Medical Journal,* 319, 13–16.

Turner, B.S. (1987) *Medical Power and Social Knowledge.* London: Sage.

Wallace, E.R. (1994) Psychiatry and its nosology: a historico-philosophical overview. In Sadler, J.Z., Wiggins, O.P. and Schwartz, M.A. (eds) *Philosophical Perspectives on Psychiatric Diagnostic Classification.* Baltimore and London: Johns Hopkins University Press.

Williams, F. (1994) Social relations, welfare and the post-Fordism debate. In Burrows, R. and Loader, B. (eds) *Towards a Post-Fordist Welfare State?* London and New York: Routledge.

Williams, F. (1995) Race/ethnicity, gender and class in welfare states: a framework for comparative analysis, *Social Politics,* Summer, 127–59.

5

Psychiatric diagnosis under conditions of uncertainty: personality disorder, science and professional legitimacy

Nick Manning

Introduction

In this chapter the question is raised of why there has been a very rapid elaboration of the category of personality disorder within psychiatric classifications over the last 20 years. The answer has been sought through a sociology of psychiatric knowledge, drawing both on recent work on the sociology of science and technology, and on the relationship between psychiatric practice and government in the late 20th century.

Personality disorder is the site of considerable psychiatric controversy. Its classification, diagnosis, and treatment are disputed not only within psychiatry, but also in closely related fields of forensic and psychological work. For severe cases, the Home Secretary in Britain has recently suggested that pre-emptive incarceration is justified, and many psychiatrists feel that personality disorder is not amenable to treatment. Since 1959 it has been separated in British legislation from the two conventional conditions of mental illness and mental disability, as a third type of mental disorder – psychopathy. However the categories of personality disorder and psychopathy are not the same and the terms are used differently in the UK, in other European countries and in the USA.

The origins of personality disorder stretch back to the beginning of the 19th century. *Manie sans délire* was originally described in France by Pinel in 1801, but the term moral insanity was commonly used across the English speaking world until the early part of the 20th century. European psychiatrists tend to use the term psychopathy to refer to all personality disorders, whereas in England this more often means one sub-type, the anti-social, or severe, personality disorder. Since 1980 the American Psychiatric Association's *Diagnostic and Statistical Manual of Mental Disorders* (DSM) has assigned a special and separate axis to the personality disorders, axis II, to differentiate them from standard psychiatric syndromes covered in axis I, and there are now eleven sub-types of personality disorder. Within the better known sub-types, such as borderline personality disorder, there are further sub-classifications, Higgit and Fonagy (1992) for example identifying seven different types of borderline psychopathology in the literature.

Not only has their classification proliferated, but personality disorders are also controversial since they do not include obvious psychological or organic malfunctioning, but are detected through their interpersonal effects – for example the trail of chaotic and distressing relationships in their wake, or the criminal records frequently incurred. This means that it is through behaviour rather than mental processes that personality disorder is detected and understood. This is an important reason for the difficulty and instability of their classification.

Psychiatric classification

The process of classification is fundamental to any science. In psychiatry, it has been so difficult to arrive at an agreed approach that in the 1960s Menninger argued that diagnostic classification should be entirely abandoned (Falmer 1997: 53). A major reason for this difficulty has been the absence of independent biological tests, or specific links between clinical features and aetiological factors. Since the 19th century much effort has gone into this problem. Although the American series of Diagnostic and Statistical Manuals of Mental Disorders (DSM) first appeared in 1952, the latest developments, starting in the 1970s, have been a massive attempt to specify operational definitions for diagnoses, leading to the American series of DSMs (now up to DSM-IV) and the World Health Organisation equivalent, Chapter 5 of the International Classification of Disease, now in its tenth edition (ICD-10).

Diagnostic categories have been sharply disputed territory, homosexuality being the most famous example for its appearance and disappearance on the classification maps. Other issues such as drug use, hyperactivity in children, and post-traumatic stress disorder press for room on a crowded stage (see for example Box 1981). Within this general area of uncertainty, the classification of personality disorders is itself often seen as the most problematic issue. Many of the disorders pressing for accession to the pantheon of DSM/ICD fame are linked to types of personality disorder, which have shot to stardom, not merely in the sense that there are now eleven sub-types identified, but that within DSM they occupy their own special axis. This is territorial expansion in the grand manner.

Within psychiatry there is both a scientific base and a technological application of that science in clinical practice. This has two consequences. First, that there is slippage between what the science is doing and what happens in clinical practice. While there are some whose work spans this wide area, many psychiatrists do not cover the entire waterfront. Second, and consequently, there are differential classifications constantly developing at the two ends of psychiatric work. This kind of uncertainty and contest over knowledge is precisely the point at which we would expect social factors to have a particular influence, or at least for us to be able to identify them more easily.

The tension between the DSM system and clinical practice was examined by Brown in 1987 in a detailed study of a community mental health centre in the US. The centre was staffed by a major university medical school, and much of the teaching centred on diagnostic work. While the imposition of inappropriate diagnoses has become the stock-in-trade of psychiatric criticism (especially since the Rosenhan 1973, study), little other detailed work on the use of diagnoses has been published, apart from Light's (1980) general study of psychiatrists in training. Brown's study particularly focused on the way in which senior and junior psychiatrists alike handled the difficulty of applying DSM criteria in the clinical situation. Indeed so pervasive was this difficulty that highly routinised interactions, designed to reduce the ensuing dissonance ('remedial activity' as Goffman (1971) called them) had developed around three strategies: humour, sarcasm and imagined alternatives. For example, in one case faced with pressure from referrers for plans for future care, a staff member quipped 'his Axis I diagnosis, we decided, was "insurance claim"' (1987: 40). The constant pressure was 'to put some DSM thing on paper'. A supervisor explained at the start of the hospital year

> We have to come up with a billable diagnosis on the first day. There are a couple of favourites you can put down to please the insurance company or Medicaid, but don't feel you have to come to closure. The computer will not accept 'diagnosis deferred'. If we disagree we can make a dissenting opinion. If we have an error, Medicaid or Medicare may make us give back money' (1987: 41).

Brown develops the observation presented by Light (1980) a decade earlier, that different diagnostic frameworks develop in relation to the differing interests of managers or therapists, to suggest that the DSM diagnostic 'revolution' has occurred in part because it has been put to work in the interests of a variety of different groups, not only serving to reintegrate psychiatry into medicine, but used in different ways by insurers, governments, professionals, patients and institutions, even where there have been tensions arising out of clinical applications.

What work is the DSM doing for these groups? One aspect is the attempt to reduce uncertainty and variability in clinical and health insurance routines; as Mirowski and Ross (1989) point out when discussing US health care, superimposing a diagnosis on a person's symptoms and situation does not add, but rather removes, information. Another aspect is the desire to detect underlying, but hidden, entities. 'A diagnosis entices us to think, talk, and act as if a hidden entity has been revealed. The mythical entity insinuates itself into the role of a named actor, and the symptoms and situation dissolve into mere signs of its presence' (1989: 12). With a simple classification, and the security of the clear detection of an identifiable disorder, boundaries for diagnostic related group (DRG) payment are drawn, drugs can be targeted, and government agencies and insurers can calculate overall liabilities and costs. This is increasingly true of the UK, as well as of the USA:

> The National Health Service reforms and the development of community-based multidisciplinary care for the mentally disordered and mentally distressed require much more than the routine collection of diagnostic information only. More comprehensive information systems are required to enable the measurements of needs and outcomes, to audit clinical practice and to address issues of service quality in the purchaser/provider, contracting process and the development of National Health Service Trust Hospitals (Falmer 1997: 63–4).

However, within psychiatry the performance of systems such as DSM has been controversial. Rapid changes in the classifications themselves are difficult to reconcile with stable underlying states. Moreover their variable performance between major social categories, such as race and gender (Loring and Powell 1988), suggest that there has been considerable room for cultural influence, either within the committee systems that have refined the classifications, or within the clinical settings in which they have been used.

Sociology, science and technology

The process of psychiatric classification and diagnosis involves the construction of *representations* of aspects of the patient in terms of a presumed underlying reality, constructed as part of biological, medical or social science. The use of these representations in clinical situations involves the practical application of scientific knowledge to solve problems as understood by psychiatrists and others in the clinical setting. The way in which scientific representations, and their technological application to clinical problems, are developed has been the subject of extensive sociological study. Where scientific knowledge and technological applications are uncertain, disputed or rapidly changing, as has been the case for personality disorder, sociological study has been able more easily to examine the way in which social factors have shaped the construction and application of knowledge. A brief review of these developments in the sociology of science and technology will help us to consider using them as explanations in the case of categorical innovation in psychiatry, particularly the rapid elaboration of the diagnosis of personality disorder.

Woolgar (1995: 159, figure 4.1) summarises sociological approaches to understanding science as having developed through four stages towards a state of ethnographic inversion, whereby taken for granted assumptions in the 'black box' of science are exposed and examined as if they were an exotic and unfamiliar landscape. While these stages have indeed developed cumulatively, there is no widespread agreement that the fourth stage is uncritically or widely accepted as correct. At stage one, the real world was understood by sociologists to be transformed into scientific representations directly, with no social influences at play, or at least with a minimum of psychological or cognitive processes, such as perception. The observation of scientific competition, error or falsification led, in stage two, to a 'sociology of error' in which social influences were seen on occasions to divert or subvert true scientific representation. Following this notion, it was a relatively small step to stage three in which not only could erroneous representation be understood to have arisen out of social or cultural influences, but, equally, true representation and knowledge might also be similarly socially situated. All knowledge, both that claimed to be true and that claimed to be false, might vary with social and cultural context. It should be noted that this argument does not suggest that true knowledge, and the external reality to which it relates, is merely a cultural artefact. Such a radical stance is reserved for the fourth stage, in which the relationship between reality and observation is reversed, and the representation is taken by some sociologists of science to *constitute* reality itself.

A common strategy for identifying social and cultural effects in science has been to focus on occasions where scientific interpretation is uncertain, contested or emergent, before the point at which a common perspective and closure of alternatives has occurred. A highly influential study was that of Latour and Woolgar's (1979) on the discovery of a substance called TRF(H) (thyrotropin releasing factor (hormone)), which regulates the way substances are released by the pituitary gland. Their study was concerned to elucidate the way that the existence of TRF(H) became stabilised as an accepted fact. They describe how the reading of and discussion about the meaning of numbers from scientific equipment was transformed over the course of a few uncertain days into the 'discovery' of a substance that was felt to exist, and always to have existed, 'out there'. In particular, they wanted to show that the process of construction 'involved the use of certain devices whereby all traces of production are made extremely difficult to detect'. This process, they argued, is centred on the splitting and inversion of statements within the laboratory context, those statements being concerned with the issue of whether a particular substance such as TRF(H) really exists – *i.e.* whether it has been 'discovered':

'From their initial inception members of the laboratory are unable to determine whether statements (about the real existence of a substance) are true or false, objective or subjective, highly likely or quite probable ... once the statement begins to stabilise, however, an important change begins to take place. The statement becomes a split entity. On the one hand, it is a set of words which represent a statement about an object. On the other hand, it corresponds to an object in itself which takes on a life of its own. It is as if the original statement has projected a virtual image of itself which exists outside the statement ... Before long, more and more reality is attributed to the object and less and less to the statement about the object. Consequently an inversion takes place: the object becomes the reason why the statement was formulated in the first place. At the onset of stabilisation, the object was the virtual image of the statement; subsequently the statement becomes the mirror image of the reality 'out there' ... small wonder that the statements appear to match external reality so exactly; they are the same thing.' (1979: 176–77).

Latour and Woolgar are nevertheless at pains to distance this argument from the totally relativist position in which facts melt into perceptions. They are merely suggesting that 'out-there-ness is the consequence of scientific work rather than its cause' (1979: 182), agreeing with Marx, whom they quote approvingly, that 'an objective truth is not theoretical but a practical question' (1979: 179).

For any particular scientific finding to be established an explanation has to work – *i.e.* to resonate with other accepted theoretical elements, to generate new soluble problems and to explain aspects of observed reality. Alternative explanations have also to be discredited legitimately, so that *closure* can be established around a scientific problem – a closure that excludes alternative explanations, and excludes the possibility of any other interesting research questions or problems in connection with that particular issue.

In these and similar studies, there is an uneasy relationship between the depiction of the influence of social factors and the obstinate resistance of reality itself. Some knowledge 'works' while other knowledge doesn't. Closure is best accomplished where knowledge truths shine through. The connection between reality and knowledge has been characterised in (largely) French social theory in terms of *actor-networks* (Callon 1989: 92 ff). This is unique in that it gives space to inanimate objects and processes in the analysis of the network of relations surrounding any particular scientific project. Both human actors and non-human factors may influence the outcome. Callon suggests that actor-networks serve to provide a manageable focus for scientific work through two processes: simplification and juxtaposition. Actors cannot handle the infinite variability of the real world without simplifying it, and any particular scientific problem is both dependent upon and impacts a variety of heterogeneous elements that are linked to it, or juxtaposed in a network of relevant relations. The motive for action is the active recruitment of the varied interests of different individuals and groups into a network in which, much as in a field of battle, 'whose "fact" is more "factual" depends on whether actors succeed in enrolling allies much as leaders enrol armies and armouries' (Fujimura 1995: 304).

For example, in psychiatry, particularly where it is concerned with personality disorder, the actor-network might include doctors, patients and home secretaries, but also drugs and drug companies, insurance schemes, prisons, surveillance technology and risks. These are juxtaposed by virtue of their varied relevance to personality disorder and are the salient elements simplified out from other potential elements, such as houses, social movements, or electricity. What is included or excluded from the network is therefore fundamental to the way the scientific issues are tackled and how the story unfolds. As we shall see, key actors in the actor-network operate to recruit other elements to bolster their interests. But the significance of the actor-network model, Callon argues, is that it can incorporate inanimate changes into sociological explanations. Thus where new drugs are identified, or surveillance technologies are developed, this can be just as significant for psychiatric science as the changing fortunes of a profession, or the state, or the public's fear of crime and sense of social risk in late-modern society.

But psychiatry includes both pure science and technological application (clinical work). Sociology here has developed relevant work through the sociology of technology. Pinch and Bijker (1989) suggest that the sociology of technology is relatively undeveloped in comparison with the sociology of science. Nevertheless, there are similar issues involved. Just as successful scientific findings depend on the closure of alternative explanations and the exhaustion of interesting problems, successful technologies have also been found to depend on the closure of alternative solutions to a technical problem and the satisfactory elimination of associated difficulties. Closure, they suggest, can be the result of either the elimination of a controversial problem through a single successful technological design, or through the redefinition of a technological problem into some other related problem for which a previously indifferent solution turns out to be spectacularly successful. They cite, for example, the difficulties of Dunlop in the 1890s of persuading cyclists that the air tyre solved vibration problems, until it transpired that the air tyre proved to have enormous advantage in cycle racing and, thence, generated widespread public support.

Clinical studies involving technological artefacts or their equivalent in terms of applying diagnostic or treatment knowledge have been growing in number (Elston 1997). An early example was reported in 1976 by Bloor. In it he showed how widely varied were the routines adopted by ENT specialists contemplating tonsillectomies with regard to clinical signs, decisions, and histories. This is not surprising since over the previous 40 years wide variations had been reported, showing that treatment varied sharply by social class, geography and even rates of circumcision, which were unlikely to reflect underlying rates of a reliably detectable medical condition. Clearly the significance of this study was the remarkable lack of closure that had occurred despite many years of clinical work. A more recent example is provided by Prout's (1996) study of the metered dose inhaler. This device had two interesting effects, both delegating biomedical work to the patient, and configuring the patient to adapt to the technical demands of the device. However, a large minority of patients were unable to adapt to the device and thus the delegation and configuration failed. Further rounds of technical innovation ensued in an attempt to circumvent the 'incompetent user'.

There are equivalents within psychiatry. We have seen how difficult it has been to settle on an effective diagnostic classification, particularly when employed as a routine technology in clinical practice. Personality disorder, discussed in detail in the next section, appears to be psychiatry's equivalent to tonsillitis – widely disputed, denied even to be a medical concern by some, yet for others lurking around every clinical corner. Similarly, the difficulty of 'configuring' schizophrenic patients living in the community to self-medicate as the pharmaceuticals require, has resulted in recent political despair and the declaration that community care has failed. Perhaps standardised diagnostic manuals themselves are in effect the delegation of medical science to clinicians, many of whom fail to become correctly 'configured' in the face of the patients that they see.

Technological development is thus deeply embedded in social and culturally specified issues and none more clearly so than in the case of science, since technological artefacts are teleological – explicitly designed rather than dis-covered – and designed to overcome problems located in an actor-network in which professional, government, business and popular interests are more salient. In clinical psychiatry, pressing daily concerns to classify and find legitimate treatment for patients referred by exasperated doctors and relatives, or by police and prison authorities, and to train junior doctors and nurses, all in a manner which sustains the mystique, status and ethical standards of general medicine, suggest a rather different actor-network than in academic psychiatry.

The case of personality disorder

There is more controversy over personality disorder than almost any other area of psychiatric practice. It is a confusing area and one that attracts very little research attention. It is an important clinical area about which we know very little (Lewis and Wessely 1997: 183).

This is the opening statement in the relevant section of the latest edition of a highly respected textbook, *The Essentials of Postgraduate Psychiatry*, published by Cambridge University Press and edited by senior members of the self-proclaimed world leader in academic psychiatry, the London Institute of Psychiatry. Conventional epidemiological assessments suggest a prevalence of all types of personality disorder of around 10 per cent of the general population, 10–30 per cent appearing in primary care settings, 50–60 per cent of suicide attempts and 20–70 per cent of prisoners (Tyrer *et al.* 1991: 467–8).

Personality disorder presents difficulties both to academic psychiatrists working on ICD/DSM classifications, and to clinical staff dealing with the typical trail of interpersonal mayhem that patients with the disorder leave in their wake. There is, in addition, a troubled relationship between academics and clinicians. Such difficulties are fruitful points of entry for sociological analysis. How do psychiatrists and others deal with these difficulties and how can we understand their scientific and clinical strategies? In *Functionalism, Exchange and Theoretical Strategy* (1971), Mulkay observed, following Kuhn, that 'difficulties' (anomalies) are the stimulus to innovation. What is 'interesting', Davis (1971) suggests, is not the conformist completion of a standard scientific or technical approach, but the development of a new line of enquiry. Who develops this and how they persuade others of its merits is the very stuff of actor-networks.

For personality disorder, the historical accretions of classifications, such as those of Kraepelin, Kretschmer, Schneider and Henderson, along with an eclectic mixture of other work, have found their way into the various personality disorder subtypes in the ICD/DSM system: paranoid, schizoid, dissocial, borderline, histrionic, dependent, avoidant, anankastic, schizotypal, narcissistic, and passive-aggressive (Tyrer *et al.* 1991). For example, the DSM regroups these into three broad types, eccentric, dramatic and anxious, highly reminiscent of Henderson's three types of aggressive, creative and inadequate. All of these are described in rather general 'trait' terms, with none of the precise operational definitions used for the standard axis I disorders. Only two of these 11 types are widely used clinically – borderline and dissocial (antisocial/sociopathic/psychopathic) – each with their own actor-network. I shall attempt to lay out three actor-networks: the academic-governmental ICD/DSM network, the network for the borderline category and the forensic network for the dissocial category.

The ICD/DSM network

During the early 20th century, mental disorder was increasingly separated into the well-known triumvirate of psychosis, neurosis and psychopath (the latter two categories dropped, incidentally, by both the ICD and DSM systems in the 1990s). While the growth of psychoanalysis in the 1930s and 1940s rendered precise classification less important, by the 1960s poor agreement between psychiatrists and the large difference in first admission rates for schizophrenia in the US and UK, not to mention the abuse of the term in the Soviet Union, stimulated a series of US/UK studies. The WHO carried these international comparisons to a wider sample of countries in the early 1970s. Both in the US and the WHO these initiatives led to substantially revised versions of psychiatric classification: the ICD-8 in 1974 and DSM-III in 1980 (Falmer 1997).

The ICD-10 system, effective in the UK since April 1994, is designed to cover the requirements of scientific research, clinical work, service development and psychiatric education. It was developed between 1984 and 1990 from a series of committee discussions and field trials to produce operational definitions. A draft version was widely circulated and field trials carried out in 110 clinical centres in 37 countries involving 700 clinicians. There has been considerable and deliberate convergence between ICD-10, Chapter 5, and DSM-IV, with ICD doing most of the accommodation. The reason is that not only is the American Psychiatric Association, as author of the DSM system, supportive of its use, but other countries, including the UK, in effect use the DSM rather than the ICD system in research and clinical work. For example, the axis II split introduced into the DSM is currently under consideration for introduction to the ICD system.

The key actors in this network, particularly with respect to the personality disorders, have been American academic psychiatry, and the US public and private insurance industry, with a secondary role played by the US psychoanalytic community. This becomes clear when we examine two of the most frequently used personality disorder categories, borderline and dissocial.

The borderline network
The 'discovery' of the borderline type exhibits a distinctive pattern. Initially it was identified in 1938 by Stern, who noticed patients in his psychoanalytic office practice who disregarded the usual boundaries of therapy, and had a personality organisation which differed from psychotic or neurotic types. However, this was not taken up widely until the 1960s in the USA, when a simultaneous but distinct pattern of discovery occurred. Simultaneous discovery in science, leading to the widely recognised pattern of competition and rivalry for recognition, has been used by sociologists to suggest that external social and cultural factors may be important harbingers of scientific advance. Examples might include commercial needs, such as to establish the measurement of longitude, or the military impetus to understand group dynamics in the UK in World War II (WWII), which led to the simultaneous but independent development of therapeutic communities (Manning 1989). In this case, the two rival worlds of private psychoanalytic therapy and academic psychiatry developed the use of the borderline type at the same time. In 1967 and 1968, Kernberg gave classic psychoanalytic definitions of the *borderline personality organisation*, followed in 1972 by Masterson's extension to adolescents, using object-relations theory. The explosion of interest was remarkable. By 1975, 50 papers had been published on this theme. By 1980, there were 300 papers and by 1985, 1,000 papers (Gundersen 1994: 13).

At the very same time, Grinker *et al.* in 1968 identified the *borderline syndrome*, describing the same type of patients, but with a tighter definition. Grinker enjoyed a particularly high status in US academic psychiatry and was, in contrast to the psychoanalysts, committed to using conventional empirical methods. This gave academic legitimacy to the syndrome and once again, the development of research studies in the field took off: two in 1975, 10 by 1980, 100 by 1985 and 300 by 1990. Between 1975 and 1980,

Gundersen and others consolidated the new borderline type through literature summaries: 'The surprising attention given to those works testified to the nascent but widespread recognition of patients with this syndrome and the hunger for knowledge about them' (Gundersen 1994: 13). Subsequent empirical research established that borderline types were not subtypes of schizophrenic or affective disorders, nor inherited, but caused by childhood trauma and neglect and DSM status was duly conferred in 1980.

What is going on here?

> The interests of these groups at first seem opposed: one is deeply rooted in the psychodynamic tradition, with concern for the structure and development of personality and intrapsychic phenomena, and the other is preoccupied with accurate and reliable descriptions of behaviour that can be fashioned into the operational criteria of a DSM diagnosis. It says a great deal for the flexibility of personality disorder as a concept that these approaches have been married successfully, whereas for other subjects, particularly the neuroses, there has been a public and bad-tempered divorce. 'Borderline' is the common key to this success. Although it is accused of being an elusive adjective only (Akiskal *et al.* 1986) and unless 'used to signify a class that borders on something, has no clinical or descriptive meaning at all' (Millon 1981: 332), it permeates the literature on personality disorder in all its contexts. Indeed, to many, 'personality disorder' is interpreted as 'borderline', illustrating the adaptability of a word that, after Lewis Carroll's *Through the Looking Glass*, could be described as a 'Humpty Dumptyism' ('when I choose a word', Humpty Dumpty said in a rather scornful tone, 'it means just what I choose it to mean, – neither more nor less') (Tyrer *et al.* 1991: 464).

In the psychoanalytic field, there appears to have been a spontaneous response to the articulation of a new type. The key element was that it focused on instability of identity. There was alienation from stable relationships and a mixture of grandiosity, contempt and dependency. Patients tended to polarise people between good and bad and attacked the links between them. Feelings of rage or shame are projected onto others. Why did this strike such a chord in the late 1960s rather than pre-war? It would appear that liberalisation of attitudes in the 1960s, the growth of inter-personal tolerance of varied lifestyles and values, the focus on personal fulfilment through close personal relationships and the movement of identity issues into the heart of popular culture, meant that those who were unable to respond to these changes would have begun to differentiate themselves and appear in the offices of private psychoanalysts. It is important to remember that within actor-network theory, both actors and non-human factors, are included as part of the network within which the scientific or technical innovation is embedded. In the psychoanalytic actor-network, the massive cultural changes of the 1960s are the key stimulus.

Turning to the world of academic psychiatry we can more easily identify Grinker as the key player. No doubt the same stranded souls, left behind by changes in the 1960s, were appearing in psychiatric clinics and hospital out-patient departments. At the same time, with the passing of the 1965 US medicare and medicaid social security amendments, there was rapidly growing concern about the control of government health spending and the desire to contain costs. In this context, Grinker was able to recruit support from academic psychiatrists and the committee system of DSM, for his newly-discovered syndrome. In both cases, the development of a new type enabled a heterogeneous group of patients that did not fit elsewhere (neither schizoid nor affective) to be *simplified* into a new category, which was *juxtaposed* with a theoretical explanation (childhood trauma), articulated with alternative theories (no evidence for heritability) and became inverted from a statement about difficult patients, to the discovery of an already pre-existing and coherent patient type: the 'borderline'.

The dissocial (antisocial/sociopathic/psychopathic) network
This category has long and classic roots, touched on earlier in this chapter, although it only appeared in psychiatric textbooks in the UK in 1956. There is considerable variation and overlap in the use of terms related to this type. In Europe the whole set of personality disorders is often grouped under the term psychopath. In the DSM system, however, the psychopathic type is just one of the 11 sub-types of personality disorder. In the UK the general term severe personality disorder has recently been used by the Home Secretary to accentuate the dangerousness of some patients in this category to justify pre-emptive incarceration. In British mental health law, the category psycho-pathic disorder is very wide, covering most types of personality disorder: 'a persistent disorder or disability of mind (whether or not including subnormality of intelligence) which results in abnormally aggressive or seriously irresponsible conduct ...'. Public interest in serial killers and fictionalised characters such as Hannibal Lecter, have influenced popular views. On the other hand long standing specialist treatment units, such as Henderson Hospital in the UK, have until recently used this term to describe their patients, whereas during the 1990s it has become clear that most of them should be classified in the borderline category (Dolan *et al.* 1997: 275). In fact, many patients classified as dissocial would be found in prison or in severe cases in the special hospitals such as Broadmoor or Rampton.

Ramon (1986) argues that the growth of psychological models of group and organisational life after WWII, followed by the 'open door' policies of many mental hospitals in the 1950s, and the decline in mental hospital population, exposed these patients as if by a falling tide, but with a widespread concern that there was no psychiatric technology (drugs, ECT, psycho-surgery) that would work for them. They were not popular with psychiatrists who felt they were largely untreatable, and their inclusion as a special category in the 1959 Mental Health Act was controversial, and famously criticised by Baroness Wootton (1959) at the time. Here we see a clear conflict of interest between the profession and the state. Why include them under mental health law? Ramon argues that:

> The answer ... is not to be found at the level of medical expertise but at the level of social regulation. The psychiatric concept of psychopathy makes possible a way of explaining conduct which would otherwise be socially unintelligible, regulating individuals who do not fit prevailing explanations of social need and their associated welfare systems, and confining persons who would otherwise fall outside the ambit of both the criminal justice system and the psychiatric system itself (1986: 227).

The solution to the distaste of conventional psychiatric services for the dissocial type, was to be the development of a medium secure unit service, situated on the psychiatric side of the medical-penal divide, but separate from either district services, or the special hospitals. These, recommended by the Butler Committee (Home Office/Department of Health and Social Security, 1975), were however very slow to materialise, partly because of the unwillingness of nurses to work in them. Ramon concluded that the categorisation of personality disorder is a useful smokescreen for detaining difficult people, because there has been no technology yet that has commanded widespread support as effective, notwithstanding the claims of therapeutic communities, such as Henderson Hospital, to be able both to contain and treat such people.

In recent years, there has been a slow but gathering movement to make the case for therapeutic community treatment. This approach, developed as a crusading and radical approach to psychiatric treatment after WWII, has been very reluctant to articulate an effective actor-network for dissocial patients (Manning 1979), particularly in terms of the conventional presentation of empirical evidence. This has allowed an assumption to develop in the psychiatric profession that 'nothing works'. However, in the last decade in the UK, research associated with the Henderson Hospital and Grendon Underwood Prison has built a sufficiently convincing case for both services to be expanded through the funding of entirely new units; and in Germany Lösel (1998) has been very active in supporting the German equivalent: the social-therapeutic institution. Similar developments have been growing quickly within the US prison system (Rawlings 1999). Recently, the High Security Psychiatric Services Commission Board responsible for the special hospitals and, in effect, charged with the management of these patients throughout the UK, commissioned a review of the evidence which showed that, indeed, the therapeutic community does appear to have a demonstrable effect (Lees *et al.* 1999) and has set up a sub-committee to evaluate the evidence further.

In the case of the dissocial type, the key actors have been the psychiatric profession, the state and the uncertain evidence of any effective technology. The general term 'psychopath' has been pared down to a more limited type, as other types of personality disorder have achieved separate categorisation, at the hands of psychoanalytic and academic innovation. Rather than the 'discovery' of a new type of disorder, there has been the steady residual-isation of a rump of supposedly untreatable, and, as far as the current Home Secretary is concerned, intolerable people.

Conclusion: science, technology and professional survival

Psychiatry is a science, a technology and a profession. All three aspects bring to psychiatry's actor-network particular opportunities, motivations and constraints. In the world of science, while there are deliberate deceptions from time to time, these are rare. More often scientific ideas have been exposed as based on historically or culturally bound perceptions, when they have made claims to universality. We can look back with the benefit of hindsight to the Copernician debate over the relative movement of earth and sun, or the more recent debates on the Darwinian theory of evolution. After the US War of Independence, Benjamin Rush identified diseases such as 'anarchia' (an excessive passion for liberty) and 'revolutiona' (continued loyalty to the British Crown) (Szasz 1971: 140). Lest this seems a cheap historical point, of no more consequence than the idea that phlogiston 'causes' fire, the similarity to the diagnosis of 'sluggish schizophrenia', often given to dissidents under Russia's Brezhnev government, is notable. In the 20th century controversy was still common in the field of psychiatry over the scientific status of mental illnesses. Trombley (1981) identified in detail the social and cultural influences on the eminent doctors who diagnosed Virginia Woolf as insane. Szasz built a whole career on the argument that mental illness was a myth, more or less over the same period that the ICD/DSM system was being painstakingly put into place.

Within psychiatry there have been few periods, if any, of 'normal science' in the Kuhnian sense. Rather the pattern has been one of continual innovation. Psychiatry is part of medicine. Psychiatrists are trained in medical schools. Psychiatric nurses learn general nursing. In medicine powerful techniques have been developed and applied to prevent and treat disease, particularly with drugs and surgical skills. Practitioners of physical medicine can point with pride to the success with which many fatal diseases have been eradicated in the 19th and 20th centuries. Psychiatrists and psychiatric nurses will have learned to expect the gratification which results from the application of general medical techniques. But psychiatry is an area which has not had the spectacular success of physical medicine. As Merton (1968) observed, such a disjunction, where goals are accepted but the existing means for their attainment are inadequate and rejected, generates great incentive for innovation. In such a situation, a cherished goal will virtually justify any means. Hence, such practices as 'ether-drip therapy', 'carbon dioxide inhalation therapy', 'brain surgery', 'electro-shock therapy' and 'insulin-coma therapy' have all been justified by the cherished goal of psychiatric treatment, even when theoretical reasons for the effects were not at all clear. Rapid innovation of the personality disorders is thus not unusual for psychiatry.

This pattern lends itself to sociological analysis. But pressure for innovation is not a sufficient explanation. Why do some ideas come to be taken up rather than others? The answer depends on the networks within which the diagnostic systems are embedded, the academic context for particular disorders and the clinical problems faced in psychiatric practice. These networks act as filters for the sifting of ideas and the matching of ideas with perceived issues and problems. Indeed, the networks appear to be quite unstable, resulting in relatively rapid promotion and exhaustion of treatments:

> Psychiatrists, as any human beings, will grasp at straws. With the introduction of insulin shock therapy, reports of 90–95 per cent cures appeared, and we were carried away with enthusiasm. Thousands of papers were written on the subject, physiological explanations for its effectiveness were propounded. Yet, where is insulin therapy today? Who can report such cures now? That which was once heralded is hardly used today, only some decades since its introduction. Electro shock treatment is not faring much differently. It is not uncommon to hear psychiatrists, who only recently waxed enthusiastic about this procedure, indicate equal enthusiasm about tranquillisers. They are turning away from shock treatment. The explanations for its effectiveness are no longer meaningful, but those for the new drugs gain credence. How long before we witness the same thing occurring with the tranquillisers which are currently capturing the scene? In the light of what has happened with the others, it would not seem far-fetched to forecast the same doom for these drugs in psychiatry (Gralnick 1969: 90).

How right this prediction turned out to be. That generation of drugs is now condemned and has been replaced by the 'new tranquillisers'. Gralnick's comment came at the end of the 1960s, just as the borderline personality disorder type was being established. It predicts perfectly the 'take-off' of the borderline idea in both psychoanalytic and academic psychiatry networks. The actors in those actor-networks were highly motivated to support new ideas and keen to be recruited into new developments. 'Borderline' patients continue to multiply. The recent rapid growth of the recognition of childhood abuse, particularly sexual abuse, which for many psychiatrists is felt to underlie borderline symptoms, is an important part of the network sustaining the spread of the personality disorder category.

Psychiatry is also a technology. As Brown's (1987) study showed, there continues to be tension in the application of these classifications at the local clinical level. Here the messy lives and histories that patients present do not fit the categories neatly. Star (1995: 104) has asked, 'where does the mess go?' when designs are juxtaposed with an intransigent reality. She was discussing the trade-offs made by computer chip designers who have to balance incorporating of-the-shelf or standard work in their designs, which is relatively undemanding, with the requirement to adjust them to local contingencies. Psychiatrists have to do the same in terms of utilising standard classifications and therapies. Star observed four strategies. The first was the freezing of formal parts of the design, so that local contingencies can be fully attended. This is the equivalent of agreeing to the ICD-10 recommendation that one, and only one, diagnostic category should be used to determine treatment for a patient, even though most cases do not fit neatly. The difficulty with this is that it can lead to 'generative entrenchment' whereby early decisions can ramify throughout treatment, and, as with embryos, small mistakes may result in monsters downstream. The second strategy was to rely on 'wizards', 'gurus', or 'tall thin' experts who can span several parts of the spectrum. These are the psychiatrists who can work both as scientists or theorists and workaday clinicians. The trouble with these is that they are scarce and their unique capacity, if not privatised, is inaccessible to all. The third strategy was to try to capture and share this tacit knowledge, but this loops back round to the initial problems that arise with the standardisation of knowledge. We have seen this in abundance in the proliferation of more and more categories and sub-categories of personality disorder. The fourth strategy is to 'denigrate the social', or to blame the actor-network for distorting the technical system, believed in itself to be sound. A famous example was the Challenger space shuttle disaster. Once the technical failure was identified, 'impurity stories' proliferated as to the social and political reasons for it. Technical failures in psychiatry might include tardive dyskinesia, institutionalisation and, now, even community care. Each of these has been blamed on the 'impure' political or economic network within which psychiatry operates.

Finally, psychiatry is a profession. This is a state-licensed occupation. This area of the actor network within which psychiatry exists often sees psychiatry as the way in which 'the mess' is to be cleared up. The British Home Secretary's announcement on 19 July, 1999, that individuals assessed as suffering *Dangerous Severe Personality Disorder* (shortened in his press release to yet another new category, of 'DSPD') could be detained indefinitely, is a clear statement that for the residual dissocial personality disorder category, the final core had been reached. There is no such category within the current ICD/DSM system to date, although the innovative term *severe personality disorder* was promulgated in 1996 by the medical directors of the specialist Henderson and Cassel Hospitals (Norton and Hinshelwood 1996) and in the time-honoured fashion taken up by psychiatric colleagues. Nevertheless, psychiatry is being called upon to undertake the 'dirty work' that Hughes (1971) described as common to all societies.

In each of these areas – science, technology and profession – there have been particular network configurations that have impacted on the recent pattern of category innovation in the personality disorders. The science has thrown up a sustained period of innovation, yet to be exhausted. The professional context has brought pressure to bear for the treatment of a group perceived to be highly troublesome. In between, clinical psychiatrists struggle to connect these two frequently incompatible parts of the psychiatric network.

References

Akiskal, H.S., Chen, S.E. and Davis, G.C. (1986) Borderline: an adjective in search of a noun. In Stone, M.S. (ed) *Essential Papers on Borderline Disorders: One Hundred Years at the Border*. New York: New York University Press.

Bloor, M. (1976) Bishop Berkeley and the adenotonsillectomy enigma: an exploration of variation in the social construction of medical disposals, *Sociology*, 10, 43–61.

Box, S. (1981) Preface. In Schrag, P. and Divoky, D. (eds) *The Myth of the Hyperactive Child and other Means of Child Control*. Harmondsworth: Penguin.

Brown, P. (1987) Diagnostic conflict and contradiction in psychiatry, *Journal of Health and Social Behaviour*, 28, 37–50.

Callon, M. (1989) Society in the making: the study of technology as a tool for sociological analysis. In Bijker, W.E., Hughes, T.P. and Pinch, T.J. (eds) *The Social Construction of Technological Systems, New Directions in the Sociology and History of Technology*. London: MIT Press.

Davis, M.S. (1971) That's interesting! Towards a phenomenology of sociology and a sociology of phenomenology, *Philosophy of the Social Sciences*, 1, 309–44.

Dolan, B., Warren, F. and Norton, K. (1997) Change in borderline symptoms one year after therapeutic community treatment for severe personality disorder, *British Journal of Psychiatry*, 171, 274–9.

Elston, M.A. (1997) (ed) *The Sociology of Medical Science and Technology*. Oxford: Basil Blackwell.

Falmer, A.E. (1997) Current approaches to classification. In Murray, R., Hill, P. and McGuffin, P. (eds) *The Essentials of Postgraduate Psychiatry*. Cambridge: Cambridge University Press.

Fujimura, J.H. (1995) Ecologies of action: recombining genes, molecularising cancer, and transforming biology. In Star, S.L. (ed) *Ecologies of Knowledge: Work and Politics in Science and Technology*. Albany: State University of New York Press.

Gralnick, A. (1969) *The Psychiatric Hospital as a Therapeutic Instrument*. New York: Brunner/Mazel.

Grinker, R., Werble, B. and Drye, R. (1968) *The Borderline Syndrome: a Behavioural Study of Ego Functions*. New York: Basic Books.

Goffman, E. (1971) *Relations in Public*. New York: Harper and Row.

Gundersen, J.G. (1994) Building structure for the borderline construct, *Acta Psychiatrica Scandinavica*, 89, Supplement 379, 12–18.

Higgit, A. and Fonagy, P. (1992) Psychotherapy in borderline and narcissistic personality disorder, *British Journal of Psychiatry*, 161, 23–43.

Home Office/Department of Health and Social Security (1975) *Report of the Committee on Mentally Disordered Offenders*, Cmnd 6244, London: HMSO.

Hughes, E.C. (1971) Good people and dirty work. In Hughes E.C. (ed) *The Sociological Eye*. Chicago: Aldine.

Kernberg, O. (1967) Borderline personality organisation, *Journal of the American Psychoanalytic Association*, 15, 641–85.

Kernberg, O. (1968) The treatment of patients with borderline personality organisation, *International Journal of Psychoanalysis*, 49, 600–19.

Latour, B. and Woolgar, S. (1979) *Laboratory Life, the Social Construction of Scientific Facts*. London: Sage.

Lees, J., Manning, N. and Rawlings, B. (1999) *Therapeutic Community Effectiveness. A Systematic International Review of Therapeutic Community Treatment for People with Personality Disorders and Mentally Disordered Offenders*, CRD Report 17. University of York: NHS Centre for Reviews and Dissemination.

Lewis, G. and Wessely, S. (1997) Personality disorder. In Murray, R., Hill, P. and McGuffin, P. (eds) *The Essentials of Postgraduate Psychiatry*. Cambridge: Cambridge University Press.

Light, D. (1980) *Becoming Psychiatrists: the Professional Transformation of Self*. New York: Norton.

Loring, M. and Powell, B. (1988) Gender, race and DSM-III: a study of the objectivity of psychiatric diagnostic behaviour, *Journal of Health and Social Behaviour*, 29, 1–22.

Lösel, F. (1998) The treatment and management of psychopaths. In Cooke, D.J. (ed) *Psychopathy: Theory, Research and Implications for Society*. Netherlands: Kluwer Academic Publishers.

Manning, N. (1979) The politics of survival: the role of research in the therapeutic community. In Hinshelwood, R.D. and Manning, N. (eds) *Therapeutic Communities, Reflections and Progress*. London: Routledge and Kegan Paul.

Manning, N. (1989) *The Therapeutic Community Movement: Charisma and Routinization*. London: Routledge.

Masterson, J. (1972) *Treatment of the Borderline Adolescent: a Developmental Approach*. New York: John Wiley and Sons.

Merton, R. (1968) *Social Theory and Social Structure*. New York: Free Press.

Millon, T. (1981) *Disorders of Personality, DSM-III: Axis II*. New York: Wiley and Sons.

Mirowski, J. and Ross, C. (1989) Psychiatric diagnosis as reified measurement, *Journal of Health and Social Behaviour*, 30, 11–25.

Mulkay, M. (1971) *Functionalism, Exchange and Theoretical Strategy*. London: Routledge and Kegan Paul.

Norton, K. and Hinshelwood, H. (1996) Severe personality disorder, *British Journal of Psychiatry*, 168, 723–31.

Pinch, T.J. and Bijker, W.E. (1989) The social construction of facts and artefacts: or how the sociology of science and the sociology of technology might benefit each other. In Bijker, W.E., Hughes, T.P. and Pinch, T.J. (eds) *The Social Construction of Technological Systems, New Directions in the Sociology and History of Technology*. London: MIT Press.

Prout, A. (1996) Actor-network theory, technology and medical sociology: an illustrative analysis of the metered dose inhaler, *Sociology of Health and Illness*, 18, 2, 198–219.

Ramon, S. (1986) The category of psychopathy: its profession and social context in Britain. In Miller, P. and Rose, N. (eds) *The Power of Psychiatry*. Cambridge: Polity Press.

Rawlings, B. (1999) Therapeutic communities in prisons, *Policy and Politics*, 27, 1, 97–112.

Rosenhan, D. (1973) On being sane in insane places, *Science*, 179, 250–8.

Star, S.L. (1995) The politics of formal representations: wizards, gurus, and organisational complexity. In Star, S.L. (ed) *Ecologies of Knowledge: Work and Politics in Science and Technology*. Albany: State University of New York Press.

Stern, A. (1938) Psychoanalytic investigation and therapy in the borderline group of neuroses, *Psychoanalytic Quarterly*, 7, 467–89.

Szasz, T. (1971) *The Manufacture of Madness*. London: Routledge & Kegan Paul.

Trombley, S. (1981) *'All that Summer She was Mad', Virginia Woolf and her Doctors*. London: Junction Books.

Tyrer, P., Casey, P. and Ferguson, B. (1991) Personality disorder in perspective, *British Journal of Psychiatry*, 159, 463–71.

Woolgar, S. (1995) Representation, cognition, and self: what hope for an integration of psychology and sociology? In Star, S.L. (ed) *Ecologies of Knowledge: Work and Politics in Science and Technology*. Albany: State University of New York.

Wootton, B. (1959) *Social Science and Social Pathology*. London: Allen and Unwin.

6

A phenomenology of fear: Merleau-Ponty and agoraphobic life-worlds

This chapter is dedicated to Jim Davidson, 1965–2000

Joyce Davidson

Agoraphobia: an introduction

Both received popular wisdom and dictionary definitions typically characterise agoraphobia as being an experience of 'dread in, and of, open spaces'[1]. However, while the experience of agoraphobia is evidently spatially mediated (as is apparent in other names for the condition such as *platzangst* in German, and *peur des espaces*, in French) this common definition is actually quite misleading (Marks 1987). As the term itself, coined by Westphal in 1871, suggests, it seems to be *social* spaces, those 'public places of assembly' epitomised by the *agora* (the ancient Greek marketplace), rather than *open* spaces that typically induce agoraphobic avoidance[2]. To paraphrase Sartre, hell, for the agoraphobic, is in fact 'other people'.

Despite sharing some features with, and often seeming to encompass social phobia, the *Diagnostic and Statistical Manual of Mental Disorders* (DSM IV) classifies agoraphobia as an identifiably separate anxiety disorder from both 'Social' and 'Simple' phobias. (American Psychiatric Association 1994). Although the APA is consistent in characterising agoraphobia in terms of the subjects' fears about being away from home and/or in social situations from which they cannot easily withdraw, the precise diagnostic criteria have altered with each edition of DSM[3]. Since 1980 (DSM III) agoraphobia has been closely associated with the new diagnostic category of 'Panic disorder', hence the current definitions of 'Panic disorder with agoraphobia' and the less common, and more contentious, 'Agoraphobia without a history of panic disorder'[4]. The occurrence of panic attacks is not only of crucial diagnostic importance, it is also a primary concern of sufferers themselves. (In my own research all those I have interviewed have, without exception, experienced panic attacks[5].) Typically, the onset of agoraphobic avoidance occurs in *women* – around 89 per cent of agoraphobics are female (Clum and Knowles 1991)[6] – following a panic attack in a public place, whether in response to stressful circumstances, or seemingly 'out of the blue'. Sufferers then begin to avoid places of a similar nature for fear they might experience another attack.

What is clear is that both the agoraphobic's difficulties in traversing social space and any accompanying panic attacks seem to entail a destabilisation, if not complete breakdown of the boundary between 'inner' self and 'outer' world (Davidson 2000). In the words of one interviewee, 'When I take a serious ... panic attack, I feel as though there's no ... no top of my head. I feel as though it's all opened up, and it's *air* '[7]. In extreme cases this is experienced as a threat to the sufferer's sense of identity, as a form of derealisation or depersonalisation[8]. In this situation, Marks writes, 'one feels temporarily strange, unreal, disembodied, cut off or far away from immediate surroundings, and one's voice sounds strange and distant' (Marks 1987: 342). The sufferer cannot *connect* with her surroundings and feels 'out of place' in a disconcertingly alien world.

Such experiences are difficult to conceptualise, but I shall argue that the philosophy of Merleau-Ponty, which seeks to elucidate the interrelations between self and others in terms of phenomenology of social space can provide valuable insights into agoraphobia.

Merleau-Ponty, space and the horizons of identity

> Every sensation carries within it the germ of a dream or depersonalisation [...] this activity takes place on the periphery of my being (Merleau-Ponty 1962: 215. Hereafter referenced as *PP*.).

Since, as Merleau-Ponty points out, our own births and deaths are 'prepersonal horizons' that cannot be experienced by us, all that remains of our existence is our apprehension of ourselves as 'already born' and 'still alive'. (*PP*: 216) But, although there are *defining* moments at our beginning and at our ending, the nature of our existence in between these points is less easily circumscribed. Modernity and modern philosophy, in keeping with Newton's solid mechanics and the possessive individualism of an emergent capitalism, have sought to impose hard and fast lines around us; to make of the individual an atom, a being-for-itself, autonomous, self-interested and introspective[9]. For Descartes, the first modern philosopher, the *cogito* provided the acid test of our continued existence – I am thinking, therefore I am ('still in existence'). In this way existence was intellectualised, equated with the activity of thinking, of bringing our being before the court of self-consciousness.

Ironically, for a materialist age, where tangibility is regarded as the *sine qua non* of the external world's existence, the Cartesian solution redefines the self in terms of a life of the mind. Subjects are thinking things (*res cogito*) who are *not of this world*, souls without material substance (*res extensa*). In this way our identity is protected only at the cost of completely separating self and world, internal and external, the subjective from the objective. We are ghosts in the body's machine, disconnected observers watching the world pass us by.

But, Merleau-Ponty argues that this cannot be. We are not a pure pre-given consciousness since consciousness is first and foremost 'intentional', it is always consciousness of some-thing[10]. What is more, this intentionality is not intellectually discovered but is something we become aware of through our *lived* experiences. Contra Descartes, consciousness is not something set apart from the world, but is itself a part of the world, it is 'a project of the world, meant for a world which it neither embraces or possesses, but toward which it is perpetually directed' (*PP*: xvii)[11]. This dissolution of the absolute Cartesian boundary between self and world has a number of important implications. First, it re-emphasises the body as integral to any understanding of the human situation. 'I am conscious of the world through the medium of my body [. . .] I am conscious of my body via the world' (*PP*: 82). The 'subject that I am, when taken concretely, is inseparable from this body and this world' (*PP*: 40). We are *incarnate*, our access to the world is by way of our bodies. Second, this obviously means that, unlike *res cogito*, we do have extension, we *take up/occupy space*. Indeed, the experience of space is fundamental to our individuality, since our identity is no longer conceived of as a pre-given essence, a soul, but as a product and projection of our unique *situation* within the world. Third, thinking can no longer inoculate us against the world's intrusion since identity and thought are relational rather than absolute. 'I am not, therefore, in Hegel's phrase, "a hole in being" but a hollow, a fold, which has been made and can be unmade' (*PP*: 215).

Philosophy, for Merleau-Ponty thus becomes an investigation into the fragility of our existence, into the complex inter-relations between body, space and self, into what it *feels* like, and what it means to be alive. Where Descartes sought understanding through the application of a philosophical method, an intellectual programme for pure thought, Merleau-Ponty directs his attention to the *phenomenology* of existence. It is not thinking but *perception* that is paradigmatic of our lived but never fully conscious experience. Rather than taking self (perceiver) or world (perceived) as given, we must begin with perceptions themselves, *i.e.* with phenomena. Perceptions are fundamental intentional states-of-being, 'the background from which all acts stand out' (*PP*: x/xi) and which the ability to act presupposes. This 'bracketing off', or suspension of judgement about the ontology of self and world so as to focus on 'experiences' is referred to as the 'phenomenological reduction' or *epoch*.

While Descartes sought introspectively to establish the existence of an inner self through a thorough-going scepticism about sensations, Merleau-Ponty regards these self-same sensations as the only access we have to our selves and our world. This is because sensations seem to occupy a liminal position. On the one hand, sensations are the means by which I tentatively 'grasp, on the fringe of my own personal life and acts, a life of given consciousness' (*PP*: 216). They are the very ground from which my self-consciousness emerges to posit itself over and against the world. But, on the other hand, sensations remain ultimately intangible, I can never experience them as *mine* since they seemingly come and go without my calling them. Sensation 'runs through me without my being the cause of it' (*PP*: 216). I never *possess* sensations and in some strange way they seem to concern 'another self which has already sided with the world' (*PP*: 216). In a way, sensations too are a kind of pre-personal horizon. Just as 'I cannot know my own birth and death. Each sensation, being strictly speaking, the first, the last and only one of its kind, is a birth and death' (*PP*: 216).

Given the modern presupposition of an identity based upon the Cartesian self I 'naturally' assume ownership of *my* conscious thoughts since they seem to be constitutive of *my* identity. But if this identity is actually predicated on the ambiguous im-personal status of sensations then it is to sensations we must look if we are to understand who and what we are. 'Truth does not inhabit only "the inner man" [sic], or more accurately there is no inner man, man is in the world, and only in the world does he know himself' (*PP*: xi). Things are perceived before they can be thought and such perceptions evidence the complex intertwining of self and world. Phenomenology thus explores the essentially *perceptual* nature of our being-in-the-world, countering the post-Cartesian abstraction of mind from matter by concentrating on our most basic experiences, those sensations which seem to span the gap between internal and external. According to Merleau-Ponty all the efforts of phenomenology 'are concentrated upon re-achieving a direct and primitive contact with the world, and endowing that contact with a philosophical status' (*PP*: vii).

It is for these reasons that Merleau-Ponty is concerned to 'offer an account of space, time and the world as we "live" them' (*PP*: vii), rather than as abstract entities. Indeed, he introduces a crucial distinction between 'objective' and 'lived' space. The former is 'the space of rulers and tape measures', also described as physical, clear, geometrical or Euclidean space. The latter is the projection of our own spatial orientation on to the world, also referred to as subjective, existential, anthropological or phenomenal space[12].

For Merleau-Ponty, the structure of *lived* space emerges from a relationship to our environs that is both perceived and produced through the activities we engage in. Lived space is 'cut up and patterned in terms of my projects' (Bannan 1967: 37). Our movement 'superimposes upon physical space a potential or human space [. . .]. The normal function which makes abstract movement possible is one of "projection" whereby the subject of movement keeps in front of him an area of free space in which what does not naturally exist may take on a semblance of existing' (*PP*: 111). Unlike geometrical space, lived space cannot be measured in metres or miles. Its distances are not fixed, but change according to our modes of existence, our moods, and environmental factors beyond our control, *e.g.* whether it is night or day[13]. 'Our reading of the world' depends on the 'season of the year, and the season of being' (Evernden 1985: 131). Our sense of being-in-the-world entails a kind of qualitative 'measurement' of lived space, a 'lived distance', which 'binds me to the things which count and exist for me, and links them to each other. This distance measures the scope of my life at every moment' (*PP*: 286).

As one would expect, Merleau-Ponty argues that lived space is mediated through the body. 'The body is the vehicle of being in the world and having a body is, for a living creature, to be intervolved in a definite environment, to identify oneself with certain projects and be continually committed to them' (*PP*: 82). To act we need a kind of bodily sense of where we are, *i.e.* a proprioceptive awareness of our physical deployment in and through space that usually operates below the level of consciousness. This unconscious awareness of our lived space comes through perception's 'operative inten-tionality', that *intending toward the world*, which "evaluates the potentialities of my whole environment, so that objects appear as graspable or out of reach, inviting or threatening, as obstacles or aids' (*PP*: 440). We perceive and *live* this world through our various senses, seeing, hearing, touching etc. each of which have their own characteristic spatiality. Because '[e]ach sense implicates the entire body, is intrinsically intersensory' (Zaner 1964: 181), these individual sense perceptions do, ordinarily, correspond and cohere, such that 'there is a unification of these spaces in one lived spatiality' (*PP*: 260). This sense of unification – of the senses, of spatiality, of existence as a whole – can, for Merleau-Ponty, largely be attributed to the workings of our intentional arc. He writes: 'the life of consciousness [. . .] is subtended by an "intentional arc" which projects round about us our past, our future, our human setting, our physical, ideological and moral situation, or rather which results in our being situated in all these respects. It is this intentional arc which brings about the unity of the senses, of intelligence, of sensibility and motility. And it is this which "goes limp" in illness' (*PP*: 136).

Lived space and perceptual problems

Lived space is then distinct from, though related to, the pre-existing and independent space of the 'objective' world. In Merleau-Ponty's own words, '[c]lear space, that impartial space in which all objects are equally important and enjoy the same right to existence, is not only surrounded, but also thoroughly permeated by another spatiality' (*PP*: 286). While objective space is 'always already there', we are involved and connected with it only by means of *lived* space, and this connection must be managed and main-tained, 'ceaselessly composed by our own way of projecting the world' (*PP*: 287).

The 'synthesis' of space by the subject is 'a task that always has to be performed afresh' (*PP*: 140), a (usually unconscious) project of mediation that can never be completed once and for all. *Only* by means of this 'composure' of space do we come to distinguish our*selves*. 'Space is the correlate to, but also negation of, subjectivity', and so our understanding and awareness of what we are, and are not, is necessarily spatially mediated. It is drawn out of our *perceptual involvement* with the 'phenomenal field', from the 'dialogue or dialectic between organism and its environment, in which each *patterns* the other' (Spurling 1977: 11). Lived space is formed by, but also actively forms, our sense of self in the world though a 'pre-thematic "patterning" of the world that is difficult to catch at work' (Spurling 1977: 18).

From a phenomenological perspective '[w]e have the experience of an *I*, not in the sense of an absolute subjectivity, but as one indivisibly demolished and remade over the course of time. The unity of either the subject or the object is not a real unity, but a *presumptive* unity on the horizon of experience' (*PP*: 219). Since our being-in-the-world must be continually negotiated, the effective construction and reconstruction of lived space requires a certain amount of 'perceptual faith' on the part of the subject. Our coherent sense of ourselves is by no means continuous or guaranteed and if we lose perceptual faith, our 'habitual' sense of ourselves in our milieu can become confused and senseless. Our *praktagnosia* (*PP*: 140), that practical bodily (rather than symbolically mediated) 'understanding', through which our body has access to its world, can be damaged or even lost. In the event, we can no longer trust that self and space will maintain normal, predictable relations, and we no longer know what to expect from the world – we might say that we have 'lost our grip' on it.

In other words, lived space is ordinarily 'taken-for-granted', produced below or beyond the level of conscious awareness, and reveals itself only as a result of dysfunction, when it is 'thrown into relief by morbid deviations from the normal' (*PP*: 286)[14]. So long as lived space is successfully maintained, we have a sense of freedom to move as we please (within the limitations of our physicality[15]), an easy relation with an environment that invites and encourages our involvement. But, if our sense of space breaks down we may find ourselves facing a repellent, unwieldy environment that restricts our freedom of movement, and threatens our sense of well*being*.

This conception of being at home in space has clear affiliations with Heidegger's notion of 'dwelling'. To dwell 'is the basic character of Being in keeping with which mortals exist' (Heidegger 1993: 362). *Wohnen* (dwelling) 'means to reside or stay, to dwell at peace, to be content' (Krell 1993: 345). Dwelling might be summarised as a form of 'sustainable personal development', of growing within and cultivating a sustaining relationship with one's environs. '[O]nly because mortals pervade, persist through, spaces by their very essence are they able to go through spaces. But in going through spaces we do not give up our standing in them. Rather, we always go through spaces in such a way that we already sustain them by staying constantly with near and remote things' (Heidegger 1993: 359). Heidegger too suggests that moods and mental states might affect our ability to negotiate space, *e.g.* that depression might engender a 'loss of rapport with things' (Heidegger 1993: 359). Merleau-Ponty goes much further, arguing that '[w]hat protects the sane man [sic] against delirium or hallucination, is not his critical powers, but *the structure of his space*' (*PP*: 291, emphasis added).

For this reason, Merleau-Ponty suggests that the best way to investigate lived space is through applying 'a new mode of analysis – existential analysis' (*PP*: 136) to the spatialities of 'deviant' modes of existence such as that associated with schizophrenia. Explaining the logic of this approach, Hammond *et al.* (1991: 181) write that, '[t]he pathological case operates as a heuristic device that shocks one into an awareness of what is taken for granted. It is a means of gaining distance from the familiar, so that one is better able to explicate it[16]. Within this context, Merleau-Ponty presents the reader with descriptions of disturbing scenes from schizophrenic life-worlds (drawn from the work of Binswanger and Minkowski) which his conceptual analysis aims to render comprehensible. 'A schizophrenic patient, in the mountains, stops before a landscape. After a short time he feels a threat hanging over him [. . .] Suddenly the landscape is snatched away from him by some alien force. It is as if a second sky, black and boundless, were penetrating the blue sky of evening. This new sky is empty, "subtle, invisible and terrifying" ' (*PP*: 287). The schizophrenic experiences a suddenly unmanageable transition within their lived space. The world becomes *unheimlich* as he seems to lose touch with the space of the objective world, and to be left alone in a now threatening and baffling subjective space.

For the schizophrenic, the world can suddenly change its physiognomy (or its 'living significance') and appear to be menacing and sinister. 'In the street, a kind of murmur *completely envelops him*; similarly he feels deprived of his freedom as if there were always people present *round about him*; at the café there seems to be something nebulous *around him* and he feels to be trembling [sic]; and when the voices are particularly frequent and numerous, the atmosphere *round him* is saturated with a kind of fire, and this produces a sort of oppression inside the heart and lungs and something in the nature of a mist round about his head' (Minkowski, quoted in *PP*: 286, emphasis in original). Here, the subject's own lived space *limits*, rather than 'makes space for' his existence. It encloses and threatens to smother him, all the while separating him off from involvement with the shared space of others. In such cases of psychosis, the subject appears to have lost their sense of connection with objective space, and feels (with)drawn into their own fragmented and frightening spatiality. The ability to synthesise a tolerable compound of lived and objective space has been lost. We might say s/he has lost the ability to maintain the necessary balance or 'communion' (Rabil 1967: 32) between lived and objective space that allows for a comfortable, unthinking rapport with the world. This communion is, of course, necessary because 'I never wholly live in varieties of human space, but am always ultimately rooted in a natural and non-human space' (*PP*: 293)[17].

Merleau-Ponty argues that the ability to construct a 'homely' lived space is vital for one's mental health. If we are to feel that we belong, and have a place in the world, then we must be able to compose a suitable space. If we cannot 'situate' ourselves comfortably in relation to other people or things, we feel, quite literally, 'misfits'. This feeling can vary according to circumstances that are never entirely within our control. 'Sometimes between myself and the events there is a certain amount of play (*Spielraum*), which ensures that my freedom is preserved while the events do not cease to concern me. Sometimes, on the other hand, the lived distance is both too small and too great; the majority of the events cease to count for me, while the nearest ones obsess me. They enshroud me like the night and rob me of my individuality and freedom. I can literally no longer breathe; I am possessed' (*PP*: 286).

This spatial understanding of mental health seems to have wider application. Consider, for example, the following instance of 'neurotic' experience:

> I felt as if I didn't fit into the world... When I saw the snow, I felt
> I couldn't cope. One day it wasn't there and the next it was. I saw it and
> it upset me and I went to pieces ... I felt I did not want to be alive
> because I was not related to anything. I just seemed totally out of
> everything and I started to cry. I couldn't cope with the hurt and the
> pain. I felt I would never feel part of anything (Sims 1983: 116).

To keep our feet on the ground we need to be at ease with the space around us, to be on familiar and perhaps even intimate terms with our environs without suffering anxious 'feelings and fears of loss of self' (Sims 1983: 114)[18].

The experience of agoraphobia: Linda's story

Merleau-Ponty's explication of the phenomenology of spatial distortions suffered in psychotic disorders (*e.g.* schizophrenia) and 'extreme states of consciousness' (*e.g.* neurological disorders and mescaline consumption) seems ideally suited for examining a spatially mediated disorder like agoraphobia. Sufferers' accounts of spatial distortions associated with agoraphobic attacks (see below), would also seem to make them perfect exemplars of Merleau-Ponty's phenomenological problematic thereby placing us in a better position to judge his theory's philosophical merits. Much more importantly, if Merleau-Ponty's understanding of the relations between space, sensations and self-identity helps to conceptualise agoraphobics' experiences and explain their symptoms then it may be of some use in suggesting therapeutic or coping strategies for sufferers.

The best way to facilitate this *mutual* dialogue is by letting sufferers speak for themselves. In what follows I therefore focus on one particular sufferer's narrative in some detail, though this respondent's account is fully supported by extensive interviews with other sufferers. (See note 5 above) My intention in presenting a single case study is to generate the theoretical equivalent of an in-depth 'existential analysis', one that might be less meaningful at a level of greater generality.

I met 'Linda' through my ethnographic involvement with the self-help group she attended at that time. Linda is a painter and a musician, and I shall suggest that she is thus especially well placed to articulate her sensory perceptions of an agoraphobic life-world. Her experiential account will, I hope, help to paint a sophisticated phenomenological picture of agoraphobia that foregrounds the relevance of 'lived space' in understanding agoraphobic and non-agoraphobic experiences.

Linda is 39 years old, single, and lives in a Scottish village with her two school age children and an assortment of cats. She paints full time, primarily to earn a living, but she also derives a great deal of pleasure from her work. Linda says that she has recently managed to strike a balance between painting that she actually enjoys and that people are willing to buy:

> for years and years I painted flowers, and things that I...och, that were very pretty, but they just weren't me. But, I think I've maybe cracked it with the balance, and it is land, it's just landscapes [laughs] and it is so ironic, 'cause I, I've got an exhibition, in this place, [...] the theme of the exhibition is travelling, [laughs...] the irony of it just makes me smile, you know really, that here's an agoraphobic woman, producing these paintings of, you know...far distant places.

As a part-time musician, Linda often appears on stage in local venues, playing a melody instrument in a dance band.

As a child, Linda's parents had moved home frequently within Scotland. She recalls often feeling uprooted and unsettled in a new town. Linda begins her narrative by describing these aspects of her childhood, and the fact that she does so suggests that the lack of a secure and stable base in her early years continues to hold a place of importance in her personal history. She explains that when she was 17 she planned to leave an area to which she had recently moved, and had few friends, to work abroad as a nanny. It was at this stage in her life that she experienced her first panic attack; 'I can remember it quite vividly, it was the night before I left home'. When asked if she could describe it, she says:

> I was lying on my bedroom floor with headphones on, really, really loud music, and em it's strange, hard to describe [...] it was just utter terror, you know, you might...you might experience if somebody had a knife at your throat, you know, that level of fear.

Linda later comes to identify this as the beginning of her agoraphobia and says 'I think, ever since then I've always been pretty miserable actually'. In Linda's mind, the original experience of panic is linked with her anxieties about leaving home. Although 'desperate' to leave, she was unsure and anxious about what this departure might entail. This ambivalence was a source of confusion, perhaps rooted in a sense of not really *belonging* anywhere.

The job abroad didn't work out, and Linda soon came back to live in various locations in England, reluctant to return to her parents' home. She continued to experience a fairly high, but variable level of background anxiety, and to develop agoraphobic avoidance of certain, mostly crowded places. 'I always had to live out in the country, I couldn't live in town, so its, I couldn't walk through... I mean I lived in Exeter, for five, six years, and I never once walked right across, right through the main street'. Although she did consult a doctor about her difficulties with negotiating social space, 'it was just a case of pull yourself together', and years passed before she came to understand what was wrong. 'I never came up with the word agoraphobia in all those years, I never knew what it meant, I just knew that I couldn't go, I couldn't get too far away from home'. When she did eventually come across the term agoraphobia, it was through her own reading: 'I know so much about it now, as much as any shrink probably, but then... I just didn't know what the hell was happening'.

Despite an inability to stray far from the security of her home, she maintained a pretence of 'normality' for some years. In the midst of much discomfort and confusion Linda managed to complete a course at art college, clearly a difficult experience. She tried not to admit that she was struggling and often adopted strategies, invented excuses, to disguise her difficulties:

> It gradually, it kinna got worse, and I was pretty miserable at art college. I hated it [...] I was like the 'awkward' student, because, you know if they went on trips for instance, to France, or London, to galleries, I always said I couldn't afford it.

At the end of this period, she says, 'I'd had enough of England and I wanted to come home'. We might interpret this 'home-sickness' as a need for stability in her life, perhaps a desire to 'put down roots', and in a sense this is what she proceeded to do.

Having returned north to Scotland, Linda says, (my emphasis):

> I think I was quite happy for a while, quite content, I had a job, and I met this chap, and eh, my life was much more *structured*, I think [...] you get, you know, really *self contained* when you have children and a partner, but then [...] after seven years, we split up, and that's really, when I went *downhill* again, my *foundations* were shaken.

Describing the early stages of the period following her return to Scotland, Linda emphasises the positive aspects of social space, how the presence of others can in fact be experienced as helpful and *consolidating*. However, things clearly take a sudden turn for the worse with the break up of her relationship. A traumatic event such as this can subject almost anyone to a period of vulnerability and insecurity. Linda herself was deeply distressed by the experience, and she uses a powerful and seemingly *spatial* metaphorics to relate this part of her story. Her usage of the concepts of structure, foundations, containment, and downwards motion relative to her environment, can be interpreted in relation to Merleau-Ponty's phenomenological framework of identity, as a description of increased stability, then sudden erosion of her 'intentional arc' in response to changes in her emotional landscape. She had suddenly become very vulnerable indeed, destitute and dispossessed of self-worth.

Shortly after Linda's break up, she had a major panic attack when she was driving, again listening to very loud music, and 'just collapsed really'. 'It was like a snowball effect, an accumulation of all those years of [...] not addressing things that were happening in my head'. She said she had been doing too much, and thinking 'keep going, I can do it, I can do it, but actually, you know, inside, you're *crumbling*... and all of a sudden, your body, mind and body and soul just, just *exploding*, and saying STOP, 'cause you're gonnae die, or you, something... you're gonnae completely, *crack*, if you don't address this'. The terms I have italicised here emphasise the confusion Linda experiences in the boundaries of her phenomenal body, an *intolerable* and unsustainable confusion of internal and external space. She clearly loses the ability to project a protective boundary around herself, and as a result, is both assaulted by external space, *crumbling* inwardly under its pressure, and unable to prevent internal space from *exploding* outwards. Both sensations indicate a lack of containment, the *crack* that permits dispersion of self into its surroundings. Her account highlights the fact that personal 'integration is always precarious, since what can be patterned or structured can also be broken up as new patterns come into existence' (Spurling 1977: 39).

So at this stage, when things had come to a head, Linda received psychiatric help, in the form of counselling and medication. Although appreciative of the attention to her problems, and relieved, to a degree, to have them out in the open, the treatment does little to alter the agoraphobic lifestyle she has maintained more or less consistently since the age of 17. When asked about the form of treatment she would liked to have received at this stage, she says:

to be honest, in some ways, if I'd been taken into a hospital, put in a bed, and cuddled by the nurses, I mean that would have been great actually [laughs] to have a month or something out of the turmoil that my life was in.

Feeling, as she does, phenomenally insecure, Linda craves the tactility of human contact, cuddles that would soothe her enervated senses and affirm her diminished sense of self. Placed in a consolatory environment, it seems she could find the time and space to re-*cover*, to strengthen her phenomenal bodily boundaries and restore her weakened intentional arc.

For Linda, there are good reasons for *accepting* the debilitating nature of her illness. To do so means easing up on the constant battle against it, 'making the best of a bad lot' rather than trying to fight something she feels can't be beaten[19]. In this way, it is possible to avert the pain of panic attacks by completely avoiding situations that would provoke them; 'but the trouble with that is your world shrinks, till it is just the one room or your bed or whatever'. Linda goes on to say; 'the thing about agoraphobia, or maybe people with similar problems, is that they just jog along. There's a lady in the village, here where I live, hasn't come out her house in 20 years'. One can then, in a sense, 'choose' just to live within one's own 'particular radius', but this inevitably results in an extraordinarily restricted lifestyle in a constricted life-world.

Linda shares the view expressed by other sufferers that it is essential to *practise* going outside your home regularly if you are to avoid becoming house-bound for extended periods of time. This is expressed in a statement also reminiscent of Evernden's earlier point, about the phenomenal, physiognomic relevance of 'seasons of the year', and 'seasons of being':

> another relevant thing is the season. You know the winter...I don't get much practice...of, you know, going out 'cause the weather's crap, or whatever, you don't go for day trips or, you know, sort of hibernate. But in the summer, you know, the spirits lift, what have you, things become a lot easier, I become happier.

At different times, Linda stresses the fact that it becomes more difficult to function outside your home, or even to *imagine* doing so, if you 'get out the habit'. Confidence is easily lost, and painful to regain, so 'practice is really important [...] I feel that I don't do enough, to be honest, but then, at the same time, I'm wary of not pushing myself too much'. There's a delicate balance to be struck in order to keep the physiognomy of your life-world relatively constant and familiar, to keep your involvement with it on anything like an even keel. Adopting Merleau-Ponty's terms, operative intentionality has to be *exercised*, you have to practise projecting and patterning lived space, with its potential for freedom of movement, to prevent its becoming hopelessly and debilitatingly contracted.

Linda recognises that what she does for a living may not be all that conducive to developing and maintaining the skills necessary for coping in difficult spaces, which tend to be those populated with other people:

Working at home [...] it's not that healthy really, it's very isolating. And
I think if you're out in an office environment, or a shop, or, you know,
that sort of thing, you know you're mixing with people just by the very
nature of the job, you're getting practice every day.

The view Linda expresses here corresponds with some sufferers' theories
about the development and exacerbation of their agoraphobic symptoms.
Women have said that being 'stuck at home', for example, during the late
stages of pregnancy, looking after young children, or in one case because of
a back injury, can, in a sense, cause you to 'forget', or lose the habitual
bodily sense (*praktagnosia*), of what's involved in going out. In a sense, you
forget how to project your own lived space, necessary for freedom of movement, over and against those of other people. In such social circumstances,
one's own lived space may need to be asserted more strongly, and defended
against the seemingly corrosive presence of the lived spaces of others. There
is then much effort, skill, confidence and (perceptual) *faith* required to
convert space into something like a dwelling or 'homely' environment.

However, despite these perceived disadvantages of extended periods
behind closed doors, the home clearly is often experienced as a place of
sanctuary, an asylum rather than a prison (but see Valentine 1998). As we
have seen, it is understandably tempting just to stay there, and avoid risking
one's stability and security in the attempt to construct and explore a non-
home-based life-world. Most agoraphobics know, to their cost, the dangers
of over-exposure to space outside the home. The world can become very
frightening very quickly and display an overwhelming physiognomy of
horror. You have to tread lightly and warily to avoid coming face to face
with the terrible reality of full-blown panic, a breakdown in relations
between lived and objective space that causes one's surroundings to become
threatening and awful. The subject of panic feels that the space they occupy
is somehow qualitatively different from that of other people around them,
they do not *belong* there and their only option is to run, usually homewards.
Having 'lost the place' in this way, home often seems to be the only
imaginable space in which to rebuild your defences, away from the prying
eyes and *presence* of others.

When asked if she can explain why the home is the most comfortable
place to be, Linda thinks carefully about her answer. What she eventually
articulates so clearly is in fact fairly typical of sufferers' views:

When I look around here, kids aside [...] it's like, almost like an
extension... of *me*...you know it's, it feels safe because...it's, it's a
shield, it's a, protective thing, you know, obviously there's walls, and
a roof em, but I would feel just as safe in my garden.

Her statement reveals that it would be simplistic to assume that the
protection is derived from the physical enclosure of the bricks and mortar

alone. While sufferers do, to an extent, *incorporate* these walls into their sense of self, to strengthen their phenomenal bodily boundaries, there is a deeper issue at stake here, relating to the structure and spatiality of our very existence. Merleau-Ponty's existential analysis reveals that home is often the centre of our lived space. It constitutes the heart of many of our life-worlds and provides a relatively stable base for us to orient ourselves in relation to. Agoraphobics, who spend so much of their time anxiously floating free from their moorings, are especially in need of this stability. At home, the subject can attempt to flex her operative intentionality, imagining lived distances opening out before her and 'gearing' herself towards them. These spaces can be physiognomically perceived as anything from an abyss that threatens to engulf, to an expanse that invites participation. The home provides relatively stable foundations from which sufferers can make judgements about their ability to cope, and to assess the prospective reliability of their intentional arc.

However, even here, as Linda discovered, there are times when the foundations turn out to be less than solid, and this realisation can be truly terrifying. To lose the protective carapace of your sense of lived space *here*, to be invaded by *unheimlich* anxiety in your own home, is devastating to your sense of self:

> [When] you're in a state of permanent anxiety, chronic, it's really quite disabling, there's *nowhere* ..., whether it's your home ..., this is the scariest thing that I discovered, when I was really ill, it was, my home wasn't enough, my bed, my pillow, my mother staying here for months [she was my rock], wasn't enough [...] nothing is, and, that's when you just lose it completely, you, there's just *nothing* there at all, you know, this fear.

What Linda seems to be expressing here is at the very heart of existential anxiety; the fear that at the root of everything is *nothing*, and that there is no place where you are safe from the threat to your existence, the loss of self, that hovers at the bounds of being. Linda survived this experience, though the level of anxiety seems to have persisted beyond what most sufferers of agoraphobia would have to endure[20].

For agoraphobics then, anxieties are generally associated with attempts to project themselves beyond the home, which is ordinarily the safe centre from which their lived space radiates outwards. Linda notes: 'I think everybody's got their own, radius, perimeter [laughs], mine is, I can go to [nearby town], it's a bit iffy if I can walk along the main street, an' stuff like, a Saturday [when it's busier] that's really pushing it'. Bannan can be seen to echo Linda's point about the home's importance (thus suggesting this is not a uniquely agoraphobic experience) when he says that 'the centre of my space is usually my home or dwelling, in terms of which I orient myself in the lived world' (Bannan 1967: 37).

One of the tactics Linda uses to extend the perimeter of her life-world beyond her home is to project a comparable sense of security onto her *car*, which she says she uses 'too much. Like when I park my car in the town, em I have to, be near the car [...] there's always got to be this place, this sanctuary, where I can go and feel safe'. Linda is able to leave the house, and the radius of her life-world, her safety zone, extends far enough to include many of the things that are important for a 'full life'. 'The only thing that is missing in my life is this, ability to, to go, to say I'll go up north, for a holiday and, you know, what the hell, go to London and see an exhibition'. When she takes herself 'out of her element' and into unpredictable social situations, she is in a sense laying herself open to intrusion from the spatial compositions of others.

Linda has a high degree of perceptual sensitivity and, while this is clearly a source of pleasure, it is also disabling, in that she cannot always keep stimuli at a safe distance from her*self*. She often feels *invaded* by sounds:

> maybe it's being a musician, I don't know, I can't read music, everything that I learn is just by ear, I've got one of these really intense, sort of listening, skills that I've got, it's a bit mind blowing at times [...] if I'm in somewhere like Princes Street, where it's just all, the noise, the buzz, the general..., I think that definitely affects my brain, my mind, and it makes you very uneasy.

As a painter, Linda is also highly attuned, and sensitive to, visual stimuli, but she says 'I wish I wasn't'. She feels unable to protect herself from their influence, or even assault: 'All my flipping senses are too acute for their own good [...] everything about me's just really acute'. Linda is decidedly not 'thick-skinned', she emphasises the close relationship between her *acute* sensitivity to sights and sounds and her inability to project a protective spatiality, or boundary. Uncalled-for sensations seem to 'flood in' despite all she might do to try to shield herself from unwelcome stimuli. This is especially so in intense (social) spaces where these sensations emanate from and are produced by others, yet seem to enter her very being in a manner completely beyond her control[21]. Here the boundaries of identity become confused and such sensations might even seem to belong to 'another self which has already sided with the world' (*PP*: 216).

Conclusion

Bryan Turner (1987: 218) has claimed that phenomenology has limited potential for the study of health and illness, as it can *describe*, but never explain the condition in question. However, Linda's account has shown that Merleau-Ponty's existential analysis provides much more than mere description. His focus on the continual construction of, and variable relations between, lived and objective space paves the way for a more *sensitive* reading of 'disordered' encounters between individuals and their life-worlds.

Merleau-Ponty presents a philosophical problematic that provides both a framework for understanding and a nuanced vocabulary capable of expressing the existential trauma and spatially mediated experiences of the agoraphobic. He also draws our attention to the vital point that those 'boundary' problems experienced by sufferers are neither so unique, nor so bizarre, if we choose to understand them in terms of a pathology of everyday life and existence. We are not Cartesian subjects. There are no fixed and immutable boundaries between self and world. The self is a project that needs to be constantly renegotiated and the senses provide the medium of this dialectic and of our orientation in social space. The experience of panic can arrive 'out of the blue' precisely because '[e]very sensation carries within it the germ of a dream or depersonalisation [... that] takes place on the periphery of my being' (*PP*: 215).

What is more, Merleau-Ponty also reminds us that we are not 'ghosts in a machine' but embodied entities. This suggests that any therapy that concerns itself merely with the mind (*res cogito*) fails to give due weight to the bodily and sensory aspects of the condition, to our 'extended' selves. What Linda wanted most was to be 'cuddled', to have her boundaries recognised and reinforced. Many other sufferers too find that they can gain a degree of security by hanging onto someone or something. (Davidson forthcoming.)

Merleau-Ponty's emphasis on the *sociality* of space also explains why we are all subject to the effusion of others' spatial compositions and how agoraphobics' characteristic and extreme discomfort in 'public' places can be indirectly derived from other people[22]. The *presence* of others and their projections can, for the agoraphobic at least, throw the stability of spatial situation into question. She can lose the essential sense that her bodily location is 'not one among many but the centre in relation to every location.' (Bannan 1967: 74) People literally *populate* space with their own presence and constructions, causing it to become charged with their noisy, odiferous, colourful and tactile spatiality. The sensory phenomena that others make manifest has to be 'handled' by those who share their surroundings, and the 'performance' of this task is ordinarily taken for granted. The sufferer from agoraphobia, however, lacks the ability to assert their own subjective spatiality in the face of the spaces of others. When subjected to high degrees of sensory stimulation, sufferers feel 'trapped'. The contesting lived spaces of others jar their senses, and they can become overwhelmed and anxious to the extent that they suffer a full-blown panic attack. This chapter has shown that Merleau-Ponty's phenomenological framework is capable of expressing and assisting such frightening aspects of agoraphobic existence.

Merleau-Ponty's philosophy has been described as

> an attitude of wonder in the face of the world, a constant questioning and desire for understanding [...] in the hope of attaining some kind of directedness or orientation. The goal of [his] philosophy is to enable each of us to rediscover his [sic] situation in the world. (Spurling 1977: 5)

As I hope to have demonstrated, Merleau-Ponty can be read as initiating at least a partial 'explanation' of agoraphobia, and his quest for orientation may have an important part to play in the sociology of mental health.

Acknowledgement

This research is funded by the ESRC (award R00429834370).

Notes

1 The Concise Oxford Dictionary. 5th Edition (1975) Oxford: Oxford University Press.
2 Westphal describes the 'impossibility of walking through certain streets or squares, or possibility of doing so only with resultant dread of anxiety'. (Quoted in Marks 1987: 323)
3 See Gelder *et al.* (1996: especially chapter 7) for a concise review of the relevant psychiatric literature, including discussion of the history of the concept of agoraphobia, its aetiology, epidemiology, diagnosis and treatment. See also Marks (1987: especially Chapter 10) and Gournay (1989).
4 Marks (1987a) suggests that panic may only be absent in some cases because the person has successfully avoided any situation that might induce it.
5 The case study on which this paper is based is part of a much wider ongoing investigation of agoraphobia, through my involvement with self-help groups for agoraphobia sufferers in Scotland. I have conducted a series of group interviews with members of one group and have regularly attended a second as a participant observer. Additionally, I have conducted in-depth, semi-structured individual interviews with twelve agoraphobic women drawn from these groups. The interviews have been audio-taped and transcribed with the participants' permission. Participants are referred to in the text by pseudonyms.
6 On agoraphobia and gender see Fodor 1974, Brehony 1983, Tian *et al.* 1990, Bordo *et al.* 1998 and Davidson 2000. On gender difference in relation to wider mental health issues, see Busfield 1984 and 1996.
7 Describing the symptoms of panic, Marks writes: '[t]he sufferer suddenly feels anxious, ill or weak; has palpitations, lightness, and dizziness in the head (as opposed to true vertigo); feels a lump in the throat and weakness in the legs; and has an illusion of walking on shifting ground. Sufferers feel unable to breathe, or breathe too rapidly or deeply; they fear they may faint, die, scream out loud, "lose control," or "go mad." Very intense panic may root the sufferer to the

same spot until it lessens, after which she or he may run to a haven of safety – a friend or the home' (Marks 1987: 334).

8   Marks (1987) claims that the phenomena *are* equivalent and tends to use the term 'depersonalization' to cover both.

9   See Irigaray 1985 and MacPherson 1979.

10   Intentionality, from the Latin *intentio*, was a medieval term reintroduced by Franz Bretano in the 19th century who argued that all states of mind were directed towards, or about some-thing. It does not necessarily imply conscious intent on the part of the thinker. (See Searle 1988: 3.)

11   This involvement of the thinking subject in a project is paramount. For Merleau-Ponty consciousness is 'in the first place not a matter of "I think" but of "I can"' (*PP*: 137).

12   'Lived space', appears first and most frequently in his *Phenomenology of Perception*. Merleau-Ponty was not in fact the first theorist to use the concept of 'lived space'; it was introduced by the psychologist Minkowski, in 1933, and incorporated some years later into the *Phenomenological Psychology* of Erwin Straus.

13   Since 'spatiality is characteristic of our being in the world, there should be a variety of types of space according to the various modes of that commitment' (Bannen 1967: 99).

14   In this sense, lived space can be conceptualised along similar lines to Leder's (1990) notion of the 'dys-appearing body', *i.e.* the body *re*-appears to conscious awareness as a result of some dys-function. (See also Csordas 1994; Williams and Bendelow 1998a and 1998b (especially Chapter 8).)

15   See Dyck 1995, Dorn 1998 and Park *et al.* 1998 for discussion of 'disabled' experiences of space.

16   Edie makes a similar point when he says that one should study extreme states of consciousness as 'it is sometimes easier to see in certain extreme cases what the normal or ordinary implies but hides' (Edie 1987: 104).

17   It is vital to reemphasise that phenomenology's emphasis on sensations is in no way indicative of idealism. Merleau-Ponty never contests the existence of a real material world. Indeed, he writes that 'phenomenology is a philosophy for which the world is always "already there" before reflection begins – as an inalienable presence' (*PP*: vii).

18   The experience of vertigo can also be understood in terms of a loss of *balance* between lived and objective space. (See Kirby 1996, Yardley 1997 and Quinodoz 1997 for accounts of 'vertiginous' experience of the world.)

19   Many sufferers share the view that agoraphobia is something you never recover from, but merely have to learn to live with; 'I don't care what anybody says, you're never cured from agoraphobia' (Carron).

20   Ordinarily, a panic attack will usually last somewhere between a few minutes and a couple of hours, though the intensity of the experience obviously makes it feel like much longer (Gournay 1989).

21   One might speculate that the contrast between the depersonalisation Linda occasionally experienced in *listening* to and being 'possessed' by recorded music, and her ability to *play* music even in public places, might be connected with the degree to which she regards herself as responsible for (and the source of) the sensations she experiences.

22   Although I use the term 'public', it is not possible to characterise agoraphobic fear and avoidance in terms of a straightforward and traditional distinction

between 'public' and 'private' space (see, for example, Lloyd 1984, Duncan 1996, Bondi and Domosh 1998). The theorisation of agoraphobic difficulties requires a more subtle approach than this problematic distinction allows.

References

American Psychiatric Association (1994) *Diagnostic and Statistical Manual of Mental Disorders* (4th Edition), Washington, DC: American Psychiatric Association.

Bannan, J.F. (1967) *The Philosophy of Merleau-Ponty*. New York: Harcourt, Brace and World Inc.

Bondi, L. and Domosh, M. (1998) On the contours of public space: a tale of three women, *Antipode*, 30, 270–89.

Bordo, S., Klein, B. and Silverman, M.K. (1998) Missing kitchens. In Nast, H. and Pile, S. (eds) *Places Through the Body*. London and New York: Routledge.

Brehony, K.A. (1983) Women and agoraphobia: a case for the etiological significance of the feminine sex-role stereotype. In Franks, V. and Rothblum, E. (eds) *The Stereotyping of Women: its Effects on Mental Health*. New York: Springer Publishing Company.

Busfield, J. (1984) Is mental illness a female malady? Men, women and madness in nineteenth century England, *Sociology*, 28, 259–77.

Busfield, J. (1996) *Men, Women and Madness: Understanding Gender and Mental Disorder*. London: Macmillan Press Ltd.

Clum, G.A. and Knowles, S.L. (1991) Why do some people with panic disorder become avoidant?: A review. *Clinical Psychology Review*, 11, 295–313.

Csordas, T.J. (ed) (1994) *Embodiment and Experience: the Existential Ground of Culture and Self*. Cambridge: Cambridge University Press.

Davidson, J. (2000) '. . . the world was getting smaller': women, agoraphobia and bodily boundaries', *Area*, 32, 1, 31–40.

Davidson, J. (forthcoming) Fear and trembling in the mall: agoraphobic women and body boundaries. In Dyck, I. (ed) *Geographies of Women's Health*. London and New York: Routledge.

Dorn, M. (1998) Beyond nomadism: the travel narratives of a 'cripple'. In Nast, H.J. and Pile, S. (eds) *Places Through the Body*. London and New York: Routledge.

Duncan, N. (1996) Renegotiating gender and sexuality in public and private spaces. In Duncan, N. (ed) *Bodyspace*. London and New York: Routledge.

Dyck, I. (1995) Hidden geographies: the changing lifeworlds of women with multiple sclerosis, *Social Science and Medicine*, 40, 307–20.

Edie, J.M. (1987) *Edmund Husserl's Phenomenology: a Critical Commentary*. Bloomington, Indianapolis: Indiana University Press.

Evernden, N. (1985) *The Natural Alien: Humankind and Environment*. Toronto: University of Toronto Press.

Fodor, I.G. (1974) The phobic syndrome in women: implications for treatment. In Franks, V. and Burtte, V. (eds) *Women in Therapy: Psychotherapies for a Changing Society*. New York: Brunner Mazel.

Gelder, M., Gath, D., Mayou, R. and Cowen, P. (eds) (1996) *Oxford Textbook of Psychiatry*. [3rd Edition] Oxford: Oxford University Press.

Gournay, K. (ed) (1989) *Agoraphobia: Current Perspectives on Theory and Treatment*. London and New York: Routledge.

Hammond, M.A., Howarth, J.M. and Keat, R.N. (1991) *Understanding Phenomenology*. Massachusetts: Basil Blackwell.

Heidegger, M. (1993) Building, dwelling, thinking. In Heidegger, M. (ed) *Basic Writings*. London: Routledge.

Irigaray, L. (1985) *This Sex Which Is Not One*. Ithaca NY: Cornell University Press.

Kirby, K.M. (1996) *Indifferent Boundaries: Spatial Concepts of Human Subjectivity*. New York: Guilford Press.

Leder, D. (1990) *The Absent Body*. Chicago: University of Chicago Press.

Lloyd, G. (1984) *The Man of Reason: 'Male' and 'Female' in Western Philosophy*. London: Methuen and Co. Ltd.

MacPherson, C.B. (1979) *The Political Theory of Possessive Individualism: Hobbes to Locke*. Oxford: Oxford University Press.

Marks, I.M. (1987) *Fears, Phobias and Rituals*. New York and Oxford: Oxford University Press.

Marks, I.M. (1987a) Agoraphobia, panic disorder and related conditions in the DSM IIIR and ICD 10, *Journal of Psychopharmacology*, 1, 6–12.

Merleau-Ponty (1962) *Phenomenology of Perception* (trans Smith, Colin). London: Routledge and Kegan Paul.

Park, D.C., Radford, J.P. and Vickers, M.H. (1998) Disability studies in human geography. *Progress in Human Geography*, 22, 2, 208–33.

Quinodoz, D. (1997) *Emotional Vertigo: between Anxiety and Pleasure*. London and New York: Routledge.

Rabil, A. (1967) *Merleau-Ponty: Existentialist of the Social World*. New York and London: Columbia University Press.

Searle, J.R. (1988) *Intentionality: an Essay in the Philosophy of Mind*. Cambridge and New York: Cambridge University Press.

Sims, A. (1983) *Neurosis in Society*. London and Basingstoke: Macmillan Press.

Spurling, L. (1977) *Phenomenology and the Social World: the Philosophy of Merleau-Ponty and its Relation to the Social Sciences*. London and Boston: Routledge and Kegan Paul.

Straus, E.W. (1966) *Phenomenological Psychology*. London: Tavistock Publications.

Tian, P.S., Wanstall, K. and Evans, L. (1990) Sex differences in panic disorder with agoraphobia, *Journal of Anxiety Disorders*, 4, 317–24.

Turner, B. (1987) *Medical Power and Social Knowledge*. London: Sage.

Valentine, G. (1998) 'Sticks and stones may break my bones': a personal geography of harassment, *Antipode*, 30, 305–32.

Williams, S.J. and Bendelow, G. (1998a) In search of the 'missing body': pain, suffering and the (post)modern condition. In Scambler, G. and Higgs, P. (eds) *Modernity, Medicine and Health: Medical Sociology Towards 2000*. London and New York: Routledge.

Williams, S.J. and Bendelow, G. (1998b) *The Lived Body: Sociological Themes, Embodied Issues*. London and New York: Routledge.

Yardley, L. (1997) *Material Discourses of Health and Illness*. London and New York: Routledge.

Zaner, R.M. (1964) *The Problem of Embodiment*. The Hague: Martinus Nijhoff.

7

Identifying delusional discourse: issues of rationality, reality and power

Derrol Palmer

Introduction

In recent years biological concepts have begun to strengthen their hold on psychiatry. One reason for this is a wave of medical technologies, such as *in vivo* neuroimaging, which have offered new insights into brain dysfunction (*e.g.* McGuire *et al.*'s 1995 study of auditory hallucinations). A practical consequence of this new knowledge is that sociological themes and concepts are becoming increasingly marginal to the field. In short, as knowledge of 'natural' factors advances, so the need for 'social' factors seems to retreat. However, regardless of this biological ascendency, there is a way in which sociology has an undiminished and central role to play within psychiatry. This is not in the area of explanation (*i.e.* aetiology) but in that of symptom recognition (*i.e.* psychopathology). Psychiatry is only possible because certain behaviours are regarded as symptoms of disorder, whereas others are not. So, the foundational issue is not to explain disorder but to describe how it is identified. That is, to specify how sanity is distinguished from insanity, perception from hallucination and belief from delusion. It is the question of how disorderly conduct can be recognised that will be addressed in this chapter.

There are two main reasons why psychopathological concerns are particularly susceptible to sociological analysis. First, disorderly conduct is identified on social rather than biological grounds. The importance of biological knowledge in this area is undermined by the fact that symptoms could be identified long before their biological origins were known. Rosen (1968: 95) reports cases of hallucination and delusion which were treated as such in Ancient Greece. Further, even if a symptom's underlying biology has been established, this knowledge does not play a role in recognising that the behaviour is 'pathological' in nature. As Gorenstein (1989: 11) observes, eye colour is determined by genetics but having green eyes is not seen as a medical condition. In short, how a symptom is recognised and what causes it are separate issues (see Jaspers 1912/68: 1318 and Sims 1995: 20 for a psychiatric acknowledgement of this point). So, if biological knowledge is not important how is the distinction between pathological and non-pathological phenomena made? At base, the judgment of 'pathology' involves ascribing *meaning* to a person's actions. In particular, it is dependent on considering how particular actions make sense in particular social settings. What this requires is an understanding of the social norms which constitute particular contexts and against which certain forms of conduct are judged abnormal. So, some actions acquire a symptomatic significance not because they contravene the laws of biological functioning but because they infringe the social order. Garfinkel (1956: 184–7) notes that as sociologists specialise in the study of social order they are also specialists in how disorder is recognised.

The second way psychopathology is amenable to sociological analysis is because of the specific 'social order' involved in symptom recognition. As Goffman (1967: 141) notes, symptoms are embodied in face-to-face interaction. Take 'psychotic' symptoms as an example. These become apparent when people report their beliefs (*i.e.* delusions) or describe their perceptions (*i.e.* hallucinations). In either case, disorderly aspects of conduct are identified by interacting with another person; by asking them questions and listening to their answers. Indeed, Goffman's observation is consistent with psychiatric research which concludes that the major influence on clinical judgment is the diagnostic *interview* (*e.g.* WHO 1975: 141). As psychopathology is embodied in interaction, microsociology is the most appropriate discipline to study it. So, not only is the distinction between symptomatic and non-symptomatic behaviours made on social grounds, but it is also embodied in a social medium (*i.e.* interaction).

My argument so far is that the foundations of psychiatry – *i.e.* how disorders are recognised – are the specialist province not of psychiatry but of microsociology. As a result, it is reasonable to expect that microsociological work on how conduct acquires a symptomatic significance would influence psychiatric practice. However, on the whole, this has not been the case. As Bowers notes:

> Although [sociological] ideas have influenced thinking within psychiatry they have by and large been rejected by the most influential and powerful professional group in psychiatry: the psychiatrists themselves (1998: 5).

Similarly, Glassner and Freedman (1979: 8–9) suggest that much of the knowledge generated by medical sociology is consumed within the discipline itself and does not affect clinical practice. Although there are clearly ways in which sociological ideas have made an impact on psychiatry (*e.g.* social theories of aetiology), this chapter focuses on a seemingly powerful form of criticism which fails to do so; that is, the radical critique which has been articulated within the social constructionist perspective. This criticism is a foundational one in that it attempts to recast the individualistic concepts of psychiatry in social terms. However, despite having foundational concerns and the potential to influence psychiatry the constructionist critique does not. Its criticisms have gained currency within microsociology but have made little impact on the very field they intended to criticise. It is this paradoxical state of affairs which the present chapter seeks to account for and move beyond. In doing so, I take debates about how delusions are identified as a case study, and examine a key way that constructionist sociology has criticised psychiatric work. Secondly, I report the results of a study into how delusions are recognised and use these to move beyond the paradox outlined above. This involves outlining a method of study which both produces a foundational criticism of psychiatry whilst retaining relevance for that discipline.

Debating delusions

The following sections outline a debate between constructionist micro-sociology and psychiatry over the nature of delusion. Of all symptoms, delusions are of central importance in psychiatry. They are found in over 75 clinical conditions and are also a hallmark of 'psychosis', namely, of the severest form of psychiatric disorder. Yet in spite of this centrality, delusions have remained largely enigmatic. Indeed, after nearly a hundred years of research, even their definition is still disputed (Cutting 1997: 194). However, despite disagreement on the specifics, a consensus has been reached that delusions are examples of *irrationality* (Gelder *et al.* 1989: 14, Busfield 1996: 69–75 and Bowers 1998: 158–60). For example, believing that The News At Ten contains coded messages about your personal life is not merely 'implausible' or 'unreasonable' but in some sense irrational. Thus the debate between psychiatry and microsociology over the nature of delusion revolves around the basis on which certain social actions can be called irrational.

Psychiatry and the issue of 'reality'
Psychiatry's official line on how delusions are irrational is found in its diagnostic manuals. These manuals specify sets of criteria which attempt to distinguish symptoms from their non-pathological counterparts. In doing so, psychiatry assumes that symptoms have intrinsic properties which are hallmarks of pathology. Since the early 1900s, just three defining criteria have been thought important for delusions. As Spitzer (1990a: 6) notes, all these are present in the following DSM-IV definition:

> Delusion. A false personal belief based on incorrect inference about external reality and firmly sustained in spite of what everyone else believes and in spite of what constitutes incontrovertible and obvious evidence or proof to the contrary (APA 1994: 765).

The first criterion is that delusions are *false* or, according to DSM-IV, they are 'incorrect inference[s] about external reality'. Secondly, delusions are held with *subjective certainty*; that is, 'in spite of what everyone else believes'. The final distinguishing mark is their absolute *incorrigibility*. In other words, delusions are utterly unshakable and cannot be changed by counter-argument or evidence. However, although there are three criteria, it is falsity alone which is the hallmark of irrationality. Subjective certainty and incorrigibility are not irrational properties of a belief if that belief is true. It is only because delusions are false that it becomes irrational to hold them with unshakable conviction. So, for psychiatry, the central criterion in establishing pathology is that of falsity. The final point to make about this criterion is that it individualises the pathological aspects of delusion. That a person's beliefs are out of touch with reality is taken to reflect a personal pathology such as poor reality testing.

Microsociology and the issue of 'power'

The microsociological approach I shall examine next has its roots in Scheff's (1966/99: 96) labelling theory, and argues that it is not falsity but power which is central to delusions. I have chosen to examine this argument because Scheff's original position has been developed by a number of different sociological schools. For example, power plays a central role in certain articulations of ethnomethodology (*e.g.* Pollner 1975), social constructionism (*e.g.* Heise 1988 and Harper 1999) and broadly Foucauldian work (*e.g.* Georgaca 1999). Despite theoretical differences between these approaches an argument emerges that, in structural terms, is independent from the school in which it is articulated. The following section will outline the key components of what I shall call 'the power argument'.

The first component of this argument is to discount psychiatry's claim that delusions have intrinsic properties. One basis for this is that certain non-pathological beliefs are strikingly similar to delusions. Scheff (1966: 93–6) and Heise (1988: 262) both give the example of prophets who, like some people with delusions, believe that they are in direct contact with God. However, prophets are not seen as delusional and may even rise in social status because of their beliefs. This point demonstrates that a belief's content is not intrinsically irrational. Secondly, microsociologists have argued that whether a belief is seen as delusional or not is largely a matter of context. As Heise (1988: 256) observes, ordinary ideas from other cultures – such as the Aztec belief that the sun required human sacrifice to rise – would be delusional if transplanted into Western society. Further, within our own culture, Goffman notes:

> ... [the] delusions of a private can be the rights of a general; the obscene invitations of a man to a strange girl can be the spicy endearments of a husband to his wife; the wariness of a paranoid is the warranted practice of thousands of undercover agents (1971: 412).

These observations point in the same direction; namely, that the types of belief considered delusional are not intrinsically irrational but are only so within a specific context. This observation shifts analytic attention from properties of the beliefs themselves to the social context in which they occur; thus effecting a shift away from psychiatry's concern with the individual to the nature of the social context in which a person is judged delusional. Having changed analytic focus in this way the key question becomes: 'what features of the social context are important?' The answer much of micro-sociology gives is 'asymmetries of power'. As I see it there are three steps to this part of the argument.

The first step is to note that delusions originate in an inter-personal *difference* over what is regarded as real. For instance, one person may think they are being followed by the CIA whereas the other does not. In Pollner's (1975: 412) words situations such as this revolve around different 'versions of reality'. Similarly, Georgaca (forthcoming) notes that delusions originate in a 'discrepancy' between two descriptions of the world and Harper (1999) that one person finds another's belief 'implausible'. The key element in all these formulations is that two people differ over what they consider real.

However, on many occasions differences such as these can be resolved by reference to shared standards which adjudicate on the correct version of reality. So, the second step in the argument is that, with delusions, there are *no shared standards* which can decide whose version of reality is correct. Pollner (1975: 418) gives a clear example of this situation involving a patient who claimed he could levitate objects. When his psychiatrist pointed out that a heavy desk he had chosen to make rise had, in fact, not moved the patient retorted 'Sir, that is because you do not see cosmic reality'. In Heise's (1988: 267) words, situations such as these are built around 'alternative realities' since both parties to the dispute have (a) their own version of reality and (b) their own standards by which to assess it. Pollner (1975: 412) makes a similar point in his discussion of 'reality disjunctures', as does Georgaca (forthcoming) when she notes that falsity cannot be definitively established. The key element here is that, for some reason, there is an absence of shared standards which could establish a definitive version of reality.

The final step in the power argument is to note that, in practice, the dispute is 'resolved' after a fashion. One person is ultimately seen as delusional whereas the other is not. It is argued that the basis on which this 'resolution' occurs is a *power asymmetry*. In situations of undecidable conflict, the most powerful party's views are counted as real and the less powerful party's are discounted as delusions. As Heise puts it:

> The thinking of one party is reified, the thinking of the other party is stigmatized, and the selection of which is which gets settled in a contest of social power, with the loser subject to social control (1988: 267).

Although these microsociological approaches agree on the centrality of power they disagree on its precise nature. For example, Harper (1999) sees power as rooted in the subject positions that constitute the institutional framework of psychiatry. However, Georgaca (1999) highlights factors which transcend the institution of psychiatry: specifically, the power differentials between competing societal 'discourses'.

In summary, the debate between psychiatry and microsociology centres on the nature of reality. Psychiatry holds a 'naïve realist' position (Harper, 1992: 360 and Cutting 1997: v) in which beliefs can be labelled false if they contrast with external reality. From sociology's point of view, however, reality itself is fractured along cultural and political lines. When people with different, self-validifying epistemologies come into conflict there are no shared standards by which to settle their dispute; no appeal to 'objective reality' as an arbitrator. As a result, it is the most powerful person whose views are counted as real. Corresponding to these two different views of reality are two different conceptions of pathology. For psychiatry, when a belief contrasts with objective reality it is the individual's problem and they who are irrational. For microsociology, delusions are inherently interpersonal phenomena which are rooted in an asymmetry of social power.

Recognising delusions: an alternative account

As noted in the introduction, although constructionist accounts such as the power argument are influential within microsociology they usually do not influence psychiatric practice. In Glassner and Freedman's (1979: 8–9) terms, such accounts rarely produce 'exodisciplinary' effects. There are many possible reasons why psychiatrists tend to ignore microsociological work on symptom recognition. For example, a commitment to natural rather than social science methodology or the preservation of a power base that constructionist work challenges. However, the following sections explore an alternative line of explanation; namely, that sociological methods generate findings which are *irrelevant* to psychiatric practice and are therefore powerless to change it. More specifically I develop an analysis of one of the main critical practices within microsociology. This practice involves starting with the problematic set by 'official' psychiatric discourse and criticising the diagnostic criteria such as falsity. Whilst this approach is intuitively correct, it is based upon a problematic assumption; namely, that diagnostic criteria adequately capture the processes by which symptoms are recognised (Coulter 1979: 147–9). However, I argue that much of the important work in recognising delusions is performed through tacit skills – what Ingleby (1982: 140) refers to as 'the invisible nine tenths of psychiatric diagnosis'. Further, these tacit skills involve processes which are significantly different from the official criteria. Indeed, psychiatry's own criterion of falsity is irrelevant to clinical practice and, as a result, criticisms of practice based on that criterion are also likely to be irrelevant.

That the falsity criterion is discrepant with the way delusions are actually recognised is appreciated by psychiatrists who have described a number of ways it fails to agree with clinical intuition (see Spitzer 1990b: 378–9 for a review). The most significant problem with defining delusions as 'false beliefs' is that sometimes they are true! As Jaspers (1959/97: 106) has noted, some delusions of infidelity have a perfectly adequate basis in real life. In other words, a person may claim that their partner is having a sexual affair and, in reality, this is so. However, even though these beliefs are true it does *not* prevent them from being diagnosed as delusions (see also Gelder *et al.* 1989: 14). This clearly demonstrates that crucial skills involved in the recognitional process are not captured by the definitional criterion of falsity. As a result, the key task facing microsociological studies in this area is to develop an analysis of the tacit skills which underpin the recognitional process but which are not captured by the diagnostic criteria.

From within the ethnomethodological tradition there has been a small body of work which has attempted to explicate the tacit skills which are involved in recognising a psychiatric disorder. As indicated in the previous paragraphs, Coulter (1979 Chapter 9) has outlined a rationale for studying the recognitional process. In particular, he points to the potential discrepancy between a symptom's official definition and the practical procedures used to identify it. However, his own work on delusions is theoretical in nature relying on an explication of Wittgenstein's later philosophy (Coulter 1973: 131–41). Although Wittgenstein's work is suggestive, it only offers the barest outline of the tacit reasoning by which disorder is recognised. For a full account of delusions to emerge Coulter's sketch needs to be developed, and reconsidered in the light of a detailed empirical analysis. This empirical focus has been explored by Smith (1978) in her analysis of the practical reasoning by which recognisable accounts of neurotic behaviour can be constructed. A crucial feature of Smith's work is that it analysed a *reconstruction* of the neurotic events (*i.e.* her materials were a person's description of their neurotic friend). Although the use of such materials does not affect the adequacy of Smith's own study it is consequential in the present context. Clinical diagnosis is not primarily based on another's reconstruction of a behaviour but on examples of the behaviour itself. So, in order to explicate the skills which are involved in symptom recognition the following study extends previous ethnomethodological work in two main ways. First, it will break new topical ground by analysing the psychotic symptom of delusion. As psychotic syndromes are qualitatively different from neurotic ones the tacit skills involved will be very different from those described by Smith. Secondly, it focuses on actual cases of delusion rather than reporting or reconstructions. In this way, direct, material access is provided to the tacit skills which underpin the recognition of delusion and which constitute the workings of psychiatry.

Recognising delusional talk: an empirical account
The following analysis describes some of the ways delusional talk can be
recognised. It is based on three recorded interviews with people who were
hospitalised with diagnoses of schizophrenia or schizo-affective disorder,
and in which delusions are expressed. It uses the principles of conversation
analysis (see Hutchby and Wooffitt 1998) to explicate the tacit skills by
which delusions are recognised. For the purposes of brevity, one case has
been selected to exemplify the general findings. As such, the analytic points
made in the analysis are generalisable to the cases of delusion from the other
interviews (see Palmer 1997: 75–138 for a full analysis). The delusional talk
is from a person whom I call R, and who is diagnosed as having schizophrenia. It was selected for analysis because the delusion is presented in a
particularly clear form. (Indeed, staff in the hospital talked of his 'classic'
presentation.) As a result, the generic issues which are involved in identifying delusional talk are particularly clear cut in this case. In the following
extract C is the interviewer and R the person with delusions (transcription
symbols are explained in the Appendix).

#1 Talk diagnosed as delusional (transcription simplified)

1	C:	So you bel<u>ie</u>ve there's an afterlife then?
2		(.)
3	R:	<u>Ye</u>:s I do no:w. No:w I've seen a god as
4		well you know. Well he doesn't call himself
5		God he calls himself Tho:r.
6		(0.8)
7	C:	Ye:ah.
8	R:	I s<u>a</u>w him on a f:- (.) I've se:en him a couple of
9		ti:mes on a f<u>ie</u>ld up in L<u>ei</u>cestershire I saw him
10		once.
11	C:	Ri:ght. ((questioning tone))
12	R:	Right out in the c<u>ou</u>ntryside where I was wo:rking.
13		(.)
14	C:	Yeah.
15	R:	I had a j<u>o</u>b as a ga:mekeeper there for Mr. B<u>u</u>rnett
16		the animal f<u>oo</u>d manuf<u>a</u>cturer.
17	C:	Uh huh.
18		(0.5)
19	R:	And e:r he visited me while I was up th<u>e</u>::re.
20		(.)
21	R:	For some re:<u>a</u>son.
22	C:	Wuh-What kind of thing does
23		What did Floor-<u>Th</u>or look like?
24		(0.8)

```
25    R:    Well he's uh quite looks qui:te impressive
26          he's gotta .hhh gotta catsuit on.
27    C:    Ri:ght.
28    R:    With an orange flas:h down the front
29          like a: flash of li:ghtning would look
30          like sometimes.
.
.           ***Lines omitted about what Thor created***
.
47    C:    Is he kind of hu:ge.
48              (0.4)
49    C:    A big bloke or?
50    R:    No: he's not hu:ge he's a biggis:h looking
51          bloke though.
52    C:    Right.
53              (0.7)
54    R:    A bih- ter:: (.) not bigger than (0.5) no:rmal
55          big men but (.) big you know.
56    C:    Ri:ght. Couldn't he:- (1.0) pahh! I don't want
57          to sound s(h)keptical but- couldn't he have just
58          beena jo:gger or something like that?
```

In this extract R reports meeting the god Thor and describes various aspects of his appearance such as his size and the clothes he wore. The central analytic question is, 'What skills enable this story to be recognised as a delusion?' Now although R believes he has met Thor, the interviewer (that is C) manifestly does not. Indeed on line 58 it is clear that C has a basis for doubt; that is, for suggesting what R saw could 'just have been a jogger.' The first point to make is that the criterion of falsity does not play a part in C's judgment. That is, C has no empirical knowledge of what 'really' happened in the field in Leicestershire and therefore cannot say that R's belief represents an 'incorrect inference about external reality.' However, he clearly has some practical basis for doubt. What this is, and what 'criteria' are involved will be the focus of my analysis.

The issue of 'evidence'
For present purposes the crucial parts of #1 are lines 22 to 58. However, to contextualise the analysis I shall make some brief comments about lines 1 to 21. The first point to note is that C asks a question on line 1 which runs 'so you believe there's an afterlife then?' On line 3, R answers by saying 'Yes I do now, now I've seen a god as well you know'. On lines 8 to 21 R expands on this claim by reporting some details of an encounter he had with the god Thor. In non-delusional accounts of paranormal activity such as those described by Woofitt (1992) a central concern is to establish the occurrence

of some supernatural happenings. In other words, descriptions of supernatural events routinely demonstrate that the event has paranormal
properties. So, in this case, we might expect R to provide some evidence
that he met the god of Thunder; for instance, he might have reported a
characteristically god-like action performed by Thor such as controlling the
weather. However, instead of providing this type of evidence R simply states
that he met Thor.

In this context I begin the analysis proper by examining the interviewer's
turn on lines 22–3 'What kind of thing does, what did Floor Thor look like?'
The first aspect of this turn to consider is the context in which it occurs.
That is, 'What did Thor look like?' is a response to R's claim that he has met
Thor. The sorts of activities people standardly do in response to a claim
involve accepting or rejecting it in some way. For instance, C could accept
that R had met Thor with a turn such as, 'Wow weren't you frightened?'
which starts with a marker of acceptance 'wow'. By contrast C's 'What did
Thor look like?' is a straight question which is not preceded by acceptance
markers. In other words, lines 22–3 *withhold* accepting R's claim that he has
met Thor. There are two key components to this withholding. First, not
accepting the claim displays that C has some reservations about the evidence
on which it is based. In other words, from C's point of view, the account on
lines 8 to 21 contains *insufficient evidence* to establish that R met Thor.
Secondly, 'What did Thor look like' gives R a chance to produce some more
evidence which might remove these reservations. In more colloquial terms,
'What did Thor look like' means something like, 'I'm not yet convinced that
you met Thor, give me some evidence that you did'.

To be confident of the preceding analysis we need to discount an
alternative way C's turn could be understood. After all, in literal terms lines
22–3 are simply an inquiry about Thor's appearance. That is, C could
merely want to know what Thor looked like and may not be seeking
evidence at all. So, how is it possible to decide if the analytic interpretation
of lines 22 and 3 is appropriate? In conversation analysis, this issue is settled
by looking at the next turn (Schegloff and Sacks 1973: 297). If R understands 'What did Thor look like?' as saying, 'Give me more evidence that
you met Thor' then presumably he will provide some evidence. So before
teasing out the key points from this analysis we need to examine R's
response on lines 25 to 30 of the following extract:

#2 Delusional talk (detail)

```
22    C:      Wuh-What kind of thing does
23            What did Floor-Thor look like?
24                    (0.8)
25  → R:      Well he's uh quite looks qui:te impressive
26  →         he's gotta .hhh gotta catsuit on.
27    C:      Ri:ght.
28  → R:      With an orange flas:h down the front
```

29 →   like a: flash of li:ghtning would look
30 →   like sometimes.

There are two main grounds for arguing that R's reply in lines 25–30 is designed to provide evidence. The first of these is its 'topic selection'. As C's 'What did Thor look like?' is an open question, it allows R to select which aspect of Thor's appearance he will describe. Indeed, an answer to this question could report any of Thor's characteristics such as his build, his hair or even the colour of his eyes. So, on what grounds does R select the catsuit? In answer, what a description of the catsuit offers is the basis for C to identify that it was Thor. In particular, the 'flash of lightning' motif is an appropriate article of clothing for Thor to wear, as it symbolises his connection with thunder storms. The second way we can identify an evidential character in this turn is through the precise way R describes the catsuit on lines 28–30. Notice here that R's turn is potentially complete on line 28. That is, 'Well he looks quite impressive, he's got a catsuit on with an orange flash down the front' is a potentially complete description of Thor's clothes. So why does R continue his description on lines 29 and 30? What these lines do is explicate the orange flash as being, 'like a flash of lightning would look sometimes'. This makes the connection between the catsuit's motif and Thor very apparent and, in doing so, gives C some evidence that it was Thor. In short, the particular aspect of Thor which R selects to describe and the way he works up that description are consistent with him presenting evidence that it was, indeed, Thor in the field.

In summary, there are two main points in the analysis so far. First, I noted that C's 'What did Thor look like?' did not accept R's claim to have met Thor. By doing so, this displays that – from C's point of view – R has given insufficient evidence to establish that it was, indeed, Thor. Secondly, this interpretation of C's turn is confirmed as R's reply is specifically built to provide more evidence. These two observations are already critical of psychiatry's position as articulated by the diagnostic criteria. The key issue in this extract is not one of empirical reality but of *evidence*. An important feature of evidencing is that it is a linguistic phenomenon which is, in principle, independent from knowledge of external reality. The strength of a person's evidence can be judged simply by listening to what they say. However, although we are in a position to make some critical comments the analysis remains incomplete as it has not described the grounds on which delusions are recognisably irrational. All it shows is that, from C's point of view, R did not provide sufficient evidence and that R supplies some more. As a result, it is necessary to continue the analysis as far as line 58. This reveals the particular type of evidence that C is seeking and, through that, a way in which delusions are identified.

A form of 'irrational' evidence
C next pursues issues of evidence on line 47 when he asks, 'Is Thor kind of huge?' The sequence this question generates is as follows

#3 Delusional talk (detail)

```
47    C:    Is he kind of hu:ge.
48              (0.4)
49    C:    A big bloke or?
50    R:    No: he's not hu:ge he's a biggis:h looking
51          bloke though.
52    C:    Right.
53              (0.7)
54    R:    A bih- ter:: (.) not bigger than (0.5) no:rmal
55          big men but (.) big you know.
56    C:    Ri:ght. Couldn't he:- (1.0) pahh! = I don't want
57          to sound s(h)keptical but- couldn't he have just
58          been a jo:gger or something like that?
```

There are two key observations to make about C's turn on line 47. First, it is the second question about Thor's appearance (the first one being 'What did Thor look like?' on lines 22 and 3). As such, line 47 pursues the issue of Thor's appearance. By asking a second, pursuit question, C implies that the answer to the first was inadequate in some way. As a result, asking 'Is Thor kind of huge' at this sequential location shows that C's reservations over whether R met Thor remain unresolved. So, line 47 displays that, from C's point of view, the report of the catsuit's orange flash is still not sufficient evidence to establish that it was Thor.

The key second observation about line 47 is that it requires R to clarify Thor's size. The important properties of this turn become most apparent when compared with other ways of asking for clarification. For example, instead of saying 'Is he kind of huge?' C could have asked 'How tall was he?' The main difference between these two ways of doing clarification is that 'Is he kind of huge' guesses at Thor's size – *i.e.* 'huge' – whereas 'How tall was he' does not. As a result of this guess, C displays an expectation that Thor is likely to be huge – in other words that Thor may have the paranormal property of enormous size. So, this particular way of clarifying provides a *hint* about the type of evidence C requires; namely, evidence that Thor was paranormal in some way.

Again, to be confident of this analysis, it needs supporting with sequential evidence. In particular, we need to establish that C's 'huge' means 'paranormally large' rather than something within the normal range. Again, the way of doing this is to examine R's next turn and ask, 'Does *he* treat "huge" as meaning paranormally large?' In this context the key feature about R's response is that on lines 54–5 he says Thor is big, 'but not bigger than no:rmal big men'. The heavy stress R puts on 'no:rmal' is a way of displaying a contrast (see Schegloff, 1998: 247–51 for a detailed analysis of this practice). That is, stressing that Thor is normal in size highlights a contrast with C's assumption that he is paranormally large. From lines 54–5 we can see that R understands 'huge' to mean something supernatural and can therefore recognise the evidential standards which are being brought to bear on his account. However, what is unusual about this turn is that although he clearly recognises the type of evidence C is seeking, he neither disputes its relevance nor provides it. For example, R could have said, 'No he wasn't huge but he did appear out of nowhere and alter the weather'. However, all he says is that Thor was 'normal' in size and does no more. Such a response is in strong contrast to the non-delusional accounts of paranormal activity that Wooffitt (1992) has studied. A theme which runs through his analysis is that people without delusions are concerned with the grounds on which their stories might be doubted and so attempt to undercut those grounds. Doing this involves substantial engagement with the other person and with their interactional concerns. It involves entering into debate with them and arguing your point of view. It is this 'outward'-looking orientation which is absent from R's talk and, as such, he appears disengaged from interactional concerns which constitute the normal social world.

In summary, from C's point of view, there are two bases on which this story can be recognised as delusional. First, R's account contravenes the logic of practical action. By this I mean that every social activity we perform has an internal logic to it. In this case, the logic is as simple as: 'When describing a paranormal entity show that something paranormal happened'. Whilst R claims to have met a god he only describes Thor in ordinary ways: as a large man, in a tracksuit with an orange flash on it. As a result, R's claims appear ungrounded and are systematically open to doubt that he mistook an ordinary phenomenon. This first basis is compounded by a second; namely, R seems unconcerned that his story is open to doubt. More specifically, in the analysis of lines 47 to 55 (*i.e.* the question 'Was he kind of huge') it became apparent that R was disengaged from key aspects of the social world. In particular, he was able to recognise the type of evidence that C required but, unaccountably, did not give it. This provides evidence of a significant disengagement from the world of normal social interaction.

Discussion

This final section teases out the implications of my analysis for the power argument in particular, and the microsociology of psychiatry more generally. A central goal of this chapter has been to account for the observation that seemingly powerful criticisms of psychiatry may be ignored by psychiatrists. Given the preceding analysis, we are now in a position to account for this paradoxical situation. In short, the power argument is ineffectual because it does not criticise the relevancies of psychiatric practice. From a clinician's perspective there are two main grounds on which this argument can be ignored. First, starting with deviance theory, microsociology has argued that delusional beliefs are not inherently pathological. In Pollner's (1975: 412) words the beliefs involved 'are not self-evidently indicative of psychopathology'. However, the clinician is faced with a world in which social activities have an intrinsic order and so can be intrinsically disordered. With respect to the type of story examined above, its internal rationality is simply 'when telling a paranormal story show that something paranormal happened'. As a result, paranormal stories can become inherently disordered and irrational if they only report ordinary events like seeing a tall man in a catsuit.

The second way in which the power argument loses its relevance for clinicians is by working with abstractions which, although not incorrect in themselves, gloss over important details of practice. Take the argument that the diagnostic context is marked by an absence of shared standards which could establish a definitive version of reality. In terms of actual practice this point is obviously correct as it was manifest that R and C did not share the same evaluative standards. However, this argument does not capture the clinically significant aspects of this difference. For a clinician the key issue is not so much the difference itself, but the *orientation* which is adopted towards it. Recognising that different standards are being applied opens up the possibilities of disputing their relevance or providing evidence which addresses them. This involves engaging with the other in debate and, in that sense, sharing a social world with them. R's talk was unusual in this respect because although he clearly recognised that evidence of the paranormal was required he neither disputed this standard nor attempted to provide that sort of evidence. In this way, he unaccountably stood outside the world of local interactional concerns. In other words, he was disengaged from the social world and therefore outside the bounds of normal interaction. In short, although the power argument makes good sociological sense it also makes practical nonsense.

The previous sections have specified two ways in which a constructionist criticism of delusion loses relevance for psychiatrists. However, from the specifics of this account we can abstract a more general point about the way that microsociology *trusts* psychiatry, despite its largely critical stance. The target of much critical work is that of psychiatry's diagnostic criteria – in this case the falsity criterion. Such a focus assumes that the brief descriptions of symptoms in manuals such as DSM-IV adequately capture the procedures which are involved in recognising a particular case. In other words, microsociology trusts psychiatrists to know and adequately describe their own practice. Hence its critical focus is frequently an official 'proxy' for practice – such as diagnostic criteria – rather than practice itself. An inherent danger in this approach is that the proxy misses crucial features of the way action is organised. This is particularly likely to be the case if tacit or practical knowledges are heavily involved. One cost of this trust, then, is that the tacit skills which psychiatrists use – and which constitute the relevant features of their world – go unexplicated and uncriticised. Sociologists are unlikely to produce effective criticisms of such knowledges by reading diagnostic manuals or even by interviewing psychiatrists themselves.

One way of overcoming this problem is to develop a distinctive sub-discipline which might be called 'clinical sociology'. By this I mean a type of sociology which starts from a point outside psychiatric discourse and allows clinical phenomena to dictate its problematic. To do so involves explicating the material workings of psychiatry in their own terms. Taking my analysis of delusions as a first attempt at this project we can see that clinical sociology would offer two ways of producing relevant criticisms of psychiatry. First, the analysis of how delusions are identified was inherently critical of psychiatry as it reveals a set of practical skills which are not recognised in the diagnostic manuals. As these skills constitute the practical basis of symptom recognition, they are directly relevant to psychiatrists and so should overcome the problems of irrelevancy outlined above. Secondly, description of these skills mean that future sociological work need not start with a proxy such as the DSM criteria, but has a critical target drawn from the workings of psychiatry.

This project is different from previous attempts to develop a clinically applied sociology, most notably by Glassner and Freedman (1979). For Glassner and Freedman clinical sociology involved the use of methods, such as ethnography, to investigate psychiatric phenomena independently. For example, they report how a case of seemingly incoherent mumbling was made understandable by discovering that the patient was a Pente-costalist who regularly spoke in tongues (Glassner and Freedman 1979: 5). Here questions about the woman's social background were able to account for her apparently incoherent speech. There is clearly scope for important work along these lines; however it offers a very limited appreciation of what clinical sociology could be. In particular, it overlooks the form of sociological reasoning which is right at the heart of psychiatry. The very symptoms psychiatry deals with are the products of shared, tacit skills. In my usage, clinical sociology does not add sociological knowledge to psychiatry but takes the more ethnomethodological path of explicating the immanent sociology of practice (Garfinkel 1967: vii). In other words instead of preserving sociology's independence a hybrid discipline is developed (see Lynch 1993: 274) which explicates psychiatry's internal sociology. It is this hybrid which offers the prospect of producing effective criticisms which are finally capable of changing psychiatry itself.

Acknowledgements

The research for this chapter was made possible by award R00429334261 from the Economic and Social Research Council.

Appendix: transcription conventions

The following transcription symbols are drawn from a system developed by Gail Jefferson. They do not represent that entire system (see Atkinson and Heritage 1984: ix–xvi for a fuller version) but only the parts of it that are used in this chapter.

1. Speech delivery

:   A colon, or colons, are used to indicate an extension of the sound which it follows. The number of colons is proportional to the length of elongation

.   A full stop indicates falling tone.

,   A comma indicates continuing intonation

?   A question mark indicates rising inflection

!   An exclamation mark indicates an animated tone.

-    A dash indicates a sound which is cut off.

2. Intervals within and between utterances

When an interval occurs within the stream of talk it is timed in 10ths of a second and inserted in the utterance at the point at which it occurs:

```
23    C:    What did Floor-Thor look like?
24              (0.8)
25    R:    Well he's uh quite looks qui:te impressive
```

Intervals which are under four tenths of a second were not timed, but are marked in the usual way except where there is a full stop inside the brackets:

```
54    R:    A bih- ter:: (.) not bigger than (0.5) no:rmal
55          big men but (.) big you know.
```

References

American Psychiatric Association (1994) *Diagnostic and Statistical Manual of Mental Disorders* (4th Edition). Washington: American Psychiatric Association.

Atkinson, J.M. and Heritage, J. (1984) *Structures of Social Action: Studies in Conversation Analysis*. Cambridge: University of Cambridge Press.

Bowers, L. (1998) *The Social Nature of Mental Illness*. London: Routledge.

Busfield, J. (1996) *Men, Women and Madness: Understanding Gender and Mental Disorder*. Basingstoke: Macmillan.

Coulter, J. (1973) *Approaches to Insanity: a Philosophical and Sociological Study*. New York: Wiley.

Coulter, J. (1979) *The Social Construction of Mind*. London: Macmillan.

Cutting, J. (1997) *Principles of Psychopathology: Two Worlds, Two Minds, Two Hemispheres*. Oxford: Oxford Medical Publications.

Garfinkel, H. (1956) Some sociological concepts and methods for psychiatrists, *Psychiatric Research Reports*, 6, 181–95.

Garfinkel, H. (1967) *Studies in Ethnomethodology*. Cambridge: Polity Press.

Georgaca, E. (1999) Factualization and plausibility in 'delusional' discourse, paper presented at the International Conference of Human Science Research, Sheffield.

Georgaca, E. (forthcoming) Psychiatry, reality and discourse: a critical analysis of the category of 'delusions', *British Journal of Medical Psychology*.

Gelder, M., Dennis, G. and Mayou, R. (1989) *Oxford Textbook of Psychiatry*. Oxford: Oxford University Press.

Glassner, B. and Freedman, J. (1979) *Clinical Sociology*. New York: Longman.

Goffman, E. (1967) *Interaction Ritual: Essays in Face-to-Face Behaviour*. London: Penguin.

Goffman, E. (1971) *Relations in Public: Microstudies of the Public Order*. London: Penguin Books.

Gorenstein, E. (1989) Debating mental illness: implications for science, medical and social policy. In Hooley, M., Neale, J. and Davison, G. (eds) *Readings in Abnormal Psychology*. New York: Wiley and Sons.

Harper, D. (1992) Defining delusion and the serving of professional interests: the case of 'paranoia', *British Journal of Medical Psychology*, 65, 357–69.

Harper, D. (1999) Reconceptualising 'delusions' as a breakdown in the discursive accomplishment of plausibility, paper presented at the International Conference of Human Science Research, Sheffield.

Heise, D. (1988) Delusions and the construction of reality. In Oltmanns, T. and Maher, B. (eds) *Delusional Beliefs*. New York: Wiley and Sons.

Hutchby, I. and Wooffit, R. (1998) *Conversation Analysis: Principles, Practices and Applications*. Cambridge: Polity Press.

Ingleby, D. (1982) The social construction of mental illness. In Wright, P. and Treacher, A. (eds) *The Problem of Medical Knowledge*. Edinburgh: Edinburgh University Press, pp. 123–143.

Jaspers, K. (1912/68) The phenomenological approach to psychopathology (trans. anonymous), *British Journal of Psychiatry*, 114, 1313–23.

Jaspers, K. (1959/97) *General Psychopathology* (trans. Hoenig, J. and Hamilton, W.). Baltimore: Johns Hopkins University Press.

Lynch, M. (1993) *Scientific Practice and Ordinary Action. Ethnomethodology and Social Studies of Science*. Cambridge: Cambridge University Press.

McGuire, P., Silbersweig, D., Wright, I., Murray, R., David, A., Frackowiak, R. and Frith, C. (1995) Abnormal monitoring of inner speech – a physiological-basis for auditory hallucinations, *Lancet*, 346, 596–600.

Palmer, D. (1997) *The Methods of Madness: Recognizing Delusional Talk*, unpublished D. Phil. thesis: University of York.

Pollner, M. (1975) 'The very coinage of your brain': the anatomy of reality disjunctures, *Philosophy of the Social Sciences*, 5, 411–30.

Rosen, G. (1968) *Madness in Society: Chapters in the Historical Sociology of Mental Illness*. London: Routledge and Kegan Paul.

Scheff, T. (1966/99) *Being Mentally Ill: a Sociological Theory*. London: Weidenfeld and Nicolson.

Schegloff, E. (1998) Reflections on studying prosody in talk-in-interaction, *Language and Speech*, 41, 235–63.

Schegloff, E. and Sacks, H. (1973) Opening up closings, *Semiotica*, 7, 289–327.

Sims, A. (1995) *Symptoms in the Mind: an Introduction to Descriptive Psychopathology* (2nd Edition), London: W.B. Saunders.

Smith, D. (1978) K is mentally ill: the anatomy of a factual account, *Sociology*, 12, 23–53.

Spitzer, M. (1990a) Why philosophy? In Spitzer, M. and Maher, B. (eds) *Philosophy and Psychopathology*. New York: Springer.

Spitzer, M. (1990b) On defining delusions, *Comprehensive Psychiatry*, 31, 377–97.

Wooffitt, R. (1992) *Telling Tales of the Paranormal: the Organisation of Factual Discourse*. London: Harvester Wheatsheaf.

World Health Organisation (1975) *The International Pilot Study of Schizophrenia*. Geneva: World Health Organisation.

8

Civil commitment due to mental illness and dangerousness: the union of law and psychiatry within a treatment-control system

Bernadette Dallaire, Michael McCubbin, Paul Morin and David Cohen

Introduction

The sociological theory of deviance centres on the notion of a social response to deviant behaviours through institutions dedicated to maintaining the social order. This perspective implies that, mirroring the main dichotomy of 'badness' (motivated criminal or delinquent acts) and 'illness' (a 'no fault' state), the institutions of justice and medicine implement specialised responses: punishment/control toward intentional deviance, and treatment/care toward deviance without responsibility. Mechanic (1978) provides a good example of this perspective in his comprehensive analysis of the field of medical sociology, which attempts to explain institutional, professional and lay responses to illness. However, this dichotomy is less applicable in the case of mental illness, first because of the unclear and contested nature of its definition as an illness and second, because of its association, for professional and lay actors, with dangerousness. From a societal point of view, this particular association places mental illness somewhere between 'badness' and 'illness': something pertaining to deviant acts as well as to deviant states, and something for which both control and treatment are needed (Szasz 1991).

Until now, most sociologists have understood the institutional response to mental illness/dangerousness through the view of an intersection between medicine/psychiatry and justice (*e.g.* Allen 1987). This view implies that, even if the treatment-control function leads to an institutional overlap, each institution retains its boundaries intact. It also implies that in some circumstances conflicts could erupt between the psychiatric and judicial systems of knowledge, orientations, interests and modes of operation. We argue in this chapter that, in the institutional response as enacted in civil court orders for confinement of citizens labelled as mentally ill (or presumed to be), this relationship between psychiatry and justice is different. Given the particular nature of mental illness/dangerousness, the institutional response to it generates a specialised cognitive and practical system.

This system, centred on the equation of treatment and control as its main *finalité*[1], operates at the civil commitment junction of psychiatry and justice. Although lacking many features of a 'classical' institution (see Dumont 1985), this system has some quasi-institutional traits[2]: (1) a shared body of norms, rules, beliefs and knowledge (both formal/codified and informal/uncodified); (2) behavioural patterns allowing for repetition and continuity of practices; (3) shared aims and interests; and (4) a central teleological orientation of treatment and control of deviance attributed to mental illness and dangerousness. Pursuing Scheff's (1999) thesis on 'systems of social control', we demonstrate that the treatment-control system enacts sets of normative expectancies and social representations through the agency of the psychiatric, judicial and lay actors involved.

Drawing upon a literature relating to various disciplines as well as our own empirical work on the concept of dangerousness in mental health and its application in civil commitment procedures, we shall illustrate how the 'in between' definition of mental illness is operationalised through the system which embodies and organises the psychiatric and judicial measures and outcomes with respect to mental illness/dangerousness. We discuss:

- the scientific issues related to the question of a relationship between dangerousness and mental illness[3];
- the nature of psychiatric opinion in the identification and prediction of danger and the relationship of that opinion with the organisation of modern psychiatry's nosological system;
- the legal application of notions of danger, or risks to the health or safety of self or others (such notions – despite variations in wording across jurisdictions – provide the criteria for civil commitment); by doing so, we shall see how civil commitment rulings constitute more than the mere translation of the legal code;
- how such issues, opinion and enactments actualise the union of the legal and psychiatric institutions within a treatment-control system handling certain persons identified as both mentally ill and dangerous to self or others – 'residual' cases regarded as problematic for society and not dealt with in another system for managing deviance, such as the criminal system.

The notion of dangerousness

In a general sense, the notion of dangerousness is used to characterise a situation, a thing or a person presenting a danger for the physical or human environment, or for oneself. This notion refers to the potential, possibility or probability of an undesirable, unrealised event; not a current event but rather a *risk* and, by extension, to the capacity to *foresee* such eventuality (Litwack 1994). In the opinion of several analysts, dangerousness and its substrate – danger – are 'fuzzy' concepts: beyond the actuarial models designed to identify and measure it, danger (and risk) is a 'fact' difficult to define, identify and, especially, to assess in a concrete situation (Slovic and Monahan 1995).

On a psychosocial level, risk and danger are closely related to unpredictability: as demonstrated by Garfinkel (1967), Goffman (1964), and Scheff (1999), the performance and organisation of everyday interactions are highly dependent on a series of normative expectancies. In situations where such expectancies are not met and in which no alternative explanation and course of action are available (*e.g.* 'strange' behaviour or 'crazy talk' from one of the agents), the order of the socially constructed experiential world is threatened.

In the context of civil commitment, dangerousness is the essential element of the civil law providing the basis for compulsory psychiatric examination or hospitalisation (hence the term *civil dangerousness*). Yet it is also a clinical concept, which may intervene in psychiatric diagnosis, prognosis and treatment plans. Finally, because it justifies and orients the processes of legal and therapeutic decision-making with respect to the assessed person, the notion of dangerousness mobilises specific sets of norms, belief systems, discourses and practices. In this sense, the notion crystalises the relations between the institutional worlds of justice and psychiatry: at this junction the domains of action and objectives are, as we shall see further, both specialised and complementary.

The question of the relationship between mental illness and dangerousness

The introduction of 'danger to self or others' as a decision criterion in civil commitment laws reveals the assumption that mental illness and dangerousness are causally related. For this reason, the critical issue – whether from a legal, medical or social point of view – resides in the association which might be detected between various manifestations of mental illness and of dangerousness, the subject of a large number of clinical and statistical studies since the 1970s. Several studies find the evidence for such a relationship, but those studies which broke down the data into characteristics like diagnosis, history, behavioural characteristics, and indicators of violence have found that the relationship would appear to hold only in specific circumstances. There is a consensus regarding statistically significant (if not strong) relationships between *severe* mental illness (especially involving marked psychotic symptoms) and criminality (one possible indicator or subset of 'dangerousness') with respect to quite specific sub-groups (Hodgins 1995). Almost all these associations involve individuals who are also classified as substance abusers (Hiday 1997). Indeed, the conclusions of the MacArthur Violence Risk Assessment Study (MacArthur Research

Network on Mental Health and the Law 2000) stress that, among people without symptoms of substance abuse, there is no difference in the prevalence of violent acts between people discharged from psychiatric hospitals and 'ordinary' members of the community.

However, some analysts emphasise the possible influence of factors which are not directly related to the patients and their behaviours. For instance, an increased emphasis upon the dangerousness criterion in emergency committals could point not only to the incidence of violent behaviours but also to changes in the application of the law, decreasing age of patients released from psychiatric institutions, a greater sensitivity of psychiatrists to the decisional consequences (especially the risk of being sued for professional error and failure in civil responsibility), and a change in community attitudes toward recourse to psychiatric internment (see McNiel and Binder 1986). Similarly, the use of compulsory detention on the ground of safety (of patients or others) could be motivated by the fact that such a measure is the only way to obtain therapeutic services, more than by the actual presence of danger, as described by Barnes (1996).

Some critics (Monahan 1992, 1998, Shea 1993–4) point on the other hand to weaknesses in the research designs that find a relationship between psychological distress and violence, and hence to limits in their validity and generalisability. These are caused by: the limited number and questionable choice of independent variables considered; the questionable choice of diagnostic categories; inadequate criteria for selection of sites as well as their limited number (several studies are mono-site); the fact that in several studies only men are included; limited or questionable generalisability due to the definition and selection of the considered populations; biases in measurement resulting from events and environments differentially affecting those who have been involved with the mental health system as opposed to the general public (*e.g.* violent acts are more likely to be detected when committed by a person in an institution or under treatment and observation in the community); and too short observational periods.

However, a more fundamental validity problem could affect almost all the studies: a possible tautology between the two poles for which associations are assessed. Not only are 'dangerous' acts more likely to be detected once a person has entered the mental health system, it is reasonable to suppose that mental illness is more likely to be diagnosed among those very individuals who pose problems to their families or communities (Scheff 1999) than among psychologically distressed persons who do not. Among such possible problems are of course violent or threatening acts – or the perception by others of a threat when it is more or less contained in the interpersonal situation and dynamics, as observed by Dallaire and Morin (1999) – and fears for the safety of the person who will become a candidate for the diagnostic process. This issue has not been raised in the dangerousness assessment literature, except recently by Arboleda-Florez *et al.* (1998). These authors characterised the problem as 'confounding by definition', which 'seriously mars any causal inferences that could be made based on empirical evidence showing a statistical association between mental illness and violence'. They further argued that the official definitions of pathology used by psychiatry, as contained in the various versions of the *Diagnostic and Statistical Manual of Mental Disorders* (DSM), have increasingly, with each new revision, incorporated language about 'violence'. Hence, 'Mental disorder and violence may be statistically related simply because of our overlapping definitions' (1998: S41).

In other words, being dangerous predisposes the likelihood of a *label* of mental illness – which 'explains' the dangerousness. Viewed from a social construction perspective, then, this causality runs not from mental illness to dangerousness, but from dangerousness to mental illness. It has not been recognised in the highly focused research that characterises the theme of 'mental illness and dangerousness' that biases possibly inherent in the research designs may simply amplify a more fundamental *social bias* to explain as mental illness otherwise inexplicable and troubling behaviour – or to capture a person 'falling through the cracks' of other social control systems. But, also viewed from a social construction perspective, causality runs from mental illness to dangerousness: acts or discourse of a person are more likely to be interpreted as indicating risks to self or others if that person has a previous psychiatric history (Cohen *et al.* 1998, Dallaire *et al.* 2000). Hence, we find that to some extent, at least, the notions of mental illness and dangerousness are so intimately related on conceptual, representational, and operational levels, as to raise the question of their actual specificity as separate notions, if any.

Although the positive associations relating mental illness to dangerousness have been characterised as at best moderate and limited (Eronen *et al.* 1998, Link *et al.* 1992, Steadman *et al.* 1998), and at worst questionable on the grounds of validity and bias as discussed above, policy debates over whether enhanced control is required over 'the mentally ill in the community' attest to a widespread perception – among the general public as well as stakeholders more involved in the mental health system as administrators, practitioners and family members – of a relationship between mental illness and violence much more broadly based than the existing literature indicates (Weitz 2000). The close association in the public's mind between mental illness and dangerousness is directly and indirectly manifested in the way that 'mental illness' and 'dangerousness' are constructed and subsequently operationalised within the mental health system.

Problems of clinical prediction: presumption of danger and presumption of illness

The scientific justification for a civil commitment system has to be based, as one of a number of necessary conditions, upon actuarial – population-level – data relating particular mental illness characteristics to indicators of dangerousness (*e.g.* a significant statistical relationship between a diagnostic category and the incidence of violent behaviours). Yet decisions to commit an individual must be individualised, the object here being to determine whether a particular individual might commit acts dangerous for self or others. The shift from statistical relationships at the population level – apart from questions of their validity and magnitude – to decisions with respect to individuals is highly problematic.

Clinical predictions by psychiatrists, presumably based upon diagnosis, case history, and behavioural signs, are commonly regarded by professional actors within the system, as well as by the public, as the prime – or only – expertise applicable to decisions to commit an individual (Pfohl 1978). This confidence is strongly contradicted by the literature however, which has abundantly criticised the applicability of such expertise, and consequently its accuracy. Clinical predictions have been found to be extremely poor, holding less acuity than prediction based purely upon actuarial data (Gardner *et al.* 1996). In 1976 Cocozza and Steadman identified a series of weaknesses preventing adequate evaluation by psychiatrists, mainly the vague character of the concept of dangerousness itself (What behaviours are classified as dangerous? Should the concern be with past, present or future acts?), and the fact that in a group of psychiatric patients, the incidence of violent acts (the base rate) is so small – only slightly more than for the general population, if that – that the occurrence of erroneous predictions of violence (false positives) is high. According to the American Psychiatric Association (APA) [2000], even in cases of patients who had *already* committed violent acts in the past, predictions were estimated to be erroneous two times out of three. On this ground, the APA states that 'psychiatrists have no special knowledge or ability with which to predict dangerous behavior' (2000: 1). This is not a new acknowledgement of the unproved value of psychiatric expertise in this area; similar conclusions were reached by APA task forces in 1974 and 1978 (described by Litwack 1994), based on a large number of studies and evaluations dating back several decades (described by Ennis and Litwack 1974).

Noting the preponderance of studies establishing important limits to the enterprise of dangerousness prediction with respect to psychiatric patients, Hughes (1996) concluded that the current state of knowledge does not permit adequate clinical predictions of violence or suicide. According to Bjorkly (1995), even those tests based on highly elaborate instruments (with scales classifying several levels of probability, drawing upon a variety of predictors and criteria) have weak predictive validity. Indeed, Faust and Ziskin (1988) found that the predictive accuracy of psychiatrists – even the most experienced – is no better than that of ordinary citizens, and that the majority of decisions would be wrong in both cases. This may seem surprising, since such an error rate is worse than chance, and worse than if predictions were based only upon the general incidence of violence in the population without any additional information about the individual case. One reason for the exceptionally high failure rate of clinical predictions may lie in the strong tendency to *over-predict* violence or danger (Hughes 1996). Besides the tautological problem raised earlier, whereby the understanding of mental illness incorporates dangerousness as an inherent part of the meaning of that term (and hence a clinical predisposition to expect danger-ousness from individuals presumed mentally ill), over-prediction might also reflect a decision rule that makes a failed prediction of danger less grave than a wrong assessment of non-danger ('better safe than sorry'). This decision rule is reinforced in many ways (Ryan 1998): by public outcries when an allegedly mentally ill person commits a particularly gruesome or 'random' violent act (with mental illness frequently *assumed* due to the inexplicable nature of the crime) [Holloway 1996]; by authorities responding to public perceptions and demands for protection (Baker 1997); and, particularly in the United States, by litigation by family members or victims when violence or suicide follows the release of a patient into the community (Appelbaum 1988). Noticeably, Scheff (1999) attributes this kind of col-lective reaction to a 'surplus emotional response to deviance'.

Some writers have placed the problem of over-prediction of danger within a larger disposition of presumption of illness (Pfohl 1978, Scheff 1978, Sjöström 1997) intimately related to contemporary clinical practice. It is partly on this ground that authors also question the value of psychiatric diagnosis itself (Kirk and Kutchins 1992). The process for current psychi-atric nosology, as officialised in the DSM (under its different revisions) of the American Psychiatric Association, and in the *International Classification of Psychological Distress and Behaviour* of the World Health Organisation, has been severely criticised for weaknesses bearing both on validity and reliability: non-exclusive pathology categories, low inter-rater agreement for several syndromes, lack of fit between empirically-derived symptom clusters and traditional diagnostic categories, inconsistency of diagnoses made at different times for the same case (Kirk 1994, Mirowski 1990). The process of inclusion and exclusion of diagnostic categories in the DSM has also been criticised for its intrinsically political nature (Caplan 1995, Kutchins and Kirk 1998).

The revisions in the symptomatology attributed to the categories can generate profound, though 'artificial' changes in the number and types of diagnosed pathologies, even severe ones (Stoll *et al.* 1993). Along with previously noted criticisms, this has led some critics, even within the psychiatric profession, also to characterise as inherently artificial virtually the entire current enterprise of psychiatric nosology (Tucker 1997). In this scenario, even if the diagnostic system is completely reliable (achieving consensus among clinicians), the validity of the diagnostic categories themselves is not strengthened: 'Anyone can achieve interrater reliability by teaching all people the "wrong" material, and getting them to all agree on it' (Brown 1990: 393).[4]

On this basis, the critique of the recourse to psychiatric expertise in criminal and civil courts and administrative tribunals has broadened to incorporate legal and ethical considerations. Whether the probity of a proof be 'beyond a reasonable doubt' (criminal cases) or the 'balance of probabilities' (civil cases), psychiatric evaluations would not meet the standard (Cohn 1998). However, some writers have taken the view that even a risk of violence less than 50 per cent can justify deprivation of liberty; that it is the responsibility of legally-mandated professionals to determine the threshold of risk or error ethically and socially acceptable (Litwack 1993). In this sense, the psychiatric experts would only have to 'do their job'. This argument presupposes, however, that courts and tribunals would explicitly assess both the actual level of risk and the minimum threshold it should attain to justify deprivation of liberty – in a process accountable to society. There is little evidence or research asking whether this is indeed the case. We have argued elsewhere (McCubbin *et al.* 1999) that researchers independent of this risk-evaluation process have been systematically impeded in efforts to cast light upon it. Such barriers could be interpreted as a sign of a reticence, on the part of those exercising state responsibility and powers with respect to civil commitment, at being observed in the course of their actual practices.

Evaluation of dangerousness in civil commitment procedures

The introduction of civil dangerousness as a decision criterion for involuntary commitment reflects a dual preoccupation in most states using it[5]. On the one hand, by specifying additional criteria for commitment, legislators aimed to protect the rights of individuals to liberty and dignity. The sole diagnosis of mental illness – or mental illness combined with need for treatment – could no longer justify commitment. On the other hand, the dangerousness criterion also fulfilled a role in protection of both the public and the committed individual – a role which must fall to the state. Hence a judge endeavouring to apply the spirit as well as the letter of the law would, in legal theory, aim to satisfy and balance these two sets of objectives, those of individual rights and the public interest (McCubbin and Cohen 2000).

Several analysts have investigated the actual factors which influence civil commitment decisions. Some have argued that the content of the laws – the legal criteria additional to diagnosis of mental illness, such as need for treatment plus danger (England and Wales) or dangerousness only (as in the United States and Québec), as well as the setting of the established terms and restrictions – would have an important impact, not only in terms of the number of commitment orders, but also in terms of the characteristics of the persons subjected to these orders (Riecher-Rossler and Rossler 1993). The weight of the evidence, however, suggests a marked gap between, on the one hand, the intention (or spirit) and often the letter of the law, and, on the other, its actual implementation. This is why Appelbaum emphasises the distinction between the law as written and the law as practised. From a perspective which is justificatory rather than critical, he writes:

> ... laws are not self-enforcing. Indeed, implementation of involuntary hospitalisation is delegated to a variety of participants in the commitment process, all of whom have the potential to affect how the law is applied. When the results of a law narrowly applied will be contrary to the moral intuitions of these parties, they will act at the margins to modify the law in practice to achieve what seem to them to be more reasonable outcomes (1997: 142).

For example, in their study of the effects of changes brought about in 1976 by the Mental Health Commitment Act of the State of Nebraska, Luckey and Berman (1979) observed a reduction in the number of involuntary admissions, but which was followed by a return to levels similar to those of the period preceding the changes. The authors explained this by evoking an 'adjustment period' during which the commitment boards familiarised themselves with the changes in content and procedure brought by the new law; the return to previous admission levels marked the end of this adaptation process. The authors hence concluded that the new legal dispositions were not in fact applied in accordance with the initial expectations. To provide another example, in a time-series analysis between 1977 and 1980, Marx and Levinson (1988) found increasing proportions of normally less assaultive populations being committed under the previous law which required assaultive behaviour, but when that requirement was changed to a health deterioration criterion, the numbers in these populations characterised as assaultive fell sharply. Roughly the same numbers of people in those populations and overall were committed before and after the change in the law. Those researchers suggested that the change in the law removed the incentive to exaggerate assaultiveness in order to justify commitment. In a wide-ranging international analysis of the different empirical tests of this phenomenon, Appelbaum (1997) observed the same evolution: the reductions in committals observed in the period immediately following legal changes were not maintained in subsequent years. He concluded that despite the introduction of 'stricter' committal criteria (based on danger to self or others), the policy changes contained in the law brought no durable changes in practice.

Such phenomena led some analysts to assert that the weight of the law is necessarily mediated, not only by the concrete interpretations that are made of them, but also by different sets of pre-existing social representations. While Hiday (1983) suggested that the 'facts' (*i.e.* the apparent signs and reports of mental illness and/or dangerousness) and the psychiatric recommendations had more impact than the attitude of judges on civil commitment outcomes, Warren (1982) emphasised that in civil commitment hearings, systems of meanings – legal, psychiatric and from common sense – defining mental illness are translated into practice. This view of a coexistence of professional and lay interpretations in systems of representations is also exposed in the analysis by Dallaire (1997) about representations of health and illness among medical and para-medical professionals: along with meanings originating from disciplinary training and knowledge and from workplace experiences, she argued, the interviewees also expressed lay-oriented interpretations about the nature, causes and consequences of health and illness.

Similarly, the study by Holstein (1993) in different American states depicted the observed hearings as processes of interpretation, where various cultural norms and 'theories of common sense' bearing on mental illness were actualised. Holstein took into account interactional and contextual aspects (the context structured by procedural rules). But, above all, he showed that the witnesses, the presentation of information, the arguments advanced and the judgment itself were part of a dynamic in which laws are used as resources: for argumentation, for the interpretation of situations, for the taking of a decision and for the justification of that decision. Such a dynamic could be characterised as rule use as opposed to rule following. In this regard Holstein emphasised that the criterion for a committal decision was not the presence of mental illness – that was taken for granted – but rather a series of preoccupations in which psychiatric opinion was primordial. They concern the nature of the madness itself, what would culturally be considered as acceptable and normal and, finally, the representations bearing on autonomy, care, supervision and compassion.

More recently, we have also demonstrated this gap between practice and the prescriptive function of law (Cohen *et al.* 1998). Analysing documents generated during 1975–93 in civil commitment appeal hearings by the Québec Social Affairs Commission (an administrative tribunal), we observed that the pertinent legal provisions appeared less as rules uniformly applied than as rhetorical instruments where the actual citation of the entire article of the law served as sole argument for the law to be applied. Furthermore, the notion of danger and the criteria for its evaluation, evoked but not formally defined in the law, were not defined by the tribunal. Indeed, in several hundred cases analysed, less than a handful of predictions of dangerousness were found. The issues raised in the hearing reports were, rather, considerations concerning *need for treatment*, the *compliance* of the patient with that treatment – especially with the medication regimen – and whether the patient's attitude (*'insight'*) was positively accepting of the diagnosis and of the necessity for following the treatment recommended by the treating psychiatrists.

Despite the fact that it concerns a different institutional locus, our study of civil commitment procedures in Montréal and Montérégie regions

(Québec, Canada) arrives at similar conclusions (Morin *et al.* 1999). First, on a quantitative level, we observed a great uniformity in the procedural characteristics and in the results of the cases. For instance, among the 1219 confinement hearings in 1996 in the civil district of Montréal, 92 per cent of the petitions were granted by the judges; the responding parties were present and questioned in only six per cent of the hearings; they were represented by an attorney in only six per cent of the cases; in comparison, the petitioning parties (*i.e.* hospitals) were represented in 99 per cent of the hearings. In sum, few of the hearings were carried out in the adversarial mode one expects from any procedure held in the formal setting of the civil court (compared to a more 'procedurally soft' setting like an administrative tribunal).

Second, our content analysis of the integral transcripts of a subsample of 20 hearings (Dallaire and Morin 1999)[6] showed that the object of the court exchanges and of the rulings was not strictly the evaluation of danger to self or others. Indeed, this analysis showed the importance of discussions concerning private and everyday life considerations (*i.e.* the person's private and social identity, situation and living conditions as male/female, old/young, husband/wife, parent, family member, community member, worker, consumer, etc.), concurrently with and inside considerations about danger. On this ground, we concluded that in the sampled cases, the assessment of dangerousness appears to be an inquiry into the *zone of confluence between the concerned individual and his/her material and social environment*. Danger was not depicted by the hearing participants as an exclusively internal characteristic of the individuals. Interestingly, this conclusion accords with the contextual model depicted by Hiday (1997), for whom both the social and material context and the larger social environment are linked to severe mental illness and violence.

In sum, several observational studies of civil commitment procedures highlight a discrepancy between the written law and the law in practice, and conclude that the actors' socially embedded agency – their perspectives, motivations and interests, as influenced by broader social representations – is the most determinant factor in civil commitment decisions. This kind of interpretation is mirrored in previous qualitative analyses concerning criminal court settings, which also point out the enacted nature of the laws. The seminal work by Sudnow (1965), followed by Atkinson and Drew (1979) equally emphasised that the application of a given law is less the product of 'rule following' than the outcome of processes of subjective evaluations based on pre-existing social representations. Furthermore, they argue, this outcome is negotiated by the actors in the course of their adversarial or non-adversarial (co-operative) formalised interactions in court.

However, criminal cases are far more visible to the public and to higher judicial authorities, than are court hearings dealing with civil commitment and, of course, even more so than cases where the decision is made by administrative tribunals or authorised individuals (*e.g.* the 'approved social worker' in the U.K.). If the professionals' roles and representations are reinforced by their exposure to other actors and the public, and by their awareness of this exposure (*e.g.* 'doing advocacy' or 'doing doctoring' according to expectations about how an attorney or a physician is supposed to act), then one could expect that in the secluded area of civil commitment, such expectancies would be less influential; that is, the agents' performance would be less oriented by their profession's norms and representations, and thus more 'polluted' by society-wide shared representations of the 'dangerous mental patient'.

To treat or to control? False contradiction and systemic *finalité*

If preoccupations touching on individual rights, public security and therapeutic need remain in relative competition in the spirit of laws concerning psychologically distressed or troubling persons (Appelbaum 1997), this competition between several aims also occurs inside the systems concerned. The double function of treatment and social control of deviance has been frequently underlined with respect to the medical institution as a whole (Conrad 1992, Freidson 1970, Zola 1972) as well as within psychiatry – notably expressed as the 'therapeutic contradiction' (Castel 1980). Concrete examples reveal the presence of this duality in clinical practice and forensic psychiatry (Bennett *et al.* 1993, Rogers 1993). The place, application, effects and, most notably, perception of coercion in psychiatric practice currently form a major research theme (Lidz and Hoge 1993). However, what has also been illustrated is the counterpart of this contradiction at the heart of the other institution involved: justice, itself also confronted with therapeutic considerations concurrently with its coercive imperatives (Wexler 1992). This 'mirror effect' has been highlighted in studies depicting the criminalisation of psychologically distressed persons (Laberge and Morin 1995, Solomon *et al.* 1995).

This view of justice and psychiatry as representing different logics in a competitive interface is less and less present in the sociological literature. Rather, an emerging perspective views this interface as one of interdependence or symbiosis (Mason and Jennings 1997, Morin 1995, Rose 1986), or, more consistent with our findings, 'convergence between the legal mind and the psychiatric concept' (Andreassen 1999: 43). Especially in this last sense, the contradictions internal to each system would only be superficial, reflecting rather a *common logic: treatment-control*. Our analysis of the treatment role and of the control role, when manifested in civil commitment, has not been able to separate them, either conceptually or in practice. The control role has relied upon the concept of dangerousness which, as our discussion above highlights, is a fuzzy concept, quite variously defined and operationalised. The treatment role relies upon the concept of 'mental illness' which, despite efforts at concrete and meaningful definition via DSM, is also said by critics to elude consensus as to what this term signifies and how mental illnesses could be categorised.

Given the failure to objectively and consensually define these two terms, our finding that the efforts to find a causal relationship between mental illness and dangerousness are tainted by a wide variety of scientific problems is not surprising. The most serious of these problems is that the concepts of 'mental illness' and 'dangerousness' have to some extent merged and, increasingly so, as reflected in changes in the DSM. Empirical studies cited here have shown that applying the criterion of dangerousness leads to the development of a series of heuristic criteria – need for help, need for treatment, lack of compliance, lack of insight, inability to take care of oneself. Some of these in practice often seem based more upon the necessity to treat than the necessity to preserve the safety of the patient or others. We therefore find a circular relationship between the separate treatment and control roles, which may be a factor in, as well as a consequence of, the merging of the concepts upon which those roles are based. We seem to have *a system which both treats in order to control and controls in order to treat*[7].

This functional and teleological union shapes the everyday practices and discourses of the actors evolving in psychiatry and justice, and especially in encounters such as civil commitment hearings where their points of view meet. Especially in our study of a sample of civil commitment hearings held in Québec (Dallaire *et al.* 2000), we observed that lawyers and judges, physicians and relatives, were operationalising the pertinent law in order to find solutions to practical problems posed by the individuals' state, behaviours and situations. Those subjected to civil commitment were 'residual cases' in the sense of Scheff (1999), insofar as solutions to the problems they posed were not sought or could not be found in incarceration, voluntary use of medical or psychosocial services, or through help from family, social networks or community. That study, as well as those of Cohen *et al.* (1998), Holstein (1993) and Warren (1982), show that even in jurisdictions where pertinent laws clearly distinguish between mental illness/need for treatment and dangerousness/control, court and administrative tribunals rulings are made mostly following an operational criterion of need for help/ need for treatment. Appelbaum (1997) interprets this discrepancy in a cultural (mostly occidental) perspective: reforms focused on the strict protection of individual rights and liberties, he argues, are inevitably confronted with resistance from those entrusted with applying them, because the laws contradict a 'social consensus' grounded in a system of values where the persons designated as mentally ill are seen as needing help and care more than freedom.

From a sociological perspective, this consensus can be viewed as a manifestation of social representations regarding mental illness. These are strongly and widely held on various levels of lay and professional representations of mental illness, both postulating an association and even an equation between 'severe' mental illness and dangerousness; of societal characterisation, which attributes an intermediate status to mental disturbance, somewhere between 'badness' deviance and 'illness' deviance; and of societal response and systemic *finalités*, through which treatment and control are also equated. In all these dimensions, where the institutions of law and psychiatry meet in operationalising civil commitment, we find one common logic and practice, reflecting the union of law and psychiatry in one treatment-control system for handling the residual deviance associated with the 'dangerous mental patient'. Because the widely shared tendency to equate mental illness with dangerousness is manifested in the rationale for, and operationalisation of, civil commitment laws, however they are written, a civil commitment system which couples mental illness with dangerousness has little or no effect on restraining committals that would otherwise be made on the basis of need for treatment. The net result of a dangerousness criterion, then, may be to manifest, reinforce, and reproduce stereotypes depicting as threats to public safety persons who experience severe psychological distress or disturbances.

We may understand the introduction of such social representations into the civil commitment process as simply a question of shared culture among the professional actors involved – as common members of a society but also of certain social classes. We might also understand the role of such representations as not inadvertent or marginal, but indeed intrinsic to the *finalités* of the civil commitment system, as a whole, as a 'treatment-control' system for the control of forms of deviance that are not subsumed under other social control systems.

Acknowledgements

Portions of this chapter had been presented to a meeting of the International Academy of Law and Mental Health (Dallaire *et al.* 1999). This chapter was developed out of funding primarily provided by the Québec Council for Social Research (CQRS). We also want to express our appreciation for financial support provided to Drs. Dallaire and McCubbin by the Institute for Public Health Research and Policy, University of Salford and by the Leverhulme Trust (UK), to Dr. Cohen by the Québec Fund in Aid of Research and Researchers (FCAR), and to Dr. McCubbin by the Canadian Institute for Advanced Research (CIAR). Our thanks to Ms Helen Busby and Mrs Angela Young, Research Fellows at the Institute for Public Health Research and Policy, University of Salford, for many fruitful exchanges during the preparation of this chapter.

Notes

1   The notion of *finalité*, a long-standing concept in the francophone philosophy, sociology, aesthetics and early biology literature, has no simple counterpart in

the English language. We understand the term to mean the teleological orientation of a system, that is, the general principle of the direction of a system. The notion of *finalité* cannot be reduced to a goal or a function: it refers to the character of something striving towards an end and implies processes through which the end is attained (*e.g.* adaptation of the means to the ends or adaptation of the parts to the whole). *Finalité* applies to a system/institution, not to its individual actors within, hence is not necessarily consistent with the expressed intent of those actors – nor with the *overt* 'objectives' of the system.

2   With respect to the mental health system, these features have been increasingly emphasised by developing thinking in sociological institutional theory, from Parsons (1974) to the 'new institutional theory' school (Scott 1993).

3   Here the discussion is limited to *severe* mental illness, frequently defined as psychosis, upon which most of the statistical analyses were centred. However, there remain several open questions concerning the more general issues regarding the meaning and application of those findings.

4   More fundamentally, a political sociology of knowledge analysis might place the development of these official classifications in a larger movement, by which psychiatry as a profession seeks to augment the scientific and clinical credibility of its uncertain base of knowledge. The uniformisation of the nosology helps to provide an objective basis for diagnosis, implicitly objectifying the syndromes as concrete and pre-existent to their classification. The marked return to the biological paradigm seen over the past two decades in psychiatry, involving persistent claims of genetic, neurological and biochemical etiologies, has provided psychiatry with some of the appearance of exactitude and 'solidity' associated with the biomedical sciences. This movement has operated to the detriment of psychological and psychosocial approaches, severely restricting the nature and results of interventions – not only in psychiatry but also, due to the dominant role of psychiatry in mental health care systems, in other mental health disciplines (psychology, nursing, social work, etc.) [McCubbin 1994].

5   For Europe, see Riecher-Rossler and Rossler 1993; for England and Wales, see Barnes 1996 and Hatfield *et al.* 1997; for the United States, see Freddolino 1990; for Canada, see Weisstub 1980: 326–340. The legislation of several countries (including England and Wales, Denmark, Norway, Sweden and Greece) incorporates the criterion of need (or necessity) for treatment in order to preserve the health or security of a person, in addition to the criterion of dangerousness with respect to oneself or others (see Appelbaum 1997). The addition of the criterion of 'need for treatment' implies a legal obligation to furnish adequate care and treatment, hence introducing the notion of 'right to treatment' for involuntary psychiatric patients (McCubbin and Weisstub 1998).

6   Our sample was atypical, designed to yield maximum information – hence restricted to cases where the petition was contested by the respondent and where the respondent was present and questioned. Even these atypical cases share some traits with the whole: for instance, 16 out of 20 ended with a granted petition for commitment or compulsory psychiatric examination.

7   Breggin (1997) and Cohen and McCubbin (1990) stress that in the case of contemporary psychiatry, mainstream treatment practices correspond to use of control over the patient; this especially because of the quasi-systematic use of medications, whose clinical 'effectiveness' comes from the fact that they pacify

the patients by altering their conscience and will. That the actual functions of the system and, hence, its implicit orientations and goals, are not merely based upon therapeutic and helping objectives but also upon the interplay of power and interests has been argued by a few critics, who have suggested that the mental health system is a profoundly *political* system (Crossley 1998, McCubbin and Cohen 1999) concerned more with social control than with health care (see Atkinson 1996, Ingleby 1985, Szasz 1994).

References

Allen, H. (1987) *Justice Unbalanced: Gender, Psychiatry and Judicial Decisions.* Philadelphia: Open University Press.

American Psychiatric Association (2000) Violence and mental illness, *APA Online* [On-line]. Available HTTP: http://www.psych.org/psych/htdocs/public_info/violen~1.htm

Andreassen, M. (1999) A comparison between legal and psychiatric statements regarding complaints about commitment: a study carried out in a Danish county 1990–1994, *International Journal of Law and Psychiatry*, 22, 37–44.

Appelbaum, P.S. (1988) The new preventative detention: psychiatry's problematic responsibility for the control of violence, *American Journal of Psychiatry*, 145, 779–85.

Appelbaum, P.S. (1997) Almost a revolution: an international perspective on the law of involuntary commitment, *Journal of the American Academy of Psychiatry and Law*, 25, 135–47.

Arboleda-Florez, J., Holley, H. and Crisanti, I. (1998) Understanding causal paths between mental illness and violence, *Social Psychiatry and Psychiatric Epidemiology*, 33, S38–46.

Atkinson, J.M. (1996) The community of strangers: supervision and the new right, *Health and Social Care in the Community*, 4, 2, 122–5.

Atkinson, J.M. and Drew, P. (1979) *Order in Court: the Organisation of Verbal Interaction in Judicial Settings.* Atlantic Highlands: Humanities Press.

Baker, E. (1997) The introduction of supervision registers in England and Wales: a risk communications analysis, *Journal of Forensic Psychiatry*, 8, 15–35.

Barnes, M. (1996) Citizens in detention: the role of the Mental Health Act Commission in protecting the rights of detained patients, *Local Government Studies*, 22, 3, 28–46.

Bennett, N.S., Lidz, C.W., Monahan, J., Mulvey, E.P., Hoge, S.K., Roth, L.H. and Gardener, W. (1993) Inclusion, motivation, and good faith: the morality of coercion in mental hospital admission, *Behavioral Sciences and the Law*, 11, 295–306.

Bjorkly, S. (1995) Prediction of aggression in psychiatric patients: a review of prospective prediction studies, *Clinical Psychology Review*, 15, 475–502.

Breggin, P.R. (1997) *Brain-Disabling Treatments in Psychiatry: Drugs, Electroshock and the Role of the FDA.* New York: Springer.

Brown, P. (1990) The name game: toward a sociology of diagnosis, *Journal of Mind and Behavior*, 11, 385–406.

Caplan, P. (1995) *They Say You're Crazy: How the World's Most Powerful Psychiatrists Decide Who's Normal.* New York: Addison-Wesley.

Castel, R. (1980) Sur la contradiction psychiatrique [on the psychiatric contradiction]. In Basaglia, F. and Basaglia-Ongaro, F. (eds) *Les Criminels de Paix* [the criminals of peace]. Paris: P.U.F.

Cocozza, J.J. and Steadman, H.J. (1976) The failure of psychiatric predictions of dangerousness: clear and convincing evidence, *Rutgers Law Review*, 29, 1084–101.

Cohen, D. and McCubbin, M. (1990) The political economy of tardive dyskinesia: asymmetries in power and responsibility, *Journal of Mind and Behavior*, 11, 465–88.

Cohen, D., Thomas, G., Dallaire, B., Morin, P., Fortier, R. and McCubbin, M. (1998) *Savoir, pouvoir et dangerosité civile: une étude des décisions de révision de cure fermée de la Commission des Affaires Sociales du Québec, 1975–1992* [Power, knowledge and civil dangerousness: a study of civil commitment appeal hearing decisions by the Québec Social Affairs Commission, 1975–93]. Research report to the Québec Council for Social Research (CQRS). Montréal: GRASP, University of Montréal.

Cohn, N.B. (1998) Navigating the bumpy road of risk assessment in pre-adjudication and civil court hearings, paper presented at *XXIIIrd International Congress on Law and Mental Health*, Paris, July.

Conrad, P. (1992) Medicalization and social control, *Annual Review of Sociology*, 18, 209–32.

Crossley, N. (1998) Transforming the mental health field: the early history of the National Association for Mental Health, *Sociology of Health and Illness*, 20, 458–88.

Dallaire, B. (1997 [1995]) Définir et reconnaître: représentations de la santé et de la maladie dans trois départements hospitaliers [to define and to recognize: representations of health and illness in three hospital departments]. *Health and Canadian Society*, 3, 1/2, 71–98.

Dallaire, B. and Morin, P. (1999) Dangerousness and the zone of confluence between the individual and his environment: an analysis of a sample of civil commitment hearings in Québec, Canada. *GRASP Working Papers Series*, 24. Montréal: GRASP, University of Montréal.

Dallaire, B., Morin, P. and McCubbin, M. (1999) The application of the 'dangerousness' criterion for civil commitment in Quebec since the reform of the Civil Code (1994): first empirical results based on systems and problem-centered approaches, paper presented at the *XXIVth International Congress on Law and Mental Health*, University of Toronto.

Dallaire, B., McCubbin, M., Morin, P. and Cohen, D. (2000) Dangerousness, personhood and the search for the traces of mental illness: an analysis of a sample of civil commitment hearings in Québec, Canada, unpublished manuscript.

Dumont, F. (1985) Le projet d'une anthropologie médicale [the project of a medical anthropology]. In Dufresne, J., Dumont, F. and Martin, Y. (eds) *Traité d'anthropologie médicale: l'Institution de la Santé et de la Maladie* [Treatise on medical anthropology: the Institution of Health and Illness]. Québec: P.U.Q., I.Q.R.C. & P.U.L.

Ennis, B.J. and Litwack, T.R. (1974) Psychiatry and the presumption of expertise: flipping coins in the courtroom, *California Law Review*, 62, 693–752.

Eronen, M., Angermeyer, M.C. and Schulze, B. (1998) The psychiatric epidemiology of violent behaviour, *Social Psychiatry and Psychiatric Epidemiology*, 33, S13–23.

Faust, D. and Ziskin, J. (1988) The expert witness in psychology and psychiatry, *Science*, 241, 31–5.

Freddolino, P. (1990) Mental health rights protection and advocacy, *Research in Community and Mental Health*, 6, 379–407.

Freidson, E. (1970) *Profession of Medicine: a Study in the Sociology of Applied Knowledge*. New York: Dodd, Mead.

Gardner, W., Lidz, C.W., Mulvey, E.P. and Shaw, E.C. (1996) Clinical versus actuarial predictions of violence in patients with mental illness, *Journal of Consulting and Clinical Psychology*, 64, 602–9.

Garfinkel, H. (1967) *Studies in Ethnomethodology*. Englewood Cliffs: Prentice-Hall.

Goffman, E. (1964) *Behavior in Public Places*. New York: Free Press.

Hatfield, B., Huxley, P. and Mohamad, H. (1997) Social factors and compulsory detention of psychiatric patients in the U.K.: the role of the approved social worker in the 1983 Mental Health Act, *International Journal of Law and Psychiatry*, 20, 389–97.

Hiday, V.A. (1983) Judicial decisions in civil commitment: facts, attitudes, and psychiatric recommendations, *Law and Society Review*, 17, 517–29.

Hiday, V.A. (1997) Understanding the connection between mental illness and violence, *International Journal of Law and Psychiatry*, 20, 399–417.

Hodgins, S. (1995) Major mental disorder and crime: an overview, *Psychology, Crime and Law*, 2, 5–17.

Holloway, F. (1996) Community psychiatric care: from libertarianism to coercion. Moral panic and mental health policy in Britain, *Health Care Analysis*, 4, 235–43.

Holstein, J.A. (1993) *Court-Ordered Insanity: Interpretive Practice and Involuntary Commitment*. New York: de Gruyter.

Hughes, D.H. (1996) Suicide and violence assessment in psychiatry, *General Hospital Psychiatry*, 18, 416–21.

Ingleby, D. (1985) Mental health and social order. In Cohen, S. and Scull, A. (eds) *Social Control and the State*. Oxford: Basil Blackwell.

Kirk, S.A. (1994) The myth of the reliability of DSM, *Journal of Mind and Behavior*, 15, 71–86.

Kirk, S.A. and Kutchins, H. (1992) *The Selling of DSM: the Rhetoric of Science in Psychiatry*. New York: de Gruyter.

Kutchins, H. and Kirk, S. (1998) *Making Us Crazy*. New York: Free Press.

Laberge, D. and Morin, D. (1995) The overuse of criminal justice dispositions: failure of diversionary policies in the management of mental health problems, *International Journal of Law and Psychiatry*, 18, 389–414.

Lidz, C.W. and Hoge, S.K. (eds) (1993) Coercion in mental health care, *Behavioral Sciences and the Law*, 11, 3.

Link, B.G., Andrews, H. and Cullen, F.T. (1992) The violent and illegal behavior of mental patients reconsidered, *American Sociological Review*, 57, 275–92.

Litwack, T.R. (1993) On the ethics of dangerousness assessments, *Law and Human Behavior*, 17, 479–85.

Litwack, T.R. (1994) Assessments of dangerousness: legal, research, and clinical developments, *Administration and Policy in Mental Health*, 21, 361–77.

Luckey, J.W. and Berman, J.J. (1979) Effects of a new commitment law on involuntary admissions and service utilization patterns, *Law and Human Behavior*, 3, 149–61.

MacArthur Research Network on Mental Health and the Law (2000) The MacArthur Violence Risk Assessment Study (1) (On-line). Available HTTP: http://ness.sys.virginia.edu/macarthur/violence.html

Marx, J.I. and Levinson, R.M. (1988) Statutory change and 'street-level' implementation of psychiatric commitment, *Social Science and Medicine*, 27, 1247–56.

Mason, T. and Jennings, L. (1997) The Mental Health Act and professional hostage taking, *Medical Sciences and Law*, 37, 58–68.

McCubbin, M. (1994) Deinstitutionalization: the illusion of disillusion, *Journal of Mind and Behavior*, 15, 35–53.

McCubbin, M. and Cohen, D. (1999) A systemic and value-based approach to strategic reform of the mental health system, *Health Care Analysis*, 7, 57–77.

McCubbin, M. and Cohen, D. (2000) Analysis of the scientific grounds for forced treatment, research paper submitted to *Little Hoover Commission on Mental Health Reform*, State of California. Available HTTP: http://www.connix.com/-narpa/cal_ioc.htm

McCubbin, M., Dallaire, B., Cohen, D. and Morin, P. (1999) Should institutions that commit patients also be gatekeepers to information about civil commitment? Implications for research and policy, *Radical Psychology* [On-line], 1, 2. Available HTTP: http://www.yorku.ca/faculty/academic/danaa/mccubbin.htm

McCubbin, M. and Weisstub, D.N. (1998) 'Meeting the needs of the mentally ill': a case study of the 'right to treatment' as legal rights discourse in the U.S.A. (*GRASP Working Papers Series*, 20), paper presented at the *XXIIIrd International Congress on Law and Mental Health*, Université René Déscartes, Paris.

McNiel, D.E. and Binder, R. (1986) Violence, civil commitment, and hospitalisation, *Journal of Nervous and Mental Disease*, 174, 107–11.

Mechanic, D. (1978) *Medical Sociology: a Comprehensive Text* (2nd edition). New York: Free Press.

Mirowski, J. (1990) Subjective boundaries and combinations in psychiatric diagnoses, *Journal of Mind and Behavior*, 11, 407–24.

Monahan, J. (1992) Mental disorder and violent behavior: perceptions and evidence, *American Psychologist*, 47, 511–21.

Monahan, J. (1998) Violence and mental health, paper presented at the *XXIIIrd International Congress on Law and Mental Health* (colloquium *Public Health Mental Health*), La Sorbonne, Paris.

Morin, P. (1995) Ordre et normes: la psychiatrie obligatoire [order and norms: the compulsory psychiatry]. In Bouchard, L. and Cohen, D. (eds) *Médicalisation et Contrôle Social* [medicalisation and social control]. Montréal: ACFAS.

Morin, P., Dallaire, B., McCubbin, M. and Cohen, D. (1999) *L'Opérationnalisation de la notion de dangerosité civile lors des audiences pour ordonnance d'examen clinique psychiatrique et d'hospitalisation psychiatrique obligatoires* [The operationalisation of the notion of civil dangerousness at hearings for psychiatric clinical examination and mandatory psychiatric hospitalisation orders]. Research report to the Québec Social Research Council (CQRS). Montréal: GRASP, University of Montréal.

Parsons, T. (1974 [1957]) The mental hospital as a type of organization. In Hasenfeld, Y. and English, R.A. (eds) *Human Service Organizations: a Book of Readings*. Ann Arbor: University of Michigan Press.

Pfohl, S.J. (1978) *Predicting Dangerousness: the Social Construction of Psychiatric Reality*. Toronto: Lexington.

Riecher-Rossler, A. and Rossler, W. (1993) Compulsory admission of psychiatric patients: an international comparison, *Acta Psychiatrica Scandinavica*, 87, 231–6.

Rogers, A. (1993) Coercion and 'voluntary' admission: an examination of psychiatric patient views, *Behavioral Sciences and the Law*, 11, 259–67.

Rose, N. (1986) Law, rights and psychiatry. In Miller, P. and Rose, N. (eds) *The Power of Psychiatry*. Cambridge: Polity.

Ryan, T. (1998) Perceived risks associated with mental illness: beyond homicide and suicide, *Social Science and Medicine*, 46, 287–97.

Scheff, T.J. (1978) Decision rules, types of error, and their consequences in medical diagnosis. In Tuckett, D. and Kaufert, J.M. (eds) *Basic Readings in Medical Sociology*. London: Tavistock.

Scheff, T.J. (1999) *Being Mentally Ill: a Sociological Theory* (3rd edition). New York: de Gruyter.

Scott, W.R. (1993) Recent developments in organizational sociology, *Acta Sociologica*, 36, 63–8.

Shea, P. (1993–4) Mental disorders and dangerousness, *International Journal of Mental Health*, 22, 71–9.

Sjöström, S. (1997) *Party or Patient? Discursive Practices Relating to Coercion in Psychiatric and Legal Settings*. Linköping: Boréa.

Slovic, P. and Monahan, J. (1995) Probability, danger, and coercion: a study of risk perception and decision making in mental health law, *Law and Human Behavior*, 19, 49–65.

Solomon, P., Rogers, R., Draine, J. and Meyerson, A. (1995) Interaction of the criminal justice system and psychiatric professionals in which civil commitment standards are prohibitive, *Bulletin of the American Academy of Psychiatry and Law*, 23, 117–28.

Steadman, H.J., Mulvey, E.P., Monahan, J., Robbins, P.C., Appelbaum, P.S., Grisso, T., Roth, L.H. and Silver, E. (1998) Violence by people discharged from acute psychiatric inpatient facilities and by others in the same neighborhoods, *Archives of General Psychiatry*, 55, 393–401.

Stoll, A.L., Tohen, M., Baldessarini, R.J., Goodwin, D.C., Stein, S., Katz, S., Geenens, D., Swinson, R.P., Goethe, J.W. and McGlashan, T. (1993) Shifts in diagnostic frequencies of schizophrenia and major affective disorders at six North American psychiatric hospitals, 1972–1988, *American Journal of Psychiatry*, 150, 1668–73.

Sudnow, D. (1965) Normal crimes: sociological features of the Penal Code in a public defender office, *Social Problems*, 12, 255–76.

Szasz, T. (1991) *Insanity: the Idea and its Consequences*. New York: Wiley.

Szasz, T. (1994) *Cruel Compassion: Psychiatric Control of Society's Unwanted*. Toronto: Wiley.

Tucker, G.J. (1997) Editorial: putting DSMIV in perspective, *American Journal of Psychiatry*, 155, 159–61.

Warren, C.A.B. (1982) *The Court of Last Resort: Mental Illness and the Law*. Chicago: University of Chicago Press.

Weisstub, D.N. (1980) *Law and Psychiatry in the Canadian Context*. Toronto: Pergamon.

Weitz, D. (2000) Who's really dangerous?: media bias – forced drugging – outpatient committal, *MadNation* [On-line], Available HTTP, http://www.madnation.org/canada/weitz.htm

Wexler, B. (1992) Putting mental health into mental health law: therapeutic jurisprudence, *Law and Human Behavior*, 16, 27–38.

Zola, I.K. (1972) Medicine as an institution of social control, *Sociological Review*, 20, 487–504.

9

Rethinking professional prerogative: managed mental health care providers

Teresa L. Scheid

American style managed care: commodification

The health care sector in the United States has undergone profound institutional change (Scott *et al.* 2000, Alexander and D'Aunno 1990) as health care systems, including mental health, have been transfigured by forces promoting corporatisation (Brown and Cooksey 1989). The pivotal forces propelling the movement to managed care are financial, namely, reduced government support for public sector health care and escalating costs in the private sector (Bazelon Center 1995, Cook and Wright 1995, Mechanic 1999, Moffic 1997). While cost containment is the primary impetus for managed care, the institutional logic is one of technical rationality and demands for efficiency. Myer (1990) conceptualises this process of rationalisation as the commodity model of organisations because organisational structures are outcomes (rather than determinants) of efficiency imperatives. Furthermore, the basis for determinations of efficiency are cost savings – consequently managed care represents a commodification of health care. Commodification is an especially apt descriptor for the private health care sector in the US, where savings often represent corporate profits (Anders 1996).

In the US managed care first emerged in the wider health care sector and began to have an impact on mental health services in the 1980s, with a greater effect in the private sector (Mechanic 1999). However, most states are turning to managed care as a means to control costs and to provide for better system co-ordination (Schlesinger and Gray 1999)[1]. While some argue that managed care provides the opportunity to reorganise and thereby improve mental health delivery systems (Boyle and Callahan 1995), the yardstick by which performance is being measured is determined by the more primary goal of cost containment (Manderscheid *et al.* 1999). Furthermore, even in managed care systems, where greater emphasis is placed upon quality care, the various mechanisms by which mental health care is managed have the potential to undermine the professional autonomy and professional prerogative of mental health care providers. Mental health care providers include psychiatrists, psychologists, social workers and nurses – with the majority of care provided by social workers and nurses who have less professional power than doctors. In both the US and the UK managed care has provided physicians with opportunities for managerial involvement and even control of managed care entities (Hafferty and Light 1995); such opportunities are far more restricted for social workers and nurses. In the UK, Griffiths and Hughes (1999) found that while the professional autonomy of health care providers was limited by various organisational structures which 'manage' care, managers rarely directly challenged clinical prerogative. However, Griffith and Hughes (1999) note that latent conflicts between purchasers and providers persist, and Rodwin (1993) has argued that managed care in the US has indeed produced a serious conflict of interest for physicians. I will argue that in the US private mental health care sector these latent conflicts represent outright contradictions between entrepreneurial standards and professional standards for care.

In 1989, the Institute of Medicine in Washington, DC defined managed care as:

> a set of techniques used by or on behalf of purchasers of health care benefits to manage health care costs by influencing patient care decision making through case-by-case assessment of the appropriateness of care prior to its provision (cited in Wells *et al.* 1995: 51).

The primary ways in which managed care controls costs are by limiting access to services and limiting the utilisation of more costly services, while encouraging the use of less costly services. Providers in both the private and public sector are subject to similar mechanisms of cost-containment which include (Mechanic 1999): gatekeeping (where access to speciality mental health care is controlled by the requirement of a referral from a primary care provider), precertification or utilisation review (where services must be authorised before a client can receive them), concurrent review or case management (ongoing review of treatment at regular intervals), and capitation (where a pre-determined fee is paid for a defined benefit with a given amount of time). Capitation provides the greatest incentive for improved cost-control and efficiency, although it is very difficult to arrive at an accurate prospective payment scheme for mental illness, especially those conditions that are chronic and/or severe (Mechanic 1999, Minkoff and Pollack 1997). Rates are set at a fraction of the fee-for-service equivalent; Freund and Hurley (1995: 482) report that this fraction is typically 95 per cent for Medicaid enrollees; private clinicians report fractions that are much lower (Tuttle and Woods 1997). Moffic (1997) found that reimbursement levels were 30 per cent below those of traditional fee-for-service. Increasingly, managed care entities are utilising case rates, where a flat rate is paid for each client for one year of care. These rates vary, but are widely considered to be very low at an average rate of between $200 to $500.00 per year (Moffic 1997, Tuttle and Woods 1997).

In order to determine if treatment is indeed cost effective, managed care must also emphasise measurable outcomes. Mental health treatment must meet standards of 'medical necessity', increasingly managed care companies will only reimburse services that have been scientifically validated as efficacious. One managed care consultant (Schreter *et al*. 1994: 57) describes utilisation review as *ideally* allowing for: (1) independent and scientific determination of the efficacy of a procedure, and (2) independent and scientific determination of the appropriateness of indicators for such a procedure. In the UK, the NHS Research and Development Initiative provides standards for 'evidence-based purchasing'; in the US private consulting firms hired by managed care companies provide the evidence upon which decisions about treatment effectiveness and efficacy are made.

An important obstacle to evaluating managed mental health care is the difficulty in assessing treatment effectiveness. The managed care consultant quoted above stated: 'to remove the emperor's clothes, *no* utilization review program has workable criteria for reviewing outpatient care' (Schreter *et al*. 1994: 58). There is little consensus about the aetiology of mental illness, nor on appropriate treatments (Mechanic 1994, Pollack *et al*. 1994, Rochefort 1989). Not only is it difficult to define the nature of the problem, but different types of treatment work with different types of clients (Cook and Wright 1995, Mechanic 1999). In terms of chronic and severe mental illness, there may not be noticeable signs of improvement, even within excellent programmes (Mechanic *et al*. 1995). Moreover, client confidentiality limits collection of, and access to, data. However, managed care companies do rely upon the assessment of client outcomes, and are propelling the development of a scientifically (as opposed to a professionally) based system of treatment and practice guidelines. A critical component of any managed care entity is an adequate information system which can organise client-level and provider-level data to allow for some assessment of treatment outcomes.

Managed care has changed the 'work' of mental health care providers as a rational business ethic, and corresponding systems of bureaucratic control have been imposed on organisations which had previously operated on the basis of a professionally determined moral foundation and ambiguous goals (Schlesinger and Gray 1999, Soderfeldt *et al*. 1996). Organisations and providers must meet the primary goal of cost containment (whether for profit-based systems, or to save 'scarce' public funds), determine the most effective means to achieve these financially determined goals, and then monitor performance to ensure that services are delivered in a cost efficient manner. In short, the current emphasis on efficiency, measurable outcomes, and cost containment is an institutional demand to which mental health care organisations must conform if they are to attain, and maintain, legitimacy in an environment where mental health care has become a commodity. Many focus on outcome assessment as the principal characteristic of managed care (Martin and Kettner 1997), and, while performance accountability may well be a good thing, it must be remembered that the yardstick by which performance is being measured (at least in the US) is determined by the more primary goal of cost containment. In terms of mental health care services, the expectation is that certain kinds of delivery systems or treatment practices will produce specific mental health care outcomes which represent a financial return. This institutional demand is difficult to meet when health care problems are chronic, and there is little agreement on appropriate treatment (Schlesinger and Gray 1999), and where the primary costs of inadequate mental health are borne by the wider community (Mechanic 1999).

In terms of mental health care providers, managed care represents a direct threat to professional prerogative in that autonomy and decision-making power are limited by third-party authorisation mechanisms. Rather than provide care, many mental health professionals find themselves in the position of having to 'sell clinical services', and decisions about care are increasingly made by business and financial specialists rather than clinical directors (Tuttle and Woods 1997). The institutional logic of commodification is in direct conflict with professionally-based logics of mental health care. The conflict is overt: 'by design, managed care is intended to alter clinical practices' (Schlesinger and Gray 1999: 441). At the core of the provider's professional logic of care is an orientation toward what I refer to as a social, rather than a medical, model of illness and treatment. The social model sees the client within a larger system and embraces a biopsychosocial philosophy of care which emphasises community integration and continual personal growth and awareness, rather than merely the relief of symptoms (the medically defined treatment goal). Mental health providers believe that medication is important, but it is not necessarily the principal basis of treatment – instead, psychotherapy, rehabilitation, or other types of therapeutic options are also seen as critical components of treatment. While both managed care entities and providers share an orientation toward improved client functioning; they differ on the extent and depth of this improvement, with managed care focusing on short-term, clearly identified outcomes and providers seeking continued improvement and long-term growth. Under managed care, services are authorised by organisational entities with a business focus; that is, treatment decisions are governed by a technocratic-rationality. However, providers are concerned with the quality of the care they provide, and adhere to a professional-rationality which is shaped by ethical standards.

In this chapter I shall examine the effect the commodification of mental health care has had on the work of mental health care providers (hereafter referred to simply as providers). I limit the discussion to providers in private practice who work primarily with clients who have their own private insurance, and treat more acute mental health problems and provide counselling services. In the US, managed care first began to have an effect on mental health services in the private sector (Mechanic 1999). Consequently, providers in private practice have had a greater period of exposure to managed care, and they are experiencing the conflict between the entrepreneurial and professional logics of care in terms of 'ethical dilemmas' as they struggle to defend established treatment practices against organisational demands for cost containment and performance-based outcomes. While my research is limited to providers in the US, mental health professionals in other systems, where care is 'managed' by bureaucratic systems of control, are likely to have similar experiences.

Methods

I began interviewing private clinicians in the spring of 1997 utilising a Directory of Professional Members developed by the local Mental Health Association for a large metropolitan city in the United States. Listing in the Directory is free, though providers must complete a short questionnaire. The Directory is then distributed throughout the community and provided to those calling the Mental Health Association for a referral or information about mental health care services (the Directory also provides information about hospitals, clinics, and public systems of mental health care). The 1997 Directory listed 44 providers, and I excluded three providers whom I knew personally, for a sampling frame of 41 providers. A stratified sample (stratified by gender and professional degree) of 15 providers was selected and 11 individuals were interviewed in depth in order to explore the various ways in which their work had changed with managed care. On the basis of information obtained from these interviews I constructed a survey instrument which was pretested on another nine providers. The questionnaire contains an equal number of open-ended and fixed-choice questions. In the autumn of 1998 another 22 providers in private practice completed the questionnaire (with a response rate of 46 per cent)[2]. A slight majority of the providers are female, and they all possessed a professional degree (either a Master's degree, a PhD, or an MD).

In this chapter I shall utilise the in-depth interviews and the open-ended questions about managed care in order to examine providers' experiences with managed care. It is important to acknowledge that the sample is small, is not necessarily representative and is limited to the experiences of those working in the US. However, the experiences of the providers interviewed is consistent with the experiences of providers in the US as articulated in the professional literature, and in the books written by providers for providers. I utilise this secondary literature as well as the qualitative data I have collected in this examination of the effect of managed care on mental health work. In the final section of the chapter I examine various efforts to counter the power of managed care to control treatment decisions of providers.

Managed care: trials and tribulations

Managed care has had a radical effect on the work of private therapists – many of the providers I interviewed were seriously considering leaving private practice if they could find ways to circumvent the restrictions imposed by managed care entities and third-party insurers. On average, about half to 80 per cent of the clients seen by providers in private practice were covered by some form of managed care. Providers reported that they dealt with an average of four to five different managed care companies. A third of the providers reported that managed care had changed the types of clients they served, and 40 per cent reported that it had changed the types of services they provide.

While some therapists acknowledged that managed care had the potential to improve both access to care and the effectiveness of that care, the prevalent sentiment was that managed care imposed a significant barrier to quality care. As one family therapist described managed care, 'it is a proven way to slow the therapeutic process down until clients get so disgruntled they leave therapy, often prematurely'. I shall first describe providers' views of the potential benefits of managed care and then turn to how managed care has changed the practices of clinicians. These changes are responsible for the overwhelming negative responses to managed care among the therapists I interviewed. It is also noteworthy that there was a great deal more acknowledgement of the potential benefits of managed care in 1997 than in 1998, by which time therapists had had more direct experience of the limitations managed care imposed on their work with clients.

A widely acknowledged benefit of managed care is the increased accountability. A number of providers whom I interviewed believed that 'there was a tremendous amount of waste and abuses... lowering the fees for doctors and therapists is not a bad thing'. Furthermore, the emphasis upon the assessment of outcomes can lead to improved standards for treatment and a more effective matching of services to individual client needs (Mechanic *et al.* 1995). One psychologist felt that managed care had made 'therapists think more about outcomes, progress, and patient satisfaction'. A PhD psychoanalyst felt it good that she now had to produce 'measurable results'; another psychotherapist felt managed care had 'produced more goal setting and follow through'.

A second, often-cited benefit of managed care is that it potentially widens access to a broader treatment population. Some of the providers in private practice found that managed care had 'allowed less financially solvent patients to come into private therapy', or that they were seeing more clients from a wider array of socio-economic groups, or more 'blue collar clients'. However, providers noted that their managed care clients had more severe problems, and were frustrated with the limits placed on their clients' treatment (I shall say more about this shortly). At the same time, many providers in private practice saw more clients who could afford to pay for their therapy; consequently their caseloads had changed to a higher income clientele.

A related benefit of managed care was that it had lowered the cost to clients, though providers were the ones to directly pick up the bill for these lower costs. However, providers did not mind earning less if this in fact produced better care; what they resented was the fact that CEOs and managed care companies were reaping in the profits at the expense of both patients and providers. As noted earlier, managed care reimburses providers at a lower rate than they charge in the traditional fee-for-service practice. Most providers reported that managed care paid at least 20 per cent less than what they had been able to charge before managed care; one master's-level counsellor reported: 'it's demoralising and demeaning to get £21.00 for sessions'. Providers make up the difference by working longer hours and seeking alternative means to augment their incomes. One psychotherapist found that his weekly working hours had increased from the average 40 hours a week 15 years ago to 60 to 70 hours, just to maintain income. Others also reported working longer hours in order to contact managed care companies for authorisation or extra sessions and to seek out new clients. However, some therapists who had opted out of managed care found that they could offer lower fees and still come out ahead, as they no longer had the administrative overhead costs associated with managed care.

> Managed care has increased the amount of paperwork and time on the phone getting authorisation for treatment or additional sessions, thereby creating 'more hoops for the client to jump through and for me [the therapist] to jump through as well'. The documentation required by managed care was felt to be 'excessive' and it took time away from not only client care, but the continuing education of the therapist as well. Not only was the amount of paperwork 'time-consuming, redundant, and unhelpful to the therapeutic process' the information requested by many managed care companies 'compromised confidentiality'.

There is a great deal of concern with the impact of managed care on the quality of the provider-client relationship (Backlar 1996). Often these concerns are described in terms of various ethical dilemmas which result when managed care entities implement various forms of oversight review to 'manage' the care provided by providers:

> My experience with managed care was very negative. I think it's totally unethical; I think it's totally coercive...One of the things I don't like about managed care is they want you to work for them. You know, they tell me – 'tell her it's in her best interests [the client], ... Tell her.' It's like, I don't work for you [the managed care company], they coerce mental health professionals as well as patients...if you want to stay on their panel you have to play their game (MSW therapist).

The overwhelming concern with managed care was with the threats to client confidentiality and quality care. Providers are no longer able to serve as advocates for their clients, or to offer those services which they feel may be most beneficial to the client. Managed care subjects the treatment decisions of providers to increased managerial, financial, and bureaucratic scrutiny. Both the quantity and quality of interaction between the provider and client may be reduced, and an emphasis on accountability interferes with the therapeutic relationship. As described by Edwards:

> The two most basic components of an analytic therapeutic process, the patient's ability to speak freely and the therapist's capacity to listen freely, are being seriously compromised ... I was further distressed with the new form that had recently been adopted by the company. It provided even less opportunity to convey the uniqueness of each person than the previous one. One had the choice of describing a patient, for example, as disheveled, bizarre, inappropriately groomed, or well groomed. None of these categories describe a patient (1997: 200 and 211).

In managed care organisations, decisions to reimburse mental health services are based upon external determinations of 'medical necessity'. If a given mental health condition meets DSM-IV criteria, results in impaired social functioning, and if treatment is effective and justified by the professional literature and can be monitored for effectiveness, then it will meet the condition of medical necessity (Birne-Stone *et al.* 1997, Mechanic 1999, Moffic 1997). The standard of medical necessity is very difficult to apply to mental health care where there is little consensus on what constitutes appropriate care (Clark *et al.* 1994). If one views mental health as a continuum (once again, the social model of care), then more mental health care is better, and meeting the conditions of medical necessity invariably means doing less for the client (Herron 1997). By adhering to a strict medical model of care, managed care companies avoid providing reimbursement for what they perceive as 'problems in living' (Schreter *et al.* 1994: 52). Several providers complained about the process of utilisation review, and denials for certain types of conditions:

> I gave her the diagnosis of adjustment disorder, and the reviewer said, what are the symptoms? And he said, it doesn't sound like an adjustment disorder ... it sounds pretty normal to me. And I had to sit there and tell the client that her services would not be covered because the insurance company didn't think she was sick.

Obviously a strident definition of medical necessity can result in dramatically lower levels of overall mental health and functioning. Managed care also raises serious questions about client confidentiality. Moffic (1997: 97) notes that managed care entities ask for more information than any other third-party purchaser, and will ask for copies of notes providers keep on patients, will perform site visits to review medical records, and may even interview patients to verify treatment. Such actions are motivated by a distrust of clinicians, and can result in patient distrust of the clinician as well (Mechanic and Schlesinger 1996). Hightech management information systems allow financial managers to track client outcomes as well as to arrive at precise provider-based costs-of-care summaries, and represent a viable threat to confidentiality. Providers faced particularly tough decisions in determining how much to divulge about a client to a managed care entity. As described by one MSW therapist in referring to information about sexual orientation:

> I just don't give that information, but then the managed care company says, this is very vague. What is going on here? I say, sorry, I'm not at liberty to say ... the client has asked me not to ... I can say this diagnosis is true, and these are the symptoms, and this is what the client needs, and I resent having to negotiate with a managed care company about stuff like that.

'Negotiating for sessions with managed care' was felt to be noxious 'because it's not about care'; rather managed care had 'control of access to mental health care' and had produced a situation where 'people are denied needed care all the time'.

> I in no way need permission or supervision to do my work. They [managed care reviewers] impose themselves onto this role as if it's needed or in the service of the client's 'needs' when it's *all* about money!

Despite the constraints of various types of oversight review, providers are bound by professional norms to act as advocates for their clients, and are held ultimately accountable for treatment practices. Thus providers are legally obliged to appeal against decisions by utilisation reviewers that could result in harm to the patient (for example, denying hospitalisation for a client whom the provider feels will attempt suicide). The provider is also in the position of having to inform the client about how the system works, though they can also be dropped from networks if they disclose such information in a disparaging manner. Tuttle and Woods (1997: 52) list 'disparagement of the managed care firm' as the second most common reason for which providers are dropped from mental health panels; the most common reason being inappropriate relationships with clients. Several providers whom I interviewed were very concerned with what to tell clients about the *actual* limits on their mental health benefits. One MSW had 'been reprimanded' (for telling a client the provider would be penalised if she asked for any more sessions), and 'the reprimand included a veiled threat that I could be sued for breach of contract, and I felt like a prostitute.'

The most notable ethical dilemma arises when the provider receives some kind of financial incentive for limiting patient care, be those incentives in the form of capitated payments or case rates, retainers for seeing a fixed number of clients, or progressively decreasing reimbursement to clinicians for longer courses of treatment (Lazarus and Pollock 1997). Obviously, if cost savings are directed back to client care (as in non-profit or public systems of care) the ethical dilemma of reduced care is diminished; it is enhanced in profit-based systems. Providers also face the very real concern that they may lose their jobs as a result of their treatment decisions (Backlar 1996); if their costs of care are viewed as 'too high' they will be dropped from panels or else fired from public agencies.

One change in treatment which is a direct consequence of managed care is the greater reliance upon psychiatric medication as opposed to more intensive forms of therapy or skills training. As described by one psychiatrist:

> It has driven us away from therapy to doing meds...the way it has changed practice in general, I think, is the tension between assuming a diagnosis means a criterion for medical necessity. There are 200 schools of therapeutic thought, there are 15 different psychotropic medications, and many anti-depressives. And the data is not in to say which is right. It's just an acute care benefit, to handle a crisis, and that's it.

While there is much disagreement over the effectiveness of psychotherapy, there are data on the clinical efficacy of different types of medications, consequently, managed care contains an inherent bias toward the use of medication as a primary means of treatment. In addition to having the legitimacy of some scientific evidence to support its effectiveness, medication offers a short term solution. This is especially the case for depression, where medication does produce an alleviation of symptoms for many clients (though the source of the depression may not have been resolved). One MSW provider was told by a managed care case manager to:

> tell the patient, convince her to go on medication because we think it will solve her problem quicker. They want to do whatever to get the patient, NOT BETTER, but in shape and shipped out, off their books.

While there is some potential for managed care to improve mental health services, it will be within a limited framework governed by standards of cost-containment and efficiency constraints. Consequently the goals of treatment have changed to reflect a more medical, as opposed to a social, model of mental illness. According to one clinician:

> outpatient psychological services have traditionally been organized around the biopsychosocial model ... Clinicians are under pressure to

abandon it (the biopsychosocial model) in favor of treatment based on efficacy. Efficacy can be translated as clinical care that takes into account cost-effectiveness and the bottom line (Schreter *et al.* 1994: 64).

A private clinician whom I interviewed was more forthright in her critique:

> I in no way need permission or supervision to do my work. They [managed care reviewers] impose themselves onto this role as if it's needed or in the service of the client's 'needs' – when it's all about money!

Managed care has also changed the types of services therapists provide to their clients. With its emphasis upon cost-containment, managed care must limit services to clients and offer less intensive services (Iglehart 1996). Consequently, managed care has resulted in the redefinition of mental health as the improvement of individual functioning (Shore and Beigel 1996: 117) with an emphasis on solving the immediate problem for which the patient requested care. The providers whom I interviewed were universal in their identification of short-term therapy as one way in which their services had changed under managed care 'they [the managed care company] say there is no difference in how you treat these people; it's all short term.' Another PhD psychologist stated that managed care reviewers 'try to convince me that long-term treatment doesn't do anything better than short-term'. One psychologist found managed care 'forces patients to only be able to do short-term immediate stress reduction, and has inhibited more ongoing work on personality patterns and long-term change.' The greatest impact of this redefinition of mental health care will be felt by those clients with long-term care needs and chronic mental illnesses for whom 'cost sharing is likely to impose barriers to care' (Mechanic and Schlesinger 1993: 125). While some argue that short-term therapy may well broaden access to care by moving more clients through the system there is little incentive for managed care organisations to seek out difficult clients (Hawthorn and Hough 1997) or to provide for the extensive needs and long-term social supports needed by individuals with chronic conditions (Bazelon Center for Mental Health Law 1995: 9). Furthermore, providers often face pressure from their managed care organisation to provide even less treatment than what is covered by a patient's benefit plan, especially when fees are capitated. One MSW provider described:

> a person who needs long-term therapy . . . there is no way I can wind this up in a couple months [in talking about a case of childhood sexual abuse by the patient's father]. I told the reviewer, that's not appropriate treatment. And they said, you don't understand, you've been seeing her for a long time, and we need to move along. I told them, do you think you could just get over it if you had been fucked by your father your whole childhood?

Another consequence of managed care is the use of fewer providers, and the reliance upon providers who provide mental health care with the lowest cost. Practically, this means use of providers with less specialised training (master's-level clinicians and social workers as opposed to PhD psychologists and psychiatrists). Psychiatrists also found their skills were devalued, according to one managed care representative (Schreter *et al.* 1994: 105) 'psychiatrists become "manpower" ... the market place will use the discipline with the lowest cost'. The primary role of the psychiatrist will be to manage medications, and in some states nurses are gaining the right to prescribe medications. Several psychologists described difficulties in getting on certain panels[3] 'because they don't want a PhD psychologist'. One managed care representative viewed 'psychotherapy as the only field of health where the patient receives the treatment the therapist is trained to provide, rather than the treatment the patient's condition requires' (Schreter *et al.* 1994: 120). Consequently, providers report that they no longer list psychotherapy as a speciality, as managed care companies have little interest in reimbursing this form of treatment (Alperin and Phllips 1997). Other professionals have redefined psychotherapy to fit into a managed care environment (Austad and Hoyt 1992, Hoyt and Austad 1992) by developing treatment modalities that are 'time sensitive, focused, and [are] oriented toward achieving clearly defined goals (Ludwig and Moltz 1997: 260). Much of this short-term, focused therapy is most effectively performed by social workers, who have had their employment opportunities expand in the managed care marketplace. Master's-level clinicians are also most likely to serve as cost containment case managers to fill other types of administrative roles in managed care companies (Schreter *et al.* 1994: 19), and the curriculum of many MSW in the US programmes is changing accordingly.

Providers have found the formation of multi-disciplinary treatment teams, or practices, allow them to survive in the managed care environment. The majority of referrals go to preferred provider groups (Tuttle and Woods 1997) whose economies of scale are preferred by managed care firms. Providers find that group models allow them to economise on the administrative overheads associated with managed care. 'We are moving toward more group practices; the individual therapist who hangs a shingle – they are going to be few and far between'. More cynically, psychiatrists and psychologists must join such multi-disciplinary practices if they are to maintain any kind of independent practice. Providers in private managed care practices are dependent on referrals from managed care entities; these entities review the number of denials for treatment, readmissions, client outcomes, therapy approach, and costs of care in deciding which providers to keep on their panels. In large speciality managed care firms (with 20,000 to 35,000 provides) nearly 80 per cent of referrals are going to only 20 per cent of the providers (Tuttle and Woods 1997) – mostly those in multi-disciplinary group practices.

In the US private sector, some providers have been able to 'opt out' of managed care; about a quarter of those interviewed, and who completed the mail questionnaire, no longer worked with managed care, though only about 15 per cent of the providers in the 1998 Directory of Professionals advertised that they did not sit on any managed care networks. Those providers who did 'opt out' found they had to market themselves to the private pay patients, or those who could afford therapy. Subsequently, these providers felt that they were no longer fulfilling a wider public good, nor were they meeting the ideals of community-based care. Other providers had developed a unique 'niche' or area of specialisation (for example, substance abuse, or sexual dysfunction) which allowed them to stay in practice. Therapists who were newer, or had less well-established practices were forced to deal with managed care – and needed to join as many panels as they could to develop a client base. Many older therapists were glad they were retiring soon, and would no longer have to deal with managed care. In general, providers in private practice felt a sense of futility:

There is a general feeling of helplessness and depression related to being in fear, and as far as I'm concerned, if people don't have their health, they don't have anything. And there is a sense of sadness and helplessness (MSW).

Evidence of countervailing power

Minkoff describes the concern among providers about 'the perceived incompatibility of managed care with community mental health ideology, and with their own deeply held principles and ideals regarding public sector service' (1997: 13). In fact, there is a body of literature, written largely by mental health care professionals and consultants, which seeks to articulate principles of managed care which provide safeguards to pre-existing philosophies of care. These responses to managed care reflect the inclination of professionals to work within the framework imposed by managed care, rather than critically to challenge the system itself. As Minkoff and Pollack observe:

We and our colleagues may feel disoriented, frightened, insecure, angry, and discouraged. Yet we can't give up. We remain committed to improving the care for people we have traditionally served ... We feel the best response to the managed care revolution is to involve ourselves in the planning and implementation of services so that our clients are protected and that the public mental health principles that we feel most strongly about are incorporated into the newly developed systems of care (1997: xi–xii).

Minkoff (1997) identifies a number of critical issues that need to be resolved for the principles of community based care to be safeguarded. First, who makes the ultimate decisions about cost versus quality? Are there external means to monitor quality? Is there some community-based control? And how is the conflict between focused, brief therapy and long-term care resolved? These questions all go to the root of the contradictions between managed care and community-based treatment ideologies, and centre on the professional prerogative of mental health care providers.

In the US there are a number of groups that have sought to safeguard standards of quality and access against the managed care bottom line of cost-control. In 1996, in response to pressures to establish a set of standards to protect the quality of care, the Institute of Medicine formed the Committee on Quality Assurance and Accreditation Guidelines for Managed Behavioral Health Care. The committee's mission was to 'develop a framework to guide the development, use, and evaluation of performance indicators, accreditation standards, and quality improvement mechanisms' (Institute of Medicine 1997: v). The National Association for Healthcare Quality (NAHQ) is another organisation that seeks, by establishing standards, to improve the quality of care to individuals in managed care organisations. In addition, the NAHQ is also seeking to promote the development of healthcare professionals. However, the providers whom I interviewed saw little political clout in their professional associations. 'We are the mediators and compromisers . . . so it's very difficult for us to take a stand'.

Another group active in seeking to guarantee care to those with severe mental illnesses is the National Alliance for the Mentally Ill (NAMI). In 1994, Laurie Flynn, the Executive Director of NAMI charged that 'few managed care organizations recognize and provide reimbursement for the full array of services required to maintain seriously mentally ill individuals in the community' (Flynn 1994: 206). In a 1997 study of nine managed behavioural health care companies, NAMI found that managed care is failing to bring the best clinical practices to those with severe mental illnesses. The primary problem was with restrictions to care, especially needed hospitalisations. The NAMI study also found that managed care firms neglected critical community support services, including housing and rehabilitation.

There have also been various legislative efforts on behalf of providers and clients. Any-willing-provider (AWP) laws force managed care firms to accept all qualified provider who agree to a company's terms, and have the potential to curb managed care's propensity to limit networks to preferred providers. While 24 states had such laws in 1996, the majority of these laws were passed before 1994. In 1995, 79 AWP laws were considered and only three passed (Tuttle and Woods 1997), reflecting the lobbying power of the managed care industry. In response, provider groups have turned to right-to-know (forcing managed care companies to state why a provider is dropped from a plan) and point-of-service measures (Tuttle and Woods 1997). Providers and consumers are also seeking to have practice guidelines made public, rightfully viewing the managed care company's control over such standards as source of great power over treatment decisions and reimbursement. There is currently (January 2000) legislation being considered at the federal level which will allow patients to directly sue the managed care company (HMO) rather than the health care provider for malpractice. The logic is that if managed care entities are making the ultimate decisions about client care (rather than the provider) they should be accountable when their decision results in personal loss or harm.

These various advocacy efforts provide some evidence of countervailing power, where various professional and community groups are seeking to control the power of managed care companies to make clinical decisions. The question remains whether these attempts to safeguard the quality of care will be enough to counter the forces behind the commodification of care.

Conclusion

Mental health professionals in the US private sector have indeed experienced a loss of professional prerogative. Managed care has changed clinical practices (with increased emphasis upon psychiatric medication and short-term focused therapeutic interventions), changed the division of labour with greater preference given to providers with lower levels of expertise and fees (preference for social workers as opposed to psychologists and psychiatrists), and in many cases now represents a serious challenge to provider-client confidentiality and trust. Mental health providers must negotiate between contradictory institutional demands in their everyday work practices; these contradictions are generally experienced as a series of ethical dilemmas. Ultimately these ethical dilemmas reflect substantial conflict over professionally based standards of care, and standards based upon a technically driven business ethic motivated primarily by fiscal savings or profit.

Managed care (whether in the private mental health sector or in public systems of health care) inevitably results in a higher level of control over clinical work practices, threatening professional prerogative. Utilisation review, and the development of various protocols to standardise treatment, directly challenge professional authority and expertise (Schlesinger *et al.* 1997, Shore and Beigel 1996). Furthermore, professional values are undermined by the substitution of entrepreneurial standards of care (Schlesinger *et al.* 1997). Commodification (*i.e.* emphasis upon cost containment and market mechanisms to make decisions about care) has indeed limited the job control and decision-making authority, as well as the input providers have into determining treatment goals (Soderfeldt *et al.* 1996). The loss of autonomy will not only produce higher levels of job dissatisfaction; it will have an effect on client outcomes as well[4].

Rather than managing care, managed care in the US private mental health care sector appears to be more about managing money – and hence exemplifies the commodification of care. Furthermore, while there is some evidence of countervailing power, providers have not directly challenged the institutional logic of commodification and its driving technocratic rationality.

There are two critical variables which will influence the countervailing power of providers which apply to all managed care systems – not just the US model. First, how much involvement do providers have in the development and implementation of managed care guidelines and clinical standards? Second, upon what standards are decisions of care being made? Is the determinant factor cost, or quality care (including access)? If providers play a major role in determinations about standards and quality of care, they are likely to seek to protect professional standards which emphasise quality care. However, if providers have a direct financial stake (as many do in the US), they will be more likely to emphasise cost savings than access or quality care.

Mental health care, in response to efficiency demands made by its environment, has indeed changed in response to 'the vicissitudes of the market' (Meyer 1990: 211). Yet both Meyer (1990) and Heydebrand (1990) view the new commodification and its concomitant technocratic rationality as unstable because of the inherent conflict between opposing forms of rationality and value orientation. In mental health care these conflicts are evidenced in debates of cost versus quality and access, short-term versus long-term therapy, treatment to provide for cure or recovery versus prevention and interventions to promote mental health and greater wellbeing, and the series of ethical dilemmas faced by providers. As Mechanic *et al.* have noted, mental health care involves 'broad social costs that are borne by families, the community, and the legal system' (1995: 25). Such costs are not taken into account by managed care companies or public entities which fund mental health care. These bodies hold the power, which in a commodity model 'accrues to those having the tools with which to maximize efficiency outcomes' (Meyer 1990: 211). Resistance, or countervailing power, must come from those who bear the social costs of mental health care: providers, clients, and the wider community.

Notes

1   Private mental health care is funded primarily by employer-based insurance plans, and by 1995 three-fourths of US workers received managed health care (Jenson *et al.* 1997). Most private plans do provide some coverage for mental health/substance abuse services, but the coverage is generally limited (Buck *et al.* 1999, Buck and Umland 1997, Jensen *et al.* 1998). Public mental health care is financed primarily through Medicaid and Medicare and provides for those lacking in private insurance, primarily individuals with chronic or long-term mental health care needs. In contrast to the private sector, mental health care

benefits in the public sector have always been to some extent managed (Lazarus and Pollock 1997) in that providers have been expected to meet the needs of geographically defined populations with limited resources.

2   The same sampling list was utilised; as would be expected, there was a good bit of change in the listing of professionals. The 1998 Directory contained 48 providers, 25 providers were listed in both 1997 and 1998, 10 providers who were listed in 1997 were no longer in the Directory (the majority of them having left private practice), and 31 providers had added their name to the list, generally in hopes of seeking additional clients.

3   A panel is a list of approved therapists or providers used by a given insurance company.

4   Aiken and Sloan (1997) found that autonomy and opportunities for authority experienced by nurses on specialised AIDS units were linked to patient outcomes.

References

Aiken, L. and Sloan, D.M. (1997) Effects of organizational innovation in AIDS care on burnout among urban hospital nurses, *Work and Occupations*, 24, 453–77.

Alexander, J.A. and D'Aunno, T.A. (1990) Transformation of institutional environments: perspectives on the corporatization of US health care. In Mick, S.S. *Innovations in Health Care Delivery*. San Francisco: Jossey-Bass Publishers.

Anders, G. (1996) *Health Against Wealth: HMOs and the Breakdown of Medical Trust*. Boston: Houghton-Mifflin.

Alperin, R.M. and Phillips, D.G. (eds) (1997) *The Impact of Managed Care on the Practice of Psychotherapy*. New York: Brunner/Mazel Publishers.

Austad, C.S. and Hoyt, M.F. (1992) The managed care movement and the future of psychotherapy, *Psychotherapy*, 29, 109–18.

Backlar, P. (1996) Managed mental health care: conflicts of interest in the provider/client relationship, *Community Mental Health Journal*, 32, 101–6.

Bazelon Center for Mental Health Law (1995) *Managing Managed Care for Publicly Financed Mental Health Services*. Washington, DC.

Birne-Stone, S., Cypres, A. and Winderbaum, S. (1997) Case management and review strategies. In Alperin, R.M. and Phillips, D.G. (eds) *The Impact of Managed Care on the Practice of Psychotherapy*. New York: Brunner/Mazel Publishers.

Boyle, P.J. and Callahan, D. (1995) Managed care in mental health: the ethical issues, *Health Affairs*, 14, 7–23.

Brown, P. and Cooksey, E. (1989) Mental health monopoly: corporate trends in mental health services, *Social Science and Medicine*, 28, 1129–39.

Buck, J.A. and Umland, B. (1997) Covering mental health and substance abuse services, *Health Affairs*, 16, 120–6.

Buck, J.A., Teich, J.L., Umland, B. and Stein, M. (1999) Behavioral health benefits in employer sponsored health plans 1997, *Health Affairs*, 18, 67–78.

Clark, R.E., Dorwart, R.A. and Epstein, S.S. (1994) Managing competition in public and private mental health agencies: implications for services and policy, *Milbank Quarterly*, 72, 653–78.

Cook, J. and Wright, E. (1995) Medical sociology and the study of severe mental illnesses: reflections on past accomplishments and directions for future research, *Journal of Health and Social Behavior*, Special Issue, 95–114.

Edwards, J. (1997) The impact of managed care on the psychoanalytic psychotherapeutic process. In Alperin, M. and Phillips, D.G. (eds) *The Impact of Managed Care on the Practice of Psychotherapy*. New York: Brunner/Mazel Publishers.

Flynn, L. (1994) Managed care and mental illness. In Schreter, R.K., Scharfstein, S.S. and Schreter, C.A. (eds) *Allies and Adversaries: the Impact of Managed Care on Mental Health Services*. Washington DC: American Psychiatric Press.

Freund, D.A. and Hurley, R.E. (1995) Medicaid managed care: contribution to issues of health reform, *Annual Review of Public Health*, 16, 473–95.

Griffiths, L. and Hughes, D. (1999) Talking-contracts and taking care: managers and professionals in the British national health service internal market, *Social Science and Medicine*, 46, 1–13.

Hafferty, F. and Light, D.W. (1995) Professional dynamics and the changing nature of medical work, *Journal of Health and Social Behavior* (Extra Issue), 132–53.

Hawthorne, W. and Hough, R. (1997) Integrated services for long-term care. In Minkoff, K. and Pollack, D. (eds) *Managed Mental Health Care in the Public Sector*. Amsterdam: Harwood Academic Publishers.

Herron, W. (1997) Restructuring managed mental health care. In Alperin, R.M. and Phillips, O.G. (eds) *The Impact of Managed Care on the Practice of Psychotherapy*. New York: Brunner Mazel Publishers.

Heydeband, W. (1990) The technocratic organization of academic work. In Calhoun, C., Meyer, M.W. and Scott, W.R. (eds) *Structures of Power and Constraint*. Cambridge: Cambridge University Press.

Hoyt, M.F. and Austad, C.S. (1992) Psychotherapy in a staff model health maintenance organization: providing and assuring quality care in the future, *Psychotherapy*, 29, 119–28.

Institute of Medicine (1997) *Managing Managed Care: Quality Improvement in Behavioral Health*. Washington DC: National Academy Press.

Iglehart, J.K. (1996) Managed care and mental health, *The New England Journal of Medicine*, 334, 131–5.

Jensen, G.A., Morrisey, M.A., Gaffney, S. and Liston, D.K. (1997) The new dominance of managed care: insurance trends in the 1990s, *Health Affairs*, 16, 125–35.

Jensen, G.A., Roos, K., Burten, R.P.D. and Bulycheva, M. (1998) Mental health insurance in the 1990s: are employers offering less to more? *Health Affairs*, 17, 201–8.

Lazarus, J. and Pollack, D. (1997) Ethical aspects of public sector managed care. In Minkoff, K. and Pollack, D. (eds) *Managed Mental Health Care in the Public Sector*. Amsterdam: Harwood Academic Publishers.

Ludwig, K., Moltz, J. and Moltz, D.A. (1997) Time-sensitive treatment in community mental health settings. In Minkoff, K. and Pollack, D. (eds) *Managed Mental Health Care in the Public Sector*. Amsterdam: Harwood Academic Publishers.

Manderscheid, R.W., Henderson, M.J., Witkin, M.J. and Atay, J.E. (1999) Contemporary mental health systems and managed care. In Horwitz, A.V. and Scheid, T.L. (eds) *A Handbook for the Study of Mental Health*. Cambridge: Cambridge University Press.

Martin, L. and Kettner, P.M. (1997) Performance measurement: the new accountability, *Administration in Social Work*, 21, 17–29.

Mechanic, D. (1994) Establishing mental health priorities, *Milbank Quarterly*, 72, 501–14.

Mechanic, D. (1999) *Mental Health and Social Policy: the Emergence of Managed Care*. Boston: Allyn and Bacon.

Mechanic, D. and Schlesinger, M. (1993) Challenges for managed competition from chronic illness, *Health Affairs* (Supplement), 12, 123–37.

Mechanic, D. and Schlesinger, M. (1996) The impact of managed care on patients' trust in medical care and their physicians, *JAMA*, 275, 21, 1693–7.

Mechanic, D., Schlesinger, M. and McAlpine, D. (1995) Management of mental health and substance abuse services: state of the art and early results, *Milbank Quarterly*, 73, 19–55.

Meyer, M.W. (1990) The Weberian tradition in organizational research. In Calhoun, C., Meyer, M.W. and Richard Scott, W. (eds) *Structures of Power and Constraint*. Cambridge: Cambridge University Press.

Minkoff, K. and Pollack, D. (eds) (1997) *Managed Mental Health Care in the Public Sector*. Amsterdam, The Netherlands: Harwood Academic Publishers.

Minkoff, K. (1997) Public sector managed care and community mental health ideology. In Minkoff, K. and Pollack, D. (eds) *Managed Mental Health Care in the Public Sector*. Amsterdam: Harwood Academic Publishers.

Moffic, H.S. (1997) *The Ethical Way: Challenges and Solutions for Managed Behavioral Healthcare*. San Francisco: Jossey-Bass Publications.

Pollack, D., McFarland, B.H., George, R.A. and Angell, R.H. (1994) Prioritization of mental health services in Oregon, *Milbank Quarterly*, 72, 515–50.

Rochefort, D. (1989) *Handbook on Mental Health Policy in the US*. New York: Greenwood Press.

Rodwin, M.A. (1993) *Medicine, Money and Morals: Physicians' Conflicts of Interest*. New York: Oxford University Press.

Schlesinger, M. and Gray, B.H. (1999) Institutional change and its consequences for the delivery of mental health services. In Horwitz, A.V. and Scheid, T.L. (eds) *A Handbook for the Study of Mental Health*. Cambridge: Cambridge University Press.

Schlesinger, M.J., Gray, B.H. and Perreira, K.M. (1997) Medical professionalism under managed care: the pros and cons of utilization review, *Health Affairs*, 16, 1, 106–24.

Schreter, R.K., Sharfstein, S.S. and Schreter, C.A. (1994) *Allies and Adversaries: the Impact of Managed Care on Mental Health Services*. Washington, DC: American Psychiatric Press.

Scott, W.R., Ruef, M., Mendel, P. and Caroneer, C.A. (2000) *Institutional Change and Organizational Transformation of the Healthcare Field*. Chicago: University of Chicago Press.

Shore, Miles F. and Beigel, A. (1996) The challenges posed by managed behavioral health care, *The New England Journal of Medicine*, 334, 116–18.

Soderfeldt, B., Soderfeldt, M., Muntaner, C., O'campo, P., Warj, L. and Ohlsom, C. (1996) Psychosocial work environment in human service organizations: a conceptual analysis and development of the demand-control model, *Social Science and Medicine*, 42, 1217–26.

Tuttle, G.McC. and Woods, D.R. (1997) *The Managed Care Answer Book for Mental Health Professionals*. Bristol, PA: Brunner/Mazel Publishers.

Wells, K.B., Astrachan, B.M., Tischer, G.L. and Unutzer, J. (1995) Issues and approaches in evaluating managed mental health care, *Milbank Quarterly*, 73, 57–72.

Notes on Contributors

Joan Busfield is Professor of Sociology at the Department of Sociology, University of Essex.

Mick Carpenter is Reader in Social Policy at the University of Warwick.

David Cohen is Professor at the School of Social Work, Florida International University, USA.

Bernadette Dallaire is Honorary Research Fellow at the Institute for Public Health Research and Policy, University of Salford.

Joyce Davidson is currently studying for a Phd. at the Department of Geography, University of Edinburgh.

Nick Manning is Professor at the School of Sociology and Social Policy, University of Nottingham.

Michael McCubbin is Associate Researcher at the FCAAR Research Centre on Social Aspects of Health and Prevention (GRASP), University of Montreal, Canada.

Paul Morin is Associate Researcher at the Monteregie Rights Defense Collective, Longueuil (Quebec), Canada.

Julie Mulvany is Head of School at the School of Social and Behavioural Sciences, Swinburne University of Technology, Australia.

Derrol Palmer is a lecturer at the Sociology Department, University of York.

Teresa L. Scheid is an Associate Professor at the Department of Sociology, University of North Carolina, USA.

Simon J. Williams is a senior lecturer at the Department of Sociology, University of Warwick.

Index